More pr
Disarming Conflict

About the author

Ernie Regehr OC is co-founder of Project Ploughshares, one of Canada's leading peace and security NGOs. He is also Senior Fellow in Arctic Security at The Simons Foundation of Vancouver, and Research Fellow at the Institute of Peace and Conflict Studies, Conrad Grebel University College, the University of Waterloo. Ernie has served as an NGO representative and expert advisor on numerous Government of Canada delegations to multilateral disarmament forums, including Review Conferences of the Nuclear Non-Proliferation Treaty and UN Conferences on Small Arms. In 1990–91 he was Canada's representative on the United Nations Group of Governmental Experts on Arms Transfer Transparency that led to the creation in 1992 of the UN Conventional Arms Register, and in 2001 was an advisor to the Government of Kenya in the development of a regional arms control agreement on small arms, known as the Nairobi Declaration. He has traveled frequently to conflict zones, especially in East Africa, contributed to Track II diplomacy efforts related to the war in southern Sudan, and is on the Board of the Africa Peace Forum of Nairobi, Kenya. He is a former Commissioner of the World Council of Churches Commission on International Affairs, where he was active in developing the WCC's position on Responsibility to Protect as adopted at the 2006 World Assembly.

Disarming Conflict

Ernie Regehr

Zed Books

LONDON

Disarming Conflict was published in 2015 by Zed Books Ltd,
The Foundry, 17 Oval Way, London SE11 5RR, UK

www.zedbooks.co.uk

First published in Canada in 2015 by Between the Lines,
401 Richmond Street West, Studio 277, Toronto, Ontario M5V 3A8.

www.btlbooks.com

Text design and page preparation by Steve Izma

Cover design by Jonathan Pelham

ISBN 978-1-78360-355-8 hb
ISBN 978-1-78360-354-1 pb
ISBN 978-1-78360-356-5 pdf
ISBN 978-1-78360-357-2 epub
ISBN 978-1-78360-358-9 mobi

Printed and bound by CPI Group (UK) Ltd, Croydon, CR0 4YY

To Nathan, Clem, Erin, and Mabel

Contents

Preface and Acknowledgements

R EADERS WILL NOT BE AT A LOSS to identify the point of view that animates this volume. You don't spend the better part of four decades in and around an organization dedicated to "beating swords into ploughshares" and then claim to come at the subject of peace and war without recourse to some pretty strong convictions. But bringing convictions to a project doesn't mean leaving the evidence behind. Peace, no less than politics, is the art of the possible. So, while a deep wariness of the utility of military force in settling highly complex political disputes certainly informs this volume and, by the way, is not out of place in any serious exploration of what underpins durable peace and stability, policy must finally be guided more by what actually works than by deep convictions about what ought to work.

A central contemporary challenge facing governments when they try to respond effectively to political conflict gone violent, or that threatens to do so, is for them to meet head on the tenacious conviction about the efficacy of war that still trumps the evidence of the past twenty-five years of armed conflict. Since the end of the Cold War the world has witnessed a succession of spectacularly failed wars, and yet public policy in far too many capitals still reflects the persistent but unsubstantiated conviction that it is the vigorous preparation for war, and from time to time the forceful prosecution of it, that produces durable peace. That the world now spends $1.7 trillion annually on armed forces – an amount roughly equal to the gross domestic output of all of Africa – is but one of the gloomier indications that assumptions about the force of arms as the final guarantor of peace and security remain prominent. But the evidence of the past twenty-five years of armed conflict points in another direction. To favour diplomacy and peacebuilding over military prowess as the more reliable means to durable peace turns out to be founded on practical realism as much as conviction.

Anecdotal evidence of the limits to force fills daily news reports, but there are also more systematic compilations of such evidence. Project Ploughshares has maintained a database on the world's wars since 1987 and it serves as a primary source for what follows. Other corroborating sources on trends in armed conflict that are consulted include the Stockholm International Peace Research Institute, the Uppsala University's

Department of Peace and Conflict Research, and the Human Security Report Project at Canada's Simon Fraser University. The definitions of war or armed conflict – these terms are used interchangeably – are drawn from the annual Project Ploughshares armed conflicts report, and conflict descriptions also rely heavily on the work of Project Ploughshares.

That means in turn that Project Ploughshares, led until mid-2015 by Executive Director John Siebert and since then by Cesar Jaramillo in the same role, tops the list of the organizations and individuals whose help has been immeasurable in completing this work. Two past chairs of the Ploughshares board, Moira Hutchison and Dona Harvey, unfailingly wise advisors and supportive friends, were especially important in supporting the idea of this project and then encouraging its completion. Dr. Jennifer Simons, President of The Simons Foundation, has also been a trusted friend and advisor, and the foundation has provided critically important financial support, both to Project Ploughshares and for this project.

I'm also especially grateful to my good friend Gerry Barr for suggesting the theme for this book and for encouraging me to stick with it. Douglas Roche, Murray Thomson, and Bev Delong are three friends and valued "comrades," not in arms, but in disarmament. We have worked together on multiple projects and their wise counsel and support on many issues and activities have been indispensable.

A special thank you to Christina Woolner for her valuable research assistance on this project. I have had the benefit of critical commentary from a number of readers of various sections of the text, and I'm indebted to Ken Epps, Cesar Jaramillo, and Tasneem Jamal, valued colleagues at Project Ploughshares, for their insights, support, and advice. I'm also especially grateful to other readers: Branka Marijan, Paul Meyer, Greg Puley, Mark Sedra, Jamie Swift, and Andrew Thompson. All offered important advice, pointed out errors, and made valuable suggestions.

All provided invaluable assistance and support, but none bears responsibility for the final product. Responsibility for all that follows, especially for all the shortcomings, is mine alone.

I'm also very grateful to the folks at Between the Lines for taking on this project and bringing it to light – Jamie Swift for his encouragement and advice, Cameron Duder for his thoughtful and careful editing, and Amanda Crocker for keeping us all on track and guiding the project through all the stages to completion.

My family has of course accompanied me and offered unfailing support through decades of attention to the issues and concerns raised here. Nancy has been my partner and colleague, not to mention first reader and constructive critic, throughout. And one brief paragraph in the "acknowledgements" section obviously doesn't begin to cover what all that support means. The dedication page lists my grandchildren – I fervently hope that they get to live in a world that has learned that peace isn't won on the battlefield.

Introduction

Fighting to Lose

A FEW OF THE RECRUITS WORE BOOTS that could pass for standard army issue. Many more wore flip flops. The rest were barefoot. Some carried the ubiquitous AK-47 automatic rifle, some had ancient single-shot Winchester rifles, others carried hastily carved representations of rifles, and still others went without. None wore uniforms. Some had camouflage trousers.

They were all trainees with the Sudan People's Liberation Army (SPLA) and their instructor was putting them through a succession of drills and callisthenic exercises in an open field surrounded by patches of bush and the thatched tukuls where they slept. On that hot and cloudless day in 1999 the SPLA was in its eighteenth year of what was by all accounts a losing fight, and these aspiring soldiers in their ragtag outfits and formations did little to lift expectations that the liberation of southern Sudan from the repressive control of the Sudanese government in Khartoum would be realized any time soon. The Government of Sudan forces outmatched the southern rebels by every measure: more fighters, more training, more guns, much better transportation and communication, and a lot more money. The government had aircraft and tanks and the petrodollars and willing suppliers to get more. The SPLA made do with their AKs and the few anti-aircraft guns, fewer artillery pieces, and occasional tanks that they managed to capture from government forces.

Throughout, the long-suffering people of southern Sudan had to endure the relentless raids of Khartoum's Antonov bombers, which by then had displaced at least two-thirds of the population of the south. Despondent tribal and community leaders in the south, though unshakable in their loyalty to the rebel cause, were asking with increasing weariness when the promised release would finally come. And as if those weren't challenges enough for the ill equipped and poorly fed cadres of the SPLA, they were also fighting against other southerners – some had split from their movement and others simply mounted opportunistic freelance militias to make mischief and to gather the meagre spoils of war in their desperately impoverished and ungoverned land.

To this visitor to the SPLA's Nimule training camp near the border with Uganda, the situation seemed, to put it generously, hopeless. The SPLA commander-in-chief was visiting the camp that day, and his well-rehearsed declarations – that all was going well, that the young men and boys out in that field would soon be joining a team of dedicated freedom fighters who were making steady progress against a corrupt and weakening government – served only to heighten the sense of unreality. The commander's name was Salva Kiir Mayardit and today he is president of the independent Republic of South Sudan.

All the vaunted military advantages held by Khartoum ultimately proved to be of no avail. From 1956 to 2006, with only brief interludes of fragile peace along the way, the Government of Sudan fought with all of its considerable weapons and political wiles to keep the south from separating. No material or human costs were spared. What Khartoum got out of it was a separated south, a new set of debilitating oil and border quarrels with the new Republic of South Sudan, and a five-decade accumulation of suspicion and enmity that will continue to be a major obstacle to the emergence of a mature and mutually beneficial relationship between the two Sudans. President Omar Hassan al-Bashir of the Republic of Sudan is now leader of a much diminished Sudan. He is also under indictment at the International Criminal Court for genocide, war crimes, and crimes against humanity, earned in Darfur in another of Sudan's multiple war zones, and he still faces a series of fights against multiple rebel groups around the country. Burdened by a combination of hubris and denial, an affliction common enough among dictators and presidents with big armies, President Bashir was in the summer of 2012 still vowing to teach President Kiir and the South Sudanese what he called "a final lesson by force" over unresolved border disputes between them.[1]

There surely are lessons to be drawn from Sudan's resort to force, but not the ones its beleaguered president was still constructing. Nor is Sudan the only source for the hard truths of contemporary warfare. The inescapable lesson of today's wars, repeatedly taught but hard to learn, is that superior military force rarely prevails when deeply rooted political conflicts become thoroughly militarized. Indeed, the lesson is more dramatic than that. The noted British military commander of a variety of collective security operations, the late General Sir Rupert Smith, described post–Cold War military actions as a succession of campaigns "that have in one way or another spectacularly failed to achieve the results intended, namely a decisive military victory which would in turn deliver a solution to the original problem, which is usually political."[2] The record of warfare over the past quarter century makes it abundantly clear that vital political objectives are these days rarely achieved through sheer military force. Military force can and frequently does record unambigu-ous tactical victories, but the durability of those apparent successes depends entirely on the strategic environment. That in turn relies on a much broader set of non-military – political/economic/social – institu-tions and responses that, if present, can be mobilized to consolidate tac-tical military gains, resolve the conflicts at the root of the fighting, and build conditions for a durable peace. If they are absent, the fighting is an exercise in futility.

Of course, utility and futility are substantially in the eye of the beholder. There is no denying the destructive power of military force, so when the objective is as simple as that, there is obvious utility in the resort to military force. Overwhelming military force does work rather well when the tactical objective is to destroy – say, when the objective is to crush a regime in Afghanistan or Iraq. And decidedly less than over-whelming force can also be, and frequently is, remarkably successful in another kind of destructive mission – say, when the objective is to render a state ungovernable, a mission at which the ill-clad and ill-equipped rebel fighters of southern Sudan excelled for some five decades. But the forces that quickly dispatched the Taliban and Saddam Hussein regimes proved impotent when it came to supporting, rather than destroying, the conditions for stable governance. And when the objectives of the rebels of southern Sudan turned from making the south ungovernable to gov-erning it, the battle proven and now better equipped and trained armed forces of the new state of South Sudan found themselves unable to learn the lesson they taught Khartoum – namely, that war is woefully unable to deliver a victory that resolves the political and economic conflicts that spawned the fighting in the first place. George W. Bush was no doubt fully persuaded of the utility of force in 2003 when he received the plaudits of troops aboard the *USS Abraham Lincoln* under the "mission accom-plished" banner. Salva Kiir was surely persuaded of the utility of force in getting him to the conference table that produced the 2005 Comprehen-sive Peace Agreement. But both men were soon to learn some hard truths about the very real limits to force.

Limits to Force

Political stability, as not only Iraq and Sudan but also the last twenty-five years of global warfare amply demonstrate, ultimately does not issue from the barrel of a gun. The resort to force, even to military force that is clearly superior in every way to that of an adversary, is predictably ineffec-tive when the objective is stable governance in a deeply divided society.

Authoritarianism of the kind practised in Khartoum cannot indefinitely hold out against the legitimacy that derives not from guns but rather the consent of the governed. Whether the objective is repressive governance or its overthrow and the restoration of democratic rule of law and the building of stable and trusted public institutions, in the long run, the effort to *force* political stability is highly destabilizing. Superior military force invariably emboldens those who possess it but just as surely it turns out not to be a reliable foundation for political stability. Indeed, one of the most difficult truths to accept about military force, including multilateral military action with peace and stability as its central objective, is that military might is not the master of its fate or destiny. Military force in the service of social/political stability is rarely capable of transcending its own social/political context and thus is not capable of producing – of forcing – predictable political outcomes where politics has become dysfunctional and public institutions are not trusted. Some of the examples of the last twenty-five years are spectacular and well known. To the notable failures of multilateral forces in Afghanistan and Iraq and to Khartoum's failure to control southern Sudan must be added Russia's utter defeat in Afghanistan and the repeated Serbian failures in the former Yugoslavia. Others, less well known but just as decisive, include the fall of the Mengistu regime in Ethiopia, the toppled regimes in El Salvador and Guatemala, and the emergence of East Timor out of Indonesia. All of these were painful, devastating episodes in the lives of the affected populations, but in the end, superior military capabilities could not force the outcomes to which the more powerful parties were committed.

The story of contemporary warfare begins on killing fields where battles are regularly won but the wars are usually lost. Nearly one hundred wars in twenty-five years, more than a quarter of them still ongoing, have been and still are largely fought to uncertain prospects. All current wars are intrastate, or civil, wars which, for the most part, begin with gradually declining trust in public institutions and political processes, escalating protest, and accompanying lawlessness, all grist for increasingly forceful opposition movements – movements that are in turn resisted with increasing shows of force by unpopular, unaccountable, and beleaguered governments. Typically, this toxic formula is ignited into active fighting by a particular crisis or triggering event, and before either opposition forces or governments are even fully aware of it, the threshold of war has been crossed. Once started, the overwhelming majority of wars, 85 per cent in the past twenty-five years, cannot be settled on the battlefield; instead most are fought to desperately hurting stalemates. Some then yield to exhaustion and gradually dissolve. The rest, the majority, are turned over to diplomats and politicians who go in search of whatever face-saving outcomes may still be available. Of the 15 per cent that are won or lost on the battlefield, rebel forces, in the case of civil wars, win as often as do governments. Of course, "winning" usually has little meaning in the circumstance. When wars finally end, whether through diplomacy or exhaustion or – unusually – on the battlefield, the state is left with the long and daunting effort to recover. Inevitably, the conditions that produced the war in the first place remain when the fighting finally ends, only more so. The main difference is that at war's end the effort to build the conditions for durable peace is undertaken in the context of seriously depleted national resources and a deeply scarred national psyche.

The wars of the past quarter century are thus most convincing as morality tales on the limits of military force. Far from offering political leaders a last resort to accomplish what could not be accomplished through politics and diplomacy, modern warfare has largely become a means of spreading or universalizing loss. Instead of winning what could not be won by other, more peaceful means, wars are most effective in ensuring that none of the stakeholders to the conflict escape its legacies of death, injury, displacement, debt, stunted economic development, and political and psychological upheaval – the effects of which continue to be felt and borne by succeeding generations.

The quick military defeats of discredited regimes in Afghanistan and Iraq in 2001 and 2003 set the stage, not for stability and prosperity, but for civil wars that well over a decade later show signs of continuing indefinitely in the manner of most contemporary wars. These ongoing, though sometimes sporadic, conflicts may not always be all-out wars of relentlessly pitched battles but nor do they allow the minimal security and stability needed to nurture basic economic activity and social development. In early 2015, Iraq, Afghanistan, and especially Syria were tragically at the relentlessly pitched battles end of the spectrum. The annual combat death toll was in the thousands in Afghanistan and Iraq, tens of thousands in Syria, and collectively in the tens of thousands in the two-dozen other wars that still plagued the planet. Despite those devastating and well-known outcomes, conventional wisdom still ignores just how rarely military force in contemporary warfare manages to deliver on its promises – the promises to vanquish an adversary, to defend freedom, to uphold national honour, to liberate a people from the yoke of oppression, and many more. When it comes to actually resolving an entrenched political conflict that has turned violent, the solution inevitably involves the same, once unsavoury compromises that would have been available before the war had the parties possessed the will or insight to pursue them at the conference table.

Of the ninety-nine wars of the past quarter century, seventy ended, but of those only ten were settled decisively on the battlefield. One of those was an interstate war (a war between countries), and of the nine civil wars fought to a battlefield victory, in only four cases did governments prevail over insurgents. In the other five, insurgents rebelling against governments prevailed. In other words, governments managed to defeat insurgents militarily in only 7 per cent of the wars they fought against their citizens. So when governments mount serious military offensives against rebel groups, the odds are overwhelmingly against them. Half of the wars ended in negotiations, and about a third gradually wound down without a clear peace settlement or a decisive outcome on the battlefield. Because most wars are fought to battlefield stalemates, from which the least humiliating path to a ceasefire and political accommodation is then the objective, rebel forces end up fighting not to "win" but to get a seat at the table – meaning that for them fighting tends to have much greater utility than it does for the governments resisting them.

In much of the public discourse surrounding the deployment of military force there is an unchallenged deference to that familiar idea of military force as a last resort – the idea that however much we may abhor military violence and the resort to war, when everything else fails, when all the political and diplomatic efforts have failed to resolve a conflict, we can if we are but powerful and clever enough still turn to military action to set things right. When diplomacy fails, according to this narrative, we can still, however reluctantly, draw the final trump of armed force to override political and social impediments to agreement and thus literally force a particular political outcome. When all else fails, we can call on the institutions and instruments of overwhelming force to solve those problems that have been proven to have no other solution. The intended point of the doctrine of last resort is clearly, and properly, to induce caution and reluctance to turn to military force, but in doing that it has also fed the myth that, in the end, force is the trump – the final arbiter in conflict. And it is a myth or conventional wisdom that endures in defiance of observable reality. The wars of the past quarter century have been singularly incapable of driving constructive political outcomes that overcome the conditions and conflicts that led to war in the first place. In other words, contemporary wars are not persuasive evidence that war is in fact a reliable last resort.

Even so, the belief in the efficiency of force thrives, and few costs are spared in building the capacity for war. Worldwide, military forces spend more in just three days, about $14 billion, than is available for the core United Nations (UN) operating budget, plus peacekeeping, for a full year ($13 billion).[3] The roughly $1.7-plus trillion the world currently spends each year on military enforcement of local and global security and stability simply cannot deliver on its ambitious promises. Indeed, it's almost as if there were an inverse relationship between the sophistication and destructive capability of a military's capacity and its utility in resolving intractable political conflicts. Nuclear weapons are the extreme case in point. They can't be used to fight and win wars, and they are impotent in the effort to prevent wars. It is important to acknowledge that the restrained and disciplined reliance on conventional national and multi-national security forces in contexts well short of war can and sometimes does help to forge new levels of stability and security a society needs to build new futures. But to do that successfully, those forces must do their work in concert with robust programs for economic development, efforts toward more equitable and inclusive governance, the provision of basic services, and the creation of trusted national institutions to sustainably deliver these social goods. Recognizing the limits to force is central to recognizing when armed security forces can or cannot be constructively deployed.

Preventing War

The effective and constructive deployment of security forces means, in particular, avoiding getting drawn into a war. The costs of war are immeasurable and the outcomes predictable – that is, wars don't produce decisive victories, they leave the conflicts that gave rise to them unresolved, and they leave the communities that must finally resolve them economically, politically, and psychically depleted. That clearly makes war prevention imperative, which in turn requires a clear understanding of the conditions that generate war. And much is known about those war-inducing conditions, knowledge that is acquired notably through the tragedy of war, aided by the work of that extraordinary band of scholars and researchers that sift through the detritus of armed conflict to glean lessons for future action. Furthermore, those lessons relevant to preventing war are most likely to come from contemporary wars – hence the focus here on the last quarter century of war. The great wars of the last century have received copious public attention and have been thoroughly mined for their lessons, but the wars of the final decade of the twentieth century and the first decades of the twenty-first bear little resemblance to those earlier conflagrations.

The question of war prevention is not the question of conflict prevention or even of unearthing the roots of conflict. The roots of conflict and grievance are many, and understanding those roots is fundamental to the political management or resolution of conflict, but the war prevention challenge is not to prevent conflict but to prevent political conflict from being transformed into armed conflict. And today that challenge is particularly daunting in the context of conflicts within rather than between states. When interstate conflicts, that is, conflicts between states, do morph into war, it is likely to be the result of deliberate decision making, however wise or foolish, but the onset of civil war, intrastate war, tends not to involve conscious, high-level decisions to opt for war. Instead, civil wars are much more likely to feature gradual descent into violence escalating to military armed conflict. As public protest grows, matched by escalating crackdowns by authorities, public order declines in contexts where neither rebels nor authorities are inclined toward compromise and where credible political processes are unavailable – rebels are typically convinced that they will have to become much more of a military threat to be taken seriously and to gain access to a serious negotiating table, and governments, when they initially respond to political protests with force, remain optimistic that they can keep that threat at bay.

Conflict analysis identifies four basic conditions that drive political conflict toward armed conflict. The first is obviously the presence of heightened political, economic, and social grievances. The point here being that the issue truly is grievance and not simply spontaneously combusted extremism disconnected from social and economic conditions. Second, when deeply held grievances become identified with particular ethnic or religious groups, or with particular regions of a country, the likelihood of the conflict turning violent increases. Third, for armed conflict to ensue, the presence of serious grievances must be bolstered by capability – that means the availability of the physical means of violence (weapons and financial backers), but also the political will or willingness of at least one of the parties to initiate the resort to overt violence. Another critical factor is the perceived absence of political alternatives and effective pathways for nonviolent conflict resolution. When the onset of war is largely "unofficial" and often unacknowledged, when it is not heralded by flags and bugles, the overt march to war is replaced by the gradual (or sometimes rapid) disintegration of order in severely troubled societies and the inexorable descent into political and criminal public violence. Indeed, "public violence" could be the most apt, though still emotionally inadequate, term for many of today's armed conflicts. Political violence is invariably linked to longstanding social and political grievances that remain chronically unaddressed and are allowed to fester and undermine confidence in public institutions and processes. When a society finds itself in that deadly combination of circumstances – pervasive grievance, loss of confidence in government, abundant supplies of user-friendly small arms, and no credible means of influencing or gaining the sympathetic ear of state authorities – descent into chaos and the kind of public violence that must finally be recognized as war becomes more and more likely.

A primary challenge to this paradigm of conflict emerging out of grievances to which authorities have too long been deaf is the rise of extremism driven by ideology and religion. Direct and outrageously vicious attacks on civilians because they support democracy or are Christians, the two primary categories of people that Boko Haram in Nigeria says it targets, have lost any meaningful link to the economic or political grievances that still define the context of such attacks. Assaults on people of the wrong stream of Islam, or because their sacrifice will hasten the establishment of a true Caliphate, the war cry of the Islamic State (IS) in Iraq and Syria, seem inspired much more by ideological or religious teaching than by the absence of an alternative to violence. Disaffection and alienations born out of social and political conditions are still lodged somewhere at the roots of these movements, but their immediate interest hardly seems to be a seat at a conference table. On the other hand, these are also not persuasive examples of the effective use of destructive military force. There are no prospects of IS and Boko Haram attacks delivering the outcomes the perpetrators claim they are pursuing – but the harm they do in the process is extraordinary. The chances of them being restrained by diplomacy are remote, but so too are the chances of them being defeated by military means. While air attacks and ground assaults may well degrade them, few military or conflict analysts now argue that there is a military solution to their challenge.

While wars emerge out of various and complex factors and circumstances, the broad strokes of armed conflict prevention are nevertheless fairly clear: being politically responsive to grievances, including the alleviation of poverty and the promotion of economic equity, employment, and education; addressing identity concerns through community-to-community engagement and trust building; controlling the arms that facilitate armed conflict; and building national institutions that have the demonstrated capacity to mediate conflict, earn the confidence of populations, and generate alternatives to both violent repression and violent rebellion. These four responses really amount to the traditional peacebuilding agenda. The last of the four, governance reform and creating genuine alternative forums for mediating entrenched conflict, needs to become much more prominent on that agenda. Dissident communities are drawn to violence, often to protect themselves from an abusive regime, but ultimately not to defeat governments but to get to a real negotiating forum. That suggests getting dissidents to a place at a table rather than forcing them to fight for it should be a key war prevention strategy. The international community has a particular role in getting disaffected communities or constituencies access to credible political or mediating forums in states with dysfunctional political systems and without the institutional means to mediate internal conflicts. Creating credible mediating mechanisms is what is meant by alternatives to violence. The international community has often done the opposite. Instead of giving voice to the aggrieved and pressuring their tormentors to address their grievances in credible forums, oppressive governments are the ones that receive the political cover from the powerful – from Mobutu in Zaire, to Saddam in pre-1991 Iraq, to Mubarak in Egypt before the Arab Spring.

War prevention is not a fool's errand. In these early years of a new millennium, wars are in fact being prevented as never before. The most notable decline has been in interstate wars. Wars between states have for the moment been eliminated. That claim is linked to some extent to how interstate war is defined, but whatever the definition, we may well be as close as the world has ever been to the fulfilment of the old Biblical prophecy that "nation will not lift up sword against nation, neither shall they learn war anymore." It is true that sustaining this phenomenon is far from guaranteed. States are still enthusiastic about learning and training for warfare, and some are in possession of nuclear arsenals that in a matter of minutes could deliver a global catastrophe that would instantly dwarf the extraordinary death toll and physical destruction of the wars of the twentieth century. Interstate war remains dangerously available, as demonstrated in the dangerous temptation to escalate and internationalize armed conflict in Ukraine and the persistent calls for attacks on Iran. However, that should not detract from the unassailable fact that in current interstate affairs, in the relationships between individual nation states, it is now the exception for two states locked in serious political or economic conflict to try to settle their dispute on the battlefield. Civil wars have also been in decline over the past quarter century, although new wars in Libya, Mali, Syria, and Ukraine had reversed that trend by 2014.

War prevention in the post–Cold War era has, from one perspective, been remarkable. Compare the past twenty-five years of warfare, each war hellish in its own way, with the seventy-five years from 1914 to 1989. There were the two world wars, the Stalinist purges, the Maoist revolution, Biafra, Pol Pot, the wars of Indochina, and many more, and together they killed on average well over two million people per year. Since the Cold War, even including the extraordinary conflicts of Sudan, the Democratic Republic of the Congo (DRC), Rwanda, and Syria, annual combat deaths and indirect deaths from war have been cut by some 80 per cent.

Disarming Conflict

But, of course, war prevention still fails too often. While the overall level of warfare is in fact declining, the Arab Spring has followed the rough pattern of armed conflict of the past twenty-five years – while there are important examples of deep political crisis not descending into sustained violence to the level of warfare, in other cases the descent to war was quick and devastating. And when prevention fails, it is neither politically nor morally acceptable for the international community to stand idly by. The impulse to "do something" is and should be powerful, and through a myriad of diplomatic, humanitarian, economic, legal, and political instruments the international community does get engaged, up to and including the multilateral deployment of military/police forces. Building the conditions for sustainable peace requires a modicum of stability and security, and in some circumstances well-trained international military and constabulary forces can restrain those who most egregiously violate the norms of decency and help to create that stability. But not always. The real challenge, when conflict dynamics are already far advanced, is to avoid exacerbating rather than mitigating violence, and instead to reliably discern when and how security forces can play a constructive role in restoring stability and protecting the vulnerable. The insertion of multilateral forces into a local conflict stands a chance of delivering desired outcomes only if key conditions prevail. There have been important lessons taught and some learned from decades of multilateral interventions, but the international community now faces the additional challenge of implementing its newly formalized commitment to protecting the most vulnerable when threatened with extreme actions that offend all public sensibility and rise to the level of crimes against humanity.

Contexts for armed combat and high levels of political violence against highly vulnerable civilian populations are by definition highly complex and extraordinarily difficult to control. Interventions can exacerbate rather than limit violence, so the international community has taken the trouble to elaborate a more reliable system of UN-based multilateral peacekeeping or peace support[4] intervention. From traditional peacekeeping that monitors ceasefires and peace agreements to armed interventions in chaotic war zones like Somalia or the DRC, the objective has been to design interventions to support a peace process rather than to defeat a party to the conflict. The challenge is, of course, to ensure that the multilateral resort to force does not become transformed from a peace support operation to participation on one side of a civil war – the record of winning such wars being less than promising. Thus the point of multilateral intervention is rarely to settle a conflict by force of arms but rather to disarm conflict by supporting and protecting the political institutions and improvised mechanisms by which the parties can pursue a political settlement. In some circumstances, this includes active combat against spoilers.

The global burden of maintaining some seventy million people in uniform and huge stores of weapons, from the smallest of side arms to nuclear-tipped missiles, all to the tune of almost $2 trillion per year, certainly militates against disarming conflict. The good news is however that the diplomatic pursuit of disarmament speaks to the growing worldwide recognition that armed force is a highly overrated investment for conflict management. But just as military forces are disproportionately promoted as guardians of security, disarmament is correspondingly still under-appreciated and under-resourced. That is at least as true of conventional disarmament as it is of nuclear disarmament. For war to be reliably prevented, conflict has to be progressively disarmed – one of the basic drivers of conflict being the ready availability of the tools of war in regions of conflict. Easy access to automatic rifles and rocket launchers and all of the paraphernalia of armed combat up to "fifth" generation fighter aircraft may not cause war, but it most certainly facilitates repression and makes combat a more readily available option. Limiting global supplies of these weapons will not end violent conflict (violence on a major scale can also be carried out with civilian tools as diverse as machetes and civilian airliners), but it would certainly make war a more distant option and much harder to sustain.

Detailed disarmament programs are increasingly available and have been set out collectively by governments, both globally and in regional contexts. The bad news is at least two-fold: the implementation deficit is formidable, a shortfall of both courage and wisdom, and those with the most military might are obviously the ones least drawn to disarmament. Indeed, in mid-2014 NATO, which already dwarfs the rest of the world's military capacity, was focused on promoting major military spending increases and mounting new symbols of military prowess and readiness.

NATO set 2 per cent of GDP as an aspirational guideline for military spending and announced a "readiness action plan," a move that would enable it to deploy a force within forty-eight hours instead of the earlier schedule of five days – although there are no known instances of NATO being politically prepared to act immediately only to have to wait five days to muster the rapid deployment force. Backed by two-thirds of the world's military spending and capacity, NATO's ineffectiveness in response to conflicts in Syria or Ukraine was not due to a lack of military capacity or readiness. The real point is that in Syria and Ukraine there neither was nor is a constructive role for partisan NATO forces – whether they were made available in five days or forty-eight hours. More capacity and more rapidly deployable forces were not about to solve those problems.

From Fighting Wars to Supporting Peace

Organized force, military and constabulary, will continue for the foreseeable future to play a prominent role in the internal peace and security affairs of individual states and relations between and among states. The repeated and predictable failure of the resort to overt force to resolve deep-seated political conflict does not negate the critical need to not only champion the rule of law but also to enforce it. The absence of any means of coercive enforcement – including the resort to lethal force by security forces – risks conflict devolving into lawless chaos that is hard to reverse, which is the most immediate and egregious offence to human security. In northeast Nigeria, the absence of trusted, reliable police and military forces allowed the extremist Boko Haram marauders almost free rein. Military and police forces do have a role to play, but it is not a contradiction to also recognize that political stability cannot be forced. Law "enforcement" is successful only when the laws are for the most part respected and voluntarily obeyed, and when enforcement focuses on isolated spoilers and criminals. In other words, military forces support stability in the context of strategic consent – when public and political institutions are trusted and voluntarily respected, and when laws and political processes are largely seen as serving justice. When minimal trust and respect are replaced by mistrust and defiance, more aggressive enforcement on its own is more likely to be destabilizing and can contribute to the escalation of violence and lawlessness.

Military force is effective, therefore, when its operations are roughly analogous to accountable police forces – when they protect public institutions and processes that enjoy public support and are seen to be in support of the political management of conflict. Police, when guided by the rule of law, bring people to justice; they don't decide on their own who the criminals are and then defeat or punish or eliminate them. Peace support forces have a similar role. The point is not to allow the purveyors of military prowess to decide winners and losers but to protect institutions and processes for politics and diplomacy. For military forces to contribute to stability and peace, they depend on, and in turn must support, an enabling political, social, and cultural context. In other words, force is not some *deus ex machina* that transcends the messy context of the day and simply reaches in and delivers a prescribed outcome. Political and social conditions matter; indeed they matter much more than do the military forces. One key lesson of the wars of the past twenty-five years is that force cannot resolve what is politically unresolvable. Syria and Ukraine are but the most recent prominent examples. Civil wars, interstate wars, and multilateral wars inevitably devolve to military stalemates that mirror the political, regional, or communal differences that spawned the fighting in the first place.

The use of force in "peace support operations" can best serve to facilitate and support stability when such interventions are clearly distinguished from warfighting operations. The distinction between peace support operations and warfighting is real and technical. The military element of peacekeeping or a peace support operation is multilaterally authorized military intervention designed to support political processes toward the settlement of conflict. Multilateral military intervention is not a way of circumventing politics – instead, it is intended to enable politics in which engagement and accommodation are pursued. Stability is the product of political accommodation, not military force, so if military force is to support stability it has to facilitate rather than circumvent political process and diplomacy. And that is the primary way in which peace support operations differ from "warfighting." Rather than facilitating or supporting the political resolution of conflict, warfighting is designed to override politics by dint of force and to impose, rather than negotiate, an outcome. And remember, in contemporary warfare the effort by states to militarily impose political objectives has been shown to fail more than 90 per cent of the time.

To be sure, that is not to claim that war never achieves the strategic objectives set for it. The one persuasive example in the past twenty-five years is the international community's action to force Iraq out of Kuwait in 1991. In that action, the international community clearly set aside political process and negotiation and Security Council diplomacy in favour of war – and it was no peace support operation. But it did uphold a key principle of international law and produce the primary desired outcome, which has proven sustainable. Of course there were important questions raised at the time: was diplomacy given its due; did the outcome justify the costs in human lives and material resources; was international humanitarian law respected in what some Americans called the "turkey shoot" that took place when coalition forces attacked retreating Iraqi forces on the highway from Kuwait back to Iraq? These are serious issues, but there is no contesting the fact that Iraqi forces were driven out of Kuwait and the country returned to the family that had controlled it, and the UN Charter principle against aggression was upheld. But in twenty-five years of post–Cold War warfare, it is the exception, not the norm.

Building Peace

The absence of war is not itself confirmation of the presence of peace. There are many countries in which war has been avoided while the conditions for war remain abundantly present. The *Global Peace Index* (GPI) recently ranked 162 countries for their peacefulness, based on indicators such as the number of violent deaths in political conflict, violent deaths due to organized crime, levels of crime more broadly, terrorist activity, relations with neighbours, police per capita, levels of military spending, the presence and availability of small arms, and other factors. Not surprisingly, the less peaceful a country is, the more likely it is to be at war, but it also shows very clearly that not all unpeaceful countries are in fact at war. Of the forty least peaceful societies in 2014, sixteen had still avoided war – North Korea and Zimbabwe being prime examples.[5] That suggests two points. The first is that war can be successfully avoided in even very unpeaceful societies. The second is that just because war has been avoided, it doesn't mean that peace prevails. Preventing war, even when conditions are driving toward war, is eminently possible, and while a war avoided does not mean peace is present, it does become the basic foundation on which peace can be progressively pursued and built. But the real lesson to which the GPI points is that civil war is unheard of when the social and economic conditions point to positive peace. None of the states in the top half of the index were at war and only one state outside the bottom quarter of the peace index (Algeria) was at war.

Disarming conflict so that peace can be built involves two essential dimensions. First is the need to actually disarm – to demilitarize and re-politicize conflict – so that even in very unpeaceful societies the destructiveness of war is avoided and the opportunity to build peace is created. Second is to take the opportunity that war avoidance creates to focus on the constitutional, political, economic, and social conditions on which peace can be built and the local and national institutions or mechanisms to mediate the political and social conflicts that all societies face. The disarming of conflict is built on the recognition that political conflicts and conditions that produce human insecurity and threaten to descend into political violence are fundamentally not amenable to military remedies. It is, above all, the wisdom to stop trying militarily to impose political outcomes that political, economic, and social conditions cannot sustain. The American academic Stephen Kinzer asks of the United States: "How can we influence the world when the instrument we wield best – military force – no longer allows us to impose our will? Successful countries of the 21st century will be those that are skillful at public diplomacy, cultural politics, and alliance-building."[6] The inability of force to impose political outcomes also applies to domestic contexts. Domestic political stability is not the product of superior force but of skills and commitments to building conditions that sustain peace and nurture the tolerance, co-operation, and interdependence that encourage constructive political compromise and avoid the descent into political violence that escalates into war.

But, of course, the realist reader, not only the sceptical reader, will properly ask whether there is anything more than wishful thinking in these formulas for peace and stability, so the following pages are an attempt to look at the evidence. And the evidence begins in the wars themselves. To start with, what are the basic facts of war of the past quarter century? How are they defined and counted (chapter 1), how did they start (chapter 2) and end (chapters 3 and 4)? Every war is its own tragic story, and its circumstances unique, but types and patterns are clearly discernable. If there is one clear pattern that emerges, it is that wars are not fought until someone wins, making peace the consequence. The evidence points to the overwhelming majority of wars ending in failure – failure defined not only as the failure to "win," but also as the failure to resolve the political conflict that led to war in the first place, and as having depleted the economic, political, and psychological resources needed for the equitable and durable resolution of those conflicts (chapter 5). The evidence of failure in turn points to the only rational response, the pursuit of another way. If armed conflict repeatedly and over decades concludes with political conflict even more deeply entrenched, with the means to resolving it seriously degraded, preparing more ardently for armed conflict in the future is unlikely to produce different results. War prevention, rather than war winning, is the strategy that commends itself, and that means rethinking the way the security dollar is spent.

Indeed, the case is made for increased security spending, as distinguished from military spending, by means of shifting the balance away from building up military capacity and toward building up the infrastructure of positive peace and the political capacity to bring relevant parties to relevant political processes (chapter 6). That in turn means reduced spending on military preparations, with more attention to conventional and nuclear disarmament (chapters 7 and 8). But it also means retaining the capacity to act when prevention fails. National governments and the international community need access to coercive force to protect vulnerable people and maintain some semblance of public order (chapter 9). That does not primarily mean access to military and police forces, but rather access to the means of building the political/social contexts in which coercive force can contribute to stability rather than to escalation of violence. And it means finally the transition from prevention to building positive peace (chapter 10).

The result sought is not perfection, but in some ways, more of the same – that is, continuing the trend toward reduced warfare worldwide. Focused attention on and amelioration of the root causes of conflict, innovative conflict resolution mechanisms, and generous funding of peacebuilding are devoutly to be wished and would make a dramatic difference in the prevalence and durability of armed conflict. The objective should be to make the current trend toward reduced warfare a more reliable and sustainable trend and to avoid the tragic relapses that traumatized the twentieth century. It means institutionalizing war prevention and war termination capabilities, removing the threat of instant global annihilation by nuclear arsenals still primed and programmed for instantaneous detonation, and offering more immediate and effective assistance to those most vulnerable when prevention fails. It means building the conditions of positive peace as if our lives depended on it.

1

A Quarter Century of Failed Warfare

THE VISIT TO THE PHILIPPINE WAR was high in the Cordillera Mountains of Luzon, and it was beautiful. Our small group of a half-dozen non-governmental observers arrived by chartered bus, slowly ascending along a winding, ever-narrowing trail. The mountains formed a wall of rock on one side and dropped sharply away on the other to valley after spectacular valley. When the bus reached the last turn-around point and could go no farther, we walked a well-worn footpath to the summit and then continued down the other side through the ancient terraces for which the region is famous and alongside the rice fields, all a luscious green. Our destination was the village deep in the valley, a small cluster of dwellings that also doubled as the front line in the decades-old war between the rebel New People's Army (NPA) and the forces of successive Philippine governments. It wasn't the only front, of course, but in the early 1980s it was one of the areas of contention in the continuing guerrilla war – a small, deceptively quiet village where they served a lunch of chicken and rice, rice wine, and war stories. Not the nostalgic tales of heroism and camaraderie from another day or the reconstruction of famous historic battles in a distant great war now consigned to fading memory and academic studies.

Their stories were the testimony, visceral and immediate, of vulnerable villagers lamenting family and community members lost, some to bullets and some to aggressive recruiters. They talked of villagers caught in the crossfire in brief but deadly skirmishes, of crops and fields trampled. The visit became an event for the whole village, and, one after the other, villagers told of lives of perpetual anxiety and ceaseless disruption – although "disruption" doesn't come close to capturing the sense of fragility that pervades lives stripped of any serious anticipation that things might soon be better. The villagers' pervasive suspicions of Manila and its "economic development" plans for the region predisposed them toward sympathy for the insurgents, but the distinctions between ally and foe had become hopelessly blurred. The serial disruptions and harassment which marked their lives came at the hands of rebel and government forces alike, making their lives an endless series of negotiations to try to balance the competing demands delivered in successive sweeps by competing armies. Pressures from the NPA to feed and shelter their cadres. Threats from government forces on regular intrusions, always looking for information, and always accusing them of being NPA sympathizers when the information wasn't forthcoming.

Weeks and even months would pass for them unmolested, but then back would come either the NPA or the Philippine Army, accusing them of being either government informants or rebel sympathizers. Through it all, access to markets was severely restricted when not cut off altogether by the uncertainty of what they would meet when they ventured out of their valley with fresh produce to sell. As we listened, far above us, across the valley, obscure forms moved through the edge of a forest. Though they were imprecise, blurry images to us, the villagers knew immediately whether they were NPA or the Army. On this occasion they were determined to be NPA, allowing the villagers to relax somewhat, relieved that they would not once again have to explain to the authorities who their visitors were that day and what they had been telling them.

The reality for their young men was to decide whether to join the government forces or the rebels, or to flee to Manila or perhaps beyond. And while uncertainty awaited anyone fleeing to the capital, the one compelling certainty it offered was the absence of any overt signs of war. Back in Manila, far from the spectacular beauty of the terraced mountains, but also far from the particular fragility that the armed conflict visited upon our hosts, the war once again seemed remote. Manila displayed all the disparities of wealth, pollution, and traffic snarls of a teeming Asian city, but it did not have the look of a war-torn country. Even on the front lines of this low-intensity war, for considerable stretches of time the word "war" would be out of place in those scenes of durable beauty and intervals of relative calm – even while war was and remains a predominant reality for affected villagers. And in the streets of Manila, anything but tranquil, the war was as remote as one could imagine it to be in a country routinely defined as being at war since the late 1960s. Questions about war certainly made sense to those with relatives and friends in the Cordilleras or in government and rebel forces, but on the streets of Manila, the Philippine wars – in addition to the marginal but persistent rebellion against the central government there is the Mindanao war for greater autonomy for the primarily Muslim region of a predominantly Christian country – lacked immediate context. Some would be surprised by the reference to "war," with very little overt mobilization or political posturing to highlight a state of war. But in fact the Philippine wars reflect much of the character of contemporary warfare. There are clearly the high intensity wars of Syria, Iraq,

Afghanistan, and parts of the Democratic Republic of the Congo (DRC), but many of the wars of the past quarter century are sporadic, often remote from the centres of power, but always debilitatingly disruptive to those who live within their pernicious orbits.

By contrast, for example, a visit to a mountain resort town in Mexico, a country not at war by the definition used here, but where the evidence of war was prominently paraded through the streets of the local town. Just a couple of hours southwest of Mexico City, on one of Valle de Bravo's seemingly endlessly sunny days, this quiet escape from the heat and bustle of the capital saw large convoys of military trucks and equipment, carrying hundreds of well-armed and outfitted troops, speeding through town and heading south to engage the cartels of Mexico's drug wars – promising another series of skirmishes in the Army's decade-old fight with the cartels. Mexico's drug war, between rival cartels as well as between government and cartel forces, has claimed tens of thousands of lives, but Mexico is not one of the ninety-nine wars listed in the quarter century of fighting of the post–Cold War era.

There is a logic to the inclusion of the Philippines and the exclusion of Mexico on the list of contemporary wars, but it does require an explanation. And the point is not to offer the "correct" definition of war; the point is to settle on a clear and consistent definition. The effort to document and understand trends in state-level violence or warfare in the post–Cold War era means it is obviously important to know what is being counted and what is not.

Defining Wars

The wars or armed conflicts of the late twentieth and early twenty-first centuries are eminently recognizable for their devastating and inevitable consequences, but that doesn't mean they are easily defined or counted.[1] Few contemporary wars are formally declared, and most do not follow from any conscious or official decision to go to war. And because fighting is frequently isolated to particular regions within a country and is often sporadic, as in the Cordilleras of the Philippines, it is not entirely obvious when a country is in fact "at war." There is no mistaking what is happening in Syria, but are Kenya and Thailand really at war? In the latter two cases, few citizens in the major population centres see or directly experience war, but after two decades of disturbances and clashes in Kenya and almost a decade of renewed fighting in southern Thailand, the human and material costs, as in other wars, are staggering. Since 1991 Kenya has seen ongoing ethnic clashes in the Great Rift

Valley, with land grievances going back to the British colonial period. In addition, there are the armed incursions by the Islamic militants from Somalia's al Shabaab. Declaring retaliation for the operations of Kenyan forces inside Somalia, al Shabaab claimed responsibility for the 2013 attack on the Westgate shopping mall in Nairobi, which killed at least 65 people and wounded more than 175, and the 2015 attack on Garissa University College in northeastern Kenya, killing 147 and wounding 79. In 2004, fighting erupted in Thailand when several armed rebel groups escalated long-standing political pressures among the southern Malay people, a population that is largely Muslim and does not identify as Thai, seeking independence from Thailand. The population in the region of instability in Thailand will understand only too clearly the sources and costs of the violence that regularly visits their communities, but the people of Bangkok are unlikely to think of their country as being at war. For Americans the war in Iraq ended the day their troops left the country; for Iraqis there is no end in sight.

So, to count and track modern warfare, and to understand trends, there needs to be a set of clear and measurable criteria for determining when a country has entered into a state of war and when the conditions of war no longer obtain.[2] The criteria used by researchers certainly vary, but the essential focus is on politically motivated conflict that reaches a certain threshold of violence. The widely respected Correlates of War Project,[3] begun in 1963 by the late J. David Singer, defines war as sustained combat that involves armed forces resulting in at least one thousand combat deaths per year.[4] The equally prominent University of Uppsala Conflict Data Program (UCDP), conducted in co-operation with the Peace Research Institute Oslo (PRIO), defines an armed conflict as "a contested incompatibility that concerns government and/or territory where the use of armed forces between two parties, at least one of which is the government of a state, results in at least 25 battle-related deaths"[5] each year, referred to as a minor armed conflict, and at least one thousand battle-related deaths per year for "war."[6] The Center for Systemic Peace (CSP) in the United States tracks "major episodes of political violence" involving more than five hundred directly related deaths.[7]

Drawing on these definitions, the *Project Ploughshares Armed Conflicts Report*[8] defines armed conflicts or wars according to four basic criteria:

1. The fighting is over a political conflict and is fundamentally in pursuit of political (as distinct from criminal) ends.
2. It involves armed combat by the armed forces of at least one state and the forces of one or more armed faction seeking a political end.

3. At least one thousand people (combatants and civilians) have been killed directly by the fighting during the course of the conflict.
4. There are ongoing combat deaths of at least twenty-five per year.

These criteria do not make a distinction between major and minor armed conflicts, but by adding a conflict to the list of current wars only after the one thousand deaths threshold is reached, the definition is weighted toward more substantial and sustained armed conflicts. The definition applies to interstate as well as intrastate conflicts.

By these criteria, at the close of 2014 there were twenty-nine wars (including Ukraine, which by mid-2014 had surpassed the one thousand deaths threshold) underway in twenty-six countries. All were intrastate armed conflicts – civil wars – and in each case combat deaths had risen beyond one thousand, armed forces were battling rebel or irregular forces of some description and capacity, and the issues over which they fought were political. In some instances, as in Syria, the violence was extreme, as combat deaths reached the tens of thousands annually, and the parties in combat were too many to count. In other cases, as in Kenya, Thailand, and the Philippines, the levels of fighting were much lower and sporadic, with combat deaths in the low one hundreds.

Levels of armed conflict or war (the terms are used interchangeably here) vary from year to year, but the objective is not to draw sharp distinctions between minor and major conflicts. Instead, the point is to include all instances in which the avenues for resolving a society's inevitable conflicts have clearly moved beyond the political realm to make armed confrontation a substantial and ongoing focus for addressing, or avoiding, political conflicts and grievances. The one thousand deaths threshold indicates there has been a major departure from political processes, and the annual twenty-five deaths threshold indicates a sustained resort to violence and force and an ongoing failure to return to nonviolent means of addressing political conflict. A war or armed conflict is taken to have ended when there is a formal ceasefire or peace agreement followed by a decline in the annual combat death toll to below twenty-five. Or, in the absence of a formal ceasefire, a war is deemed over after two years of dormancy, defined as two successive years in which the combat death toll is fewer than twenty-five per year.

The terms "war" and "armed conflict" obviously cover a very wide range of levels of violence and the counting method used here is bound to understate the overall level of global political violence. In Guinea-Bissau, for example, a series of upheavals in the late 1990s left hundreds dead and many tens of thousands displaced from their homes. Many analysts referred to the upheavals as a "civil war" and there is no doubt that those directly affected experienced it as war. The conflict prompted diplomatic and military interventions by the Economic Community of West African States,[9] but because it did not reach the threshold of one thousand combat deaths it is not included here among the wars or armed conflicts of the past twenty-five years. The intense five-day war in 2008 between Russia and Georgia over the territories of South Ossetia and Abkhazia is not recorded as a war because the known death toll did not reach one thousand, even though tens of thousands of people were displaced from their homes. Under the counting rules used here, a political armed conflict could continue for eight to nine years with annual combat deaths around the one hundred mark, which would obviously indicate a country mired in chronic political instability and experiencing grave threats to public safety, but it would still not be included on the list of wars. Any definition of war inevitably becomes arbitrary at the margins, so the objective is to be consistent – to adopt a definition that can be applied over time (in this case, the quarter century since the end of the Cold War) and thus tell us something about conflict trends.

Consistency is a greater challenge than one might expect, so it's worth acknowledging some additional definitional complications. Though the basic criterion for "war" is that the fighting is over political disputes, the term "political conflict" obviously falls well short of technical precision. The distinction between political and criminal violence is nevertheless discernable and, more to the point, important, even though in current civil wars the distinction is often obscured. It is common, for example, for armed bands or factions, as well as some government forces, to take advantage of extreme political instability and the "fog of war" to engage in criminal activity (e.g., theft, looting of natural resources, notably blood diamonds, extortion, ransom payments, and so on). In some instances these activities are pursued in order to fund political/military campaigns, whereas sometimes they are pursued primarily for personal enrichment, and the point at which they become predominantly criminal is obviously a matter of some judgment. For example, all of these kinds of criminal activity were present among both pro-government and anti-government forces in the long-running north-south civil war in Sudan that led ultimately to the separation of South Sudan. But throughout that war, it was still clear that the fundamental conflict was a political one in which the future shape and governance of the country was contested – it was not fundamentally a case of criminal behaviour motivated by greed.

On the other hand, there are also clear instances in which purely criminal violence not linked to political conflict escalates to the point that it takes on significant political overtones and complications. The

Mexican drug "war" already mentioned is perhaps the most prominent case in point. The fundamental dispute between the government and the drug lords is not political – it certainly engages politics, but the core dispute is not about contesting political visions or control of the country's governance apparatus. The drug war, even though it has killed many more people than some long-running wars have, nevertheless remains an extreme example of law enforcement authorities confronting organized crime, and the involvement of Mexico's armed forces is really an example of military aid to the civil law enforcement authority. Rising drug-related violence obviously reflects a weakened state and a deficient law enforcement capacity, and thus the conflict could also be seen as a failed state war (a category discussed later),[10] but the resulting violence is not a response to political grievance and is not guided by a political program or a set of politically motivated or defined objectives.

There are, however, other and quite different instances when major law enforcement challenges become defined as war, notably when they involve communal, that is, political, responses to failed state structures. Armed violence among pastoralist cattle herding communities in various parts of the Horn of Africa region regularly flares up in the absence of effective state law enforcement, but the community responses are politically defined efforts to establish communal security and territorial integrity. Among pastoralist groups in the Horn, cattle rustling is part theft and part tradition, but it is also heavily linked to communal identity and well-being. And inasmuch as it is a tradition that has been weaponized through the ready access to automatic weapons, violent clashes over cattle sometimes escalate to the level of warfare, with commensurate consequences. Disputes among pastoralist groups also inevitably involve issues of access to pasture lands and water for their cattle, and while such disputes should and would be settled by the rule of law if the central governments had the capacity for the administration of justice in remote regions, they frequently don't. Pastoralist groups find they have to pursue these disputes on their own. These are conflicts that engage questions of basic political rights, communal identity and well-being, and the role of such communities within the national political framework. Consequently, such conflicts, when they pass the threshold of one thousand combat deaths, are included in lists of armed conflicts or wars.

So, while political and criminal violence cannot always be neatly separated, the dynamics of each are quite different. Even where criminal violence is closely linked to political conflict and violence – as in the emergence of piracy off the Somali coast – the political violence inevitably has very different roots, and thus calls for very different remedies.

Counting Wars

In line with the definition used here – wars being political conflicts that have turned violent, involve state military forces, have reached a threshold of one thousand combat deaths, and have continued at the rate of at least twenty-five combat deaths per year – ninety-nine wars were fought in the past twenty-five years (twenty-nine of which, as already noted, are still ongoing in early 2015). These precise numbers, as will become clear, imply much more precision than is actually possible. At the beginning of this period, 1989 and the ending of the Cold War, there were thirty-five wars underway, belying, by the way, the notion that the Cold War presided over a more stable global political order. How we got from thirty-five hot wars at the end of the Cold War to the current twenty-nine (a modest but noteworthy decline of 17 per cent) is a long tale of extraordinary suffering that continues. The statistics are straightforward. In the twenty-five years from 1989 through 2014, sixty-four new wars began, roughly 2.5 per year on average, adding to the thirty-five wars already underway and bringing the total to ninety-nine. Of those, seventy ended, bringing the total of remaining wars down to twenty-nine (ten of the sixty-four new wars were restarts of wars that had ended earlier).

Recall some of the thirty-five armed conflicts that were underway back in 1989 (on the territories of thirty countries). Europe's sole war at the time was in the United Kingdom – namely the "troubles" in Northern Ireland, clearly a politically motivated conflict that involved the armed forces of the state and had claimed well over one thousand lives. In Africa, political conflicts had reached armed conflict status in, among other places, Chad, the DRC, Mozambique, Somalia, and Sudan. Chad's long-running war finally ended in 2013. Mozambique came to a negotiated peace in 1993, the start of a period of economic growth and political stability. The other three wars, plus seven others, continue in Africa. In the Middle East, wars against the Kurds were underway in Iran and Iraq in 1989. The Iran-Iraq War had been underway throughout the 1980s, but was finally coming to an end, while the Lebanese civil war continued for more than another decade, though at reduced levels of intensity in the late 1990s. The Israel-Palestine War, begun in 1948, was still underway and obviously continues to this day (continuing to see combat deaths well beyond the war-defining threshold of twenty-five per year – in 2013 it was more than two thousand), with periodic escalations, as in the summer of 2014. There were two wars in Indonesia at the end of the Cold War, a number that swelled to six separate internal wars (East Timor, West Papua, Molucca Island, Aceh, Kalimantan, and Sulawesi) by the turn of the millennium. Fortunately, that story doesn't end there. By 2005, every one of those wars had ended, and Indonesia now enjoys a level of stability not seen in the previous three decades. Afghanistan was also deep into war in 1989, and its story does not follow Indonesia's trajectory (more on Afghanistan in chapter 9).

The Western Hemisphere is another compelling story of wars ending. In 1989, there were five wars underway (Colombia, El Salvador, Guatemala, Nicaragua, and Peru). Two years later, Panama was added briefly to the list, and five years later Haiti was added. Today, only Colombia remains at war in the Western Hemisphere, and in early 2015 the main opposition movement, the Farc, undertook a cessation of hostilities, and the government agreed to talks toward a mutual ceasefire.[11] Haiti, in particular, illustrates the truth that the absence of war does not guarantee the presence of peace. The most recent manifestation of war ended in 2007, but in 2010 came the earthquake. Well over two hundred thousand people died and more than that were injured, and much of the country's modest infrastructure and housing was in ruins. And then came cholera – notably brought on by peacekeeping forces.

There was a spike in new wars in the first post–Cold War decade, with total armed conflicts peaking at forty-four in the mid-1990s – the focus being states formerly within the orbit of the Soviet Union (Albania, Armenia-Azerbaijan, Georgia) and linked to the break-up of Yugoslavia. Since then there has been a fairly steady decline in global warfare, going from forty-one in 2000 to twenty-four in 2010. In 2011, the total moved up to twenty-six as a result of the Arab Spring and the addition of Libya and Syria to the list of states at war. In 2013, the Central African Republic, Mali, and Egypt all passed the one thousand deaths threshold and were thus added to the list of conflicts, but Chad was removed from the list following two years of conflict deaths staying below twenty-five, bringing the total at the end of 2013 to twenty-eight. Then in 2014 the conflict in Ukraine escalated to war status, bringing the count to twenty-nine wars in twenty-six states. The Philippines is the location for two wars, and India has three separate wars on its territory; hence the number of wars is higher than the number of states in armed conflict. Almost one-quarter of the armed conflicts that were underway in 1989 are still active today, testifying to the longevity of contemporary war. Of the current twenty-nine conflicts, eleven have been active for less than a decade, but eighteen have been underway for more than a decade – and of those, twelve have been ongoing for more than two decades, and six for more than three decades.

Of the ninety-nine wars fought during the past quarter century, thirty-five were in Africa, twenty-seven in the Asia-Pacific region, eleven in Europe, eight in the Western Hemisphere, and eighteen in the Middle East. As a percentage of states at war in a particular region, the Middle East was the most conflict intensive region. In 2015 the global distribution of warfighting stood at ten in Africa, nine in Asia, two in Europe (the Russian Caucasus and Ukraine), one in the Western Hemisphere, and seven in the Middle East (still the most conflict intensive region).

Several organizations and research groups compile data on contemporary wars and there is, as one should expect, broad agreement on current conflict trends, with differences in numbers largely explained by varying definitions of when a war is to be counted. The CSP examines the performance of the global system through three fundamental themes: governance, development, and conflict.[12] A particularly telling measure of global system performance is obviously the level of political violence and the trends in armed conflict. The CSP offers an overall measure of the magnitude of warfare through a complex evaluation of each conflict's "comprehensive effects on the state or states directly affected by the warfare, including numbers of combatants and casualties, affected area, dislocated population, and extent of infrastructure damage." CSP research shows a significant and steady increase in "societal warfare," essentially civil wars, during the Cold War. This steady increase in the magnitude of civil war since the 1950s is largely explained by the interference of superpowers, which provided military or material support and in turn led to "a general tendency toward longer, more protracted, wars during that period." But the CSP reports that by its figures the overall magnitude of warfare globally has decreased by over 60 per cent since peaking in the mid-1980s, falling by 2010 to its lowest level since 1961.[13] Its count of individual wars (which it defines as political violence that has produced more than five hundred directly related deaths) indicated that at the end of 2013 there were twenty-four "countries experiencing major armed conflicts within their territory" – all of which were societal (intrastate) warfare. The CSP, like other sources, saw a post–Cold War peak in wars in the early 1990s, when "nearly thirty per cent of the countries in the world were experiencing some form of major political violence." In mid-2014, there were twenty-three countries experiencing major armed conflict within their territories – that represents about 12 per cent of states. The CSP also confirms the relatively low level of interstate, as opposed to intrastate, wars, although it records more interstate wars since it includes decolonization wars and some internationalized civil wars as interstate wars.

The Human Security Report (HSR) at Canada's Simon Fraser University has been reporting a significant drop in the number of wars, relying on data from the University of Uppsala Conflict Data Program (UCDP):

"During 2012 – the most recent year for which there are data – the number of conflicts being waged around the world dropped sharply, from 37 to 32.[14] High-intensity conflicts have declined by more than half since the end of the Cold War, while terrorism, genocide and homicide numbers are also down." The HSR confirms the overall decline in armed conflicts since the early 1990s. From a peak of just over fifty armed conflicts at the start of the 1990s, the number declines to just under forty by 2011 (about a 20 per cent drop). In fact, though the numbers are fairly volatile, HSR shows a slight increase in the total number of conflicts since 2002, from thirty to the upper thirties by 2011, but this is due primarily to the way in which the data counts low-intensity conflicts. The HSR shows a higher total number of wars than does the Ploughshares data primarily relied on here, due in particular to the way conflicts are counted by the UCDP. It records a state-based low-intensity conflict for a given calendar year if there were twenty-five or more battle deaths in that year, even if the thousand deaths threshold has not been reached. Thus, the UCDP data identifies more conflicts than does the Ploughshares data, the latter requiring the cumulative total of deaths to reach one thousand before it is recorded as a war. In the case of high-intensity conflicts, those with one thousand battle deaths per year, the UCDP data shows them to be in sharp decline since the late 1990s (more than a 50 per cent drop).

The HSR/UCDP data also shows that globally, battle deaths from state-based conflicts have reduced sharply since the mid-1990s when they reached a total of about eighty thousand in a single year to just over twenty thousand in 2011. But after 2011 those numbers increased significantly due to wars in Syria and Libya. The HSR includes a category of "internationalized intra-state conflicts" – conflicts that involve foreign troops. The number has increased, although there were still fewer than ten in 2011. Locations included Afghanistan, Iraq, Rwanda, Somalia, Uganda, and Yemen.

For 2012, the UCDP reports thirty-two armed conflicts (minimum of twenty-five combat deaths) in twenty-six locations, down from thirty-seven in 2011.[15] Six of those wars had more than one thousand battle deaths (the same as in 2011). Combat deaths were estimated at 37,941. Syria accounted for 15,055 of those, although annual combat deaths in Syria averaged well over fifty thousand in subsequent years. "Overall, the 2000s has been the least conflict-ridden decade since the 1970s," says the Uppsala project. While the Ploughshares data shows ninety-nine armed conflicts since the end of the Cold War, the UCDP shows a total of 141. Of these, ninety-two were minor and forty-nine (35 per cent) were major. The annual number peaked at fifty-two in 1991 and 1992 but then declined to thirty-two in 2012. Of these twenty-six were minor and six (just under 20 per cent) were major. The total numbers are higher than those reported by Ploughshares because of Ploughshares' higher threshold for the onset of a war (cumulatively one thousand combat deaths), but the overall trend shown is the same – the numbers peak in the early 1990s (due largely to conflicts related to the break-up of the former Soviet Union and the former Yugoslavia), then decline steadily to 2011–12, when the trend reverses.

Civil Wars

By far the most common type of contemporary war is the *intrastate war*, which is a war internal to a particular state (a civil war) and involves the armed forces of that state in battle against rebel or insurgent forces. Of the ninety-nine wars fought in the past quarter century, ninety-three were wars within states – and all wars at the end of 2014 were civil wars.

Some civil wars have seemed more like international wars, with heavy fighting by American and other forces in Iraq and Afghanistan, for example, but all civil wars have significant international dimensions, and a few have a lot more than others. In a civil war, many states other than the one directly in conflict are typically also involved, sometimes heavily so. Neighbouring states sometimes give sanctuary to insurgents or assist them with financial aid and support them in other ways. Outside states supply arms, either to the government or the insurgents. International humanitarian agencies assist victims. The current wars in Afghanistan and Iraq are counted as civil wars, even though both obviously had major interstate episodes when US-led coalitions attacked Afghanistan and Iraq respectively in 2001 and 2003. In both cases, the wars transitioned back to civil wars with extraordinary and continuing levels of outside intervention. But they are not international wars between states, and they are also not strictly civil wars with only the usual level of international involvements. Hence, they are characterized here as multilateral wars – a category that also includes multilateral engagements in Kuwait-Iraq, Bosnia-Herzegovina, Serbia over Kosovo, Haiti, and Libya. These multilateral operations are distinct from multilateral peacekeeping (a distinction to which we will return in chapter 5).

In civil wars the fighting is typically intermittent and of widely varying levels of intensity. Afghanistan, Iraq, and Syria are obviously not in that category; they experience persistent and high levels of armed clashes and attacks. Rwanda went from political tension to unprecedented levels of violence and back down again in a very short period. The two wars in the Philippines are examples of ongoing but low-level conflicts, with annual combat deaths often below one hundred – but, of course, with political, economic, and social disruption well out of proportion to the intensity of action on their actual battlefields.

Civil wars follow three basic types: state control, state formation, and state failure wars.[16] In state control wars the focus of the fighting is obviously to gain control of the state – rebels fight to overthrow the existing regime and replace it with new rulers or to open up the political process to permit elections (the wars in Syria, Afghanistan, and Iraq are state control wars). In state formation wars the objective is either to change the shape of the state through secession and the establishment of a new state (South Sudan and Eritrea and the new states that emerged out of the former Yugoslavia), or to change the way a state functions by seeking a measure of autonomy, recognition, or self-rule for particular regions or communities within it (the conflict over Kashmir, earlier Shia uprisings in Iraq, the fighting in Mindanao). State failure wars typically involve domestic chaos and armed violence, frequently localized and with neither state control nor state formation aims. Sometimes they are brought on by persistent and debilitating state control and/or state formation wars. State failure wars are thus conflicts in which the armed conflict is about more local issues and disputes involving violence in the absence of effective government control and services.

The term state failure, or more commonly "failed state" is not without controversy. A failed state is generally understood as a state experiencing advanced deficiencies in governance, law enforcement, security, and the delivery of basic services, combined with and resulting in a broad sense of the illegitimacy of the government of the day and public institutions. The controversy stems in part from the implication that the failure is all due to an internal lack of will or competence. In fact, such conditions have multiple roots, many of them external, regional and international, and due to systems and practices stacked to the advantage of external actors. The point of the "state failure war" designation in this context is to identify armed conflicts that are not linked to efforts to gain control of the state or to re-shape it but are focused instead on efforts to manage or exploit local conflicts which derive from the lack of effective state management or a state presence due to lack of capacity.

Thus, as already noted, pastoralist communities in East Africa, for example, often live well beyond the reach of the state. There are virtually no state security services or institutions present and no political means of mediating disputes over access to grazing lands and water or of settling disputes related to cattle raiding. Communities come into conflict and, with access to small arms, there is an almost inevitable escalation of violence – it is political violence (and clearly distinct from criminal violence and organized crime), but it is violence over local issues, and the parties do not have state control or state formation objectives. In Sudan, the decades-long, largely north-south civil war led to state failure conflicts between and within major ethnic communities due in large part to the complete absence of the rule of law. In some cases, there is more than one type of armed conflict present within a country. In Syria, for example, in addition to the central conflict over who controls the state, there are plenty of internecine conflicts and battles in a war zone with hundreds of armed groups. In other words, the Syrian conflict is essentially a state control conflict, but with obvious state failure elements. Similarly, the primary violence in the DRC is about control of the government, but there are also localized violent clashes based on local ethnic or territorial disputes – hence the war in DRC is part state control and part state failure conflict. In the Philippines, the resistance of the NPA is a state control conflict, but the secessionist campaign of rebels in Mindanao is a state formation conflict.

Half of all intrastate wars in the past twenty-five years were and are fought primarily in pursuit of state control objectives, a third focused on state formation objectives, and just under a quarter reflected failed state conditions. That comes to more than 100 per cent because at least 10 per cent of wars fit more than one of the three basic categories. Of the twenty-nine wars ongoing at the end of 2014 (by the definition used here), thirteen were state control, eleven state formation, and five failed state wars, but of those, nine included a combination of these elements.

With ten African states involved in intrastate war in 2014, one in five African states was at war – a devastatingly high level of armed conflict, but still the lowest level of any time in the past quarter century. In five of those the fighting was primarily over control of the state (Algeria, Central African Republic, DRC, Somalia, Sudan). Three were explicitly failed state wars (Kenya, Nigeria, South Sudan) in which the fighting linked more clearly to the lack of capacity of the state to maintain order and politically mediate local conflicts than to any broad objective of either regime change or state re-formation. Notably, only two of Africa's current wars (Ethiopia and Mali) can be said to be about state formation. This is especially noteworthy because Africa has typically been regarded as a continent carved up into states with boundaries to suit imperial interests rather than local coherence, with the assumption that this colonial legacy is behind much of its enduring conflict. But in fact only Ethiopia, which faces a small, for the moment, rebellion from its Ogaden Somali population seeking greater autonomy, and Mali, facing a Tuareg secessionist or autonomy movement in the north, are now the locations of overtly state formation conflicts. The conflict in Somalia also includes state formation elements – the northern part of the country has since 1991 functioned as an independent state (Somaliland) – though it is not internationally recognized as a state. Puntland in the northeast also functions autonomously, and it is not clear how these quasi-separatist states will link to Somalia as a whole once the fighting ends. Until recently Sudan was a further example, but South Sudan has successfully separated, and while war conditions continue in both Sudanese states, elements of the conflicts are now interstate (ongoing border and other disputes with Sudan) and state failure (factional fighting within the south due largely to the new government's lack of capacity to maintain order, address local grievances, and be convincingly inclusive). But in several instances, state control and state formation conflicts also included state failure elements. Thus in seven cases (DRC, Ethiopia, Kenya, Nigeria, Somalia, Sudan, and South Sudan) state failure was a factor.

Asia's nine wars in early 2015 (Afghanistan, Burma, Pakistan, Thailand, two in the Philippines, and three in India) also include all three types. State control is the primary agenda in Afghanistan, the rebellion of the NPA in the Philippines, and the Maoist uprisings in India. State formation objectives were primary in the conflicts in Kashmir and the northeast of India, in Mindanao in the Philippines, and in south Thailand. In Burma the government signed a ceasefire agreement with the Kachin Independence Organization, the last major rebel holdout in a state formation conflict, but continued violence against Muslims (a state failure dynamic) meant that combat deaths still crossed the twenty-five per year threshold so that the state of war has existed since 1988, but at a greatly diminished rate.

In the Middle East, five conflicts centred on state control (Egypt, Iraq, Libya, Syria, and Yemen) and in the other two (Israel and Turkey) the primary issue was state formation. Conflicts in Europe in the Caucasus region of Russia and Ukraine were state formation wars. The only remaining war in the Western Hemisphere, in Colombia, focused on state control, but it appeared to be winding down toward a ceasefire and ongoing talks, although clashes still produced deaths beyond the twenty-five deaths threshold.

It is easy to convey the sense that civil wars are orderly affairs, each with two sides and fitting nicely into one, or perhaps two, of the conflict categories. But, of course, the opposite is the reality. Any country experiencing regular political violence, even at the low end of the levels that meet the definition of war, is a country in political turmoil, or at least with regions in a very bad state. Behind every killing is a high level of political dysfunction, visceral enmity, communal suspicion, and debilitating levels of public insecurity in affected regions. And rarely are the conflicts neatly divided into two sides – the government and the rebels. Governments battling insurgencies are rarely of a single mind, and often they are not of a single force as pro-government but largely independent and undisciplined militias abound. Governments are also typically politically factionalized as some want a harsher crackdown on dissidents and others want to explore more political engagement. And opposition movements are typically fractured in multiple ways. Sometimes they form their own coalitions of the willing to operate as united fronts, sometimes each group pursues its particular agenda, and sometimes they fight each other rather than the government. Forging peace out of these disparate forces and interests is obviously daunting – helping to explain why wars last as long as they do.

Global terrorism is routinely described as the focus of a "war on terror," but terrorism is not identified here as a type of war. Terrorism is a tactic used in many armed conflicts or wars in very specific locations and settings, sometimes by governments and sometimes by non-state groups, and there are also terror attacks in non-war contexts, again by both non-state and state actors. Deliberate attacks on civilians that are designed to intimidate or to spread a sense of terror throughout the civilian population are violations of the laws of war and the laws of any jurisdiction with even the most minimal commitment to the rule of law. The term "war on terror" was used by Washington at one time to signal an overall military-centred strategy for countering or preventing anti-Western acts of terror in many parts of the world. The scholar Melissa Zisler makes the essential point that those who carry out acts of terror in urban non-war settings commit murder, including mass murder, by any standard of law, and they ought not, even implicitly, be accorded the status of "enemy" combatants in a war – the very status they are seeking – afforded by the term "war on terror." To commit terrorism is in non-war settings to commit criminal acts that need to be confronted as such, through policing and intelligence operations.[17]

Most acts of terror are committed in war settings. In the first week of January 2015, the week of the *Charlie Hebdo* attack in Paris that killed twelve and dominated the news, Boko Haram in Nigeria kidnapped forty boys and young men in the town of Malari,[18] two suicide bombers of the Islamic State attacked a mosque in the Iraqi town of Al-Jubba, killing twelve in the initial blast and at least as many in the firefight that followed,[19] and a suicide bomber detonated explosives alongside a military convoy in Mogadishu killing four Somali soldiers.[20] In another attack out-side a war zone in that same week, a suicide bomber in Istanbul detonated her explosive outside a police station, killing herself and a police officer.[21]

The Global Terrorism Index report for 2013 says 17,958 people were killed in terrorist attacks in 2013, a 61 per cent increase over 2012, and 82 per cent of the total in 2013 occurred in five countries (all at war): Afghanistan, Iraq, Nigeria, Pakistan, and Syria. Four groups were the pri-mary perpetrators: the Taliban, Boko Haram, Islamic State, and al Qaeda. The CSP reports that there have been 32,000 people killed in high casu-alty terrorist bombings since the 9/11 attacks in the United States. Almost 60 per cent of those killings occurred in Iraq. Afghanistan, Pak-istan, Syria, and Nigeria account for most of the rest. Islamist militants have carried out extraordinarily brazen attacks of mass murder in Europe, but they have not established a "global reach" and the over-whelming majority of their attacks have occurred within the Middle East and along the Muslim/non-Muslim fault lines in Africa. Of course, terror-ism is to some extent in the eye of the beholder – and some behold drone attacks that kill civilians in that light. For example, the CSP reports that in Pakistan from 2009 to 2011 there were sixty-nine high casualty terror-ist bombs that killed 2,642 people. In the same period in Pakistan, there were thirty-two "high casualty drone attacks" that killed 798 people.[22]

Combatting terrorism in non-war settings mandates the attention of civilian police and homeland security agencies and institutions, as well as diplomatic, intelligence, and social policy institutions. Whether such agencies are sufficiently resourced is a question that gets resolved through the usual domestic process of choosing among competing demands for public resources. Combatting terrorism in war settings, its most prominent manifestation, requires, to put it perhaps too simply, accelerated attention to war prevention and war termination. But to label the struggle to eradicate or reduce terrorism in either context as a "war on terror" does not make that struggle more effective.

Interstate Wars

Wars between states can be divided into two basic types. The term *inter-state war* is used here to indicate a war in which two or more states, unable or unwilling to settle their differences through diplomacy, elect to go to war with each other to override diplomacy and force a political outcome that each state hopes will turn out to be advantageous. There were only six such wars in the past quarter century: Eritrea-Ethiopia, Vietnam-Cambodia, Armenia-Azerbaijan, Iran-Iraq, Iraq-Kuwait, and

Israel-Lebanon. In other words, less than 10 per cent of all wars were fought between states. Today there are no exclusively state-to-state wars, and there have not been any such wars since the 1999–2000 Eritrea-Ethiopia War – and to say that particular war resolved nothing and cost what neither could afford is to seriously understate the futility of that episode of mutual destruction.

But naming the Eritrea-Ethiopia War as the last interstate war ignores the attacks by the United States on Afghanistan in 2001 and Iraq in 2003 or operations such as the NATO attacks on Libya in 2011. The initial American attacks on Afghanistan and Iraq, supported by other states, were certainly attacks by one state on another in order to deal with a dispute between them, but they both came in the context of civil wars and thus quickly transitioned to quite another kind of war. Neither of the succeeding wars was fought to settle disputes between and among countries. Instead, they both became efforts by a group of states, via multilateral coalitions of the willing, to shape the course of events within states caught up in chronic internal political and armed conflict – and the "spectacular" failure of both wars is the most dramatic current measure of the limits to force. These kinds of multilateral wars are distinct from UN-mandated and UN-commanded peacekeeping or peace support operations in support of ceasefires or peace agreements. While the ad hoc coalitions of the willing that conduct multilateral wars do sometimes operate with the explicit consent of the United Nations Security Council (as in Afghanistan *after* the initial invasion), they sometimes do not (as in NATO's air war in the former Yugoslavia on behalf of Kosovo).

Multilateral wars have been both prominent and highly controversial. The 1990 Iraq-Kuwait War gave way to Operation Desert Storm in early 1991 in order to expel Iraq from Kuwait. The 2001 US attack on Afghanistan became a multilateral operation in 2002 after the UN authorized the establishment of the International Security Assistance Force to support the new post-Taliban Afghan government (although some US Forces continued to operate independently in Afghanistan). The US 2003 invasion of Iraq was a multilateral war inasmuch as other states joined the US in military operations in support of the new post-Saddam government. There were the two NATO operations in the former Yugoslavia, bombing on behalf of Bosnia-Herzegovina and Kosovo, two separate military operations in Haiti, and the NATO-led Libya bombing campaign – for a total of eight in the past quarter century.

War and Global Armed Violence

The devastation of war takes its place within the broader panoply of human on human violence. Politically driven armed conflict or war is but one manifestation of armed violence. Organized crime, gang violence, murder, and suicide collectively far outpace war in producing violent deaths (even global traffic deaths are many times higher than direct combat deaths in wars[23]). Though deaths by murder substantially exceed war deaths,[24] the comparison fails to consider the full impact of war. While its political and social benefits are obviously few (though there is no denying the economic benefits of war and war preparations to selective industries and sectors), war's economic and human costs are literally immeasurable (more on this in chapter 5). Whereas annual combat deaths are counted in the tens of thousands, the indirect violent deaths due to war are counted in the hundreds of thousands. Millions of people are displaced by war, livelihoods for others are cut off, healthcare is nonexistent for large elements of war-affected populations, and among all these, death rates escalate significantly. Measured in premature deaths, wasted resources, deferred economic development, political instability, human rights abuses that escalate in civil war situations, and enduring psychological harm, all war remains a special kind of premeditated, politically directed inhumanity toward humanity that is different from all other forms of violence and requires its own particular remedies. The overall rate of warfare in the past quarter century is much reduced from the rates of slaughter in the first seven decades of the twentieth century, yet war persists in a variety of types and places, leaving a wake of destruction and debilitation that exacts a literally incalculable price.

2

Wars and Rumours of Wars

How Wars Start

CIVIL WARS ARE HARD TO START. It happened on average more than twice a year in the quarter century from 1989 through 2014, but when governments try to shut down political opposition through force, or when dissidents try to sustain violent confrontation of governments, the challenges are formidable. At least initially, governments have the advantage. They, after all, hold the monopoly on the resort to force and are thus already in possession of the basic means to exercise it, but the political and social/psychological foundations for mounting major police and military operations against their own citizens are not as readily constructed. On the other hand, dissidents trying to build popular support within a citizenry that is likely to retain a core deference toward the state, even an oppressive state, may find it just as daunting to establish the legitimacy of rebellion to the point of violent revolution.

The first order of business is to try to control the political discourse. Richard Jackson, an internationally recognized New Zealand expert and scholar in peace and conflict studies, summarizes research on controlling the discourse of conflict.[1] The process naturally involves the creation of the "other" and the reinterpretation of history to highlight differences and rivalries. In some cases, "ethnic entrepreneurs" set out to develop a "discourse of imminent threat and danger" directed toward particular ethnic, geographic, or religious communities. Part of the objective is "overcoming social and cultural inhibitions and norms that prohibit political and personal violence." The more claims of threat and danger draw on long-held and widely understood grievances, the more they resonate. Distrust and suspicion based on ethnicity, religion, or class are already likely to be present in any context of rising tension and are thus available to be exploited in any campaign to justify and build sustained support for either violent repression or resistance.

Governments are inclined to default to the conventions of official propaganda and portray all opposition forces as "criminal elements," "foreign elements," or "terrorists" and to question the loyalty of particular communities or organizations. Civil opposition groups in turn portray their governments as undemocratic, autocratic, and, especially, prejudiced against a particular region, ethnicity, or religion. The charge of government prejudice appeals not only to opposition to the government, but also to support for and loyalty toward one's own community. Both sides are at pains to persuade their respective constituencies that there are no alternatives, that the other side is illegitimate and understands only the language of force, and that honour and survival itself now demand direct action.

Along with the work of social/psychological/political persuasion, there is the daunting job of assembling the physical capacity to fight. States turn to loyal standing forces. Dissidents face the greater challenge of trying to muster material support – money, supplies of basic arms, and the particular challenge of acquiring steady supplies of munitions – but access to the latter two is made easier by the refusal of states to impose any real restraint on the international arms market. Dissidents also need to develop a disciplined command structure and introduce mechanisms for effective communication with, and at least minimal accountability to, their constituency. Of course, in some cases there is the convenience of being accountable only to God. But in most states and temporal communities, where putative leaders haven't yet convincingly equated their own interests and desires with the will of their particular deity, the leadership's appeal is to the people and that usually requires some means of involving the people and continuing to persuade them that the leadership acts in the service of their interests.

Capacity for sustained fighting also requires the support of neighbours. States fighting insurgencies depend on their neighbours to at the very least not actively support the dissidents. But insurgents need and solicit help from neighbouring states. That may be as simple as relying on the inability of a neighbouring state to manage effective border controls, thus not preventing people and materiel from crossing borders. More active support from neighbours can come in other ways, including safe haven for fighters, munitions pipelines, and financial backing.

Wars take effort, resources, political co-operation, and a range of leadership and logistical skills. Having these all come together at the right time and in the right places to spawn civil strife to the point of producing one thousand combat deaths is not easy. Yet over the past quarter century, there has been a steady string of such "successes" (success in mounting a fight, but certainly not in prevailing in that fight).

Though wars and rumours of war are ubiquitous, the particular conditions that cause wars or, more accurately, allow political conflict to be transformed into violent armed conflict are impossible to isolate. The general conditions out of which wars regularly erupt are common enough, but in most cases those conditions still do not lead to war. Gareth Evans, the former Australian Foreign Minister and former head of the International Crisis Group, cautions against universalizing the roots and causes of armed conflict. The actual circumstances that give rise to particular instances of armed violence are always context specific. "For every case of religious or ethnic or linguistic difference erupting in communal violence," he says,

> there are innumerably more cases around the world of people and groups of different cultures and backgrounds living harmoniously side by side; for every economic grievance that erupts in catastrophic violence there are innumerably more that don't; for every instance of economic greed – for control of resources or the levers of government – generating or fuelling outright conflict, there are innumerably more that don't.[2]

War and peace are not driven by an unseen hand of political/military determinism. The language of "root causes" warrants a generous measure of caution – not caution about identifying the roots of war, but about assigning specific causation. At the same time, of course, if governments are to develop policies and practices for war prevention, they need to be in possession of some reasonably clear evidence and understanding regarding the sources of war. In other words, they need to have some means of identifying the conditions and circumstances under which war is more likely to occur and persist. That means trying to develop a consistent and reasonably objective capacity to isolate the structural and social/political/economic conditions that heighten the risks of war and, conversely, to identify the conditions that should be fostered in order to significantly reduce the risks of war. So the relevant question about the Arab Spring is not only what were the conditions that led to revolt and political upheaval in Egypt, Libya, and Syria, but also why did political revolt lead quickly to war in Libya and Syria but not in Egypt? Under what conditions are political instability and deep social cleavages most likely to tip political conflict and violent clashes into levels of violence that warrant the designation of "war"?

As a broad generalization, perhaps the kind that Gareth Evans warns against, research suggests that armed conflict is more likely to occur when communities are imbued with deeply held dissatisfaction with the status quo, when they have access to physical and political/social resources for violence, and when they are convinced or can credibly claim that such violence is their only real hope for change. The late Thomas Ohlson of the Stockholm International Peace Research Institute put it this way: "The onset of intra-state armed conflict requires a combination of three things: Reasons in the form of motivating grievances, Resources in the form of capabilities and opportunity, and Resolve in the form of a perception that nothing short of violence will allow you to achieve your goals."[3] Alex J. Bellamy of the University of Queensland and the Asia Pacific Centre for the Responsibility to Protect adds issues of identity – when political grievances are linked to particular communities and regions, the intensity of the grievances is deepened, and calculations about their capacity for force are more optimistic.[4] Hence, these four broad categories offer a useful framework through which the drivers of armed conflict can be addressed:

1. the presence of heightened political, economic, and social grievances (grievance);
2. intergroup competition and conflict that reflects deep cleavages or disunity within a society (identity);
3. political/psychological preparedness and physical capacity for systematically violating human rights and for a sustained resort to force and violence (capacity); and
4. the perceived absence of effective mechanisms through which to credibly air grievances and advance collective objectives, and thus for non-violent conflict management and accommodation (the lack of alternatives).

The combination of grievance, identity, capacity, and lack of alternatives does not speak to the broad range of sources of political conflict; instead, these four conditions mark the transition from political conflict to sustained violent confrontation. So the question of how wars start is a not a question about the myriad sources of political conflict, but is instead the question of how political conflict that is ubiquitous and present in generous measure in all societies is converted in particular instances into violent armed conflict.

Grievances

Prosperity, or rather the lack of it, turns out to be one of the most reliable indicators or predictors of armed conflict.[5] Quite simply, says Thania Paffenholz, a senior researcher at the Centre on Conflict, Peacebuilding, and Development at the Graduate Institute of International and Development Studies, "the lower the GDP per capita in a country, the higher the likelihood of armed conflict."[6] That's not a claim that poverty *causes* conflict, only that there is a correlation between them. As Paffenholz also points out, there are a lot more low-income countries that are not at war than are. Some low-income countries experience precipitous economic decline without suffering the kind of turmoil that has sometimes visited more economically successful countries. Part of the difference is the resilience of the "social compact." She points to the presence of formal and informal mechanisms to address grievances in ways that allow them to be resolved or managed without recourse to violence. Countries with that kind of institutional infrastructure can experience economic crises and still avoid violence because they also maintained credible alternatives to it. One brief review of the literature on economics and armed conflict indicates the complexity and imprecision of the question, "Does poverty cause conflict?" While many of the "world's poorest countries are riven by armed conflict," and while poverty, conflict, and underdevelopment set up a cycle of dysfunction in which each element of the cycle is exacerbated by the other, it is also the case that internal conflict can afflict more affluent countries – like Northern Ireland and the former Yugoslavia. Since many poor countries are not at war, it's clear that poverty is not inevitably destabilizing. In fact, "economic growth can destabilize, as the wars in countries afflicted by an abundance of particular natural resources appear to show."[7]

Other reviews of the literature make the general point that countries recently burdened by armed conflict are more vulnerable to renewed conflict when economies falter. That has particular implications for Africa, where economic deprivation and recent armed conflict are both present in a relatively high number of states, making the continent especially vulnerable when economic shocks occur. It's not surprising that weak economies might result in weak state structures with reduced capacity to manage conflict and increased risk of violent conflict. When that happens, economic growth is further impeded and the cycle is reinforced. A high reliance on the export of primary commodities also heightens the risk of violent conflict. And when economic growth stalls and unemployment rises, young men may find more opportunity in rebel groups than in the labour market.[8]

Of the ninety-four countries in the bottom half of the 2014 *Human Development Index*, forty-eight, or just over 50 per cent, experienced war on their territory at some point in the past twenty-five years (but, of course, almost half did not). Only 20 per cent of the ninety-three countries in the top half of the index (including all the states caught up in armed conflict as a result of the break-up of the Soviet Union and Yugoslavia) experienced war in the past quarter century. And only three countries (Israel, the United Kingdom, and Croatia) out of the forty-seven ranked "very high" on the index experienced war. The overwhelming majority of contemporary wars have been fought on the territories of states at the low end of the human development scale (Libya and Ukraine being notable recent exceptions).

A country's income level is a very strong indicator of its risk of being involved in persistent armed conflict. Low-income countries lack the capacity to create conditions conducive to the social, political, and economic welfare of their people. They notably lack the means to establish public institutions of participatory governance capable of reliably addressing grievances and mediating conflict. And when economic inequality is linked to differences between identity groups, the correlation to armed conflict is even stronger. Group based inequalities are especially destabilizing.[9] It's important to emphasize, however, that while the emergence of armed conflict is closely tied to local conditions, those local conditions are heavily shaped by external factors. International economic conditions and trends, regional security conditions, and the interests and actions of the major powers (in short, globalization)[10] combine with internal economic/social/political/communal circumstances to create conditions conducive to both political and armed conflict.

Both scarcity and abundance in natural resources can increase the risks of armed conflict. Resource scarcity in some instances foments violent competition. For example, the impact of climate change is evident in Somalia and Sudan (i.e., Darfur) where the boundaries between arid and semi-arid or cultivatable lands are shifting and producing conflicts – in competition for that declining land resource and also because communities are forced to leave their traditional home areas and encroach upon the traditional homelands of other groups. The point is not that climate change "causes" armed conflict. Resource scarcity can, after all, also lead to conflict that elicits co-operation. States of the Nile River basin, for example, have certainly experienced multiple differences and political conflicts related to water, but co-operative, if complicated and conflict ridden, management of Nile waters has been a more or less constant feature of the region. A March 2015 agreement by Egypt, Sudan, and Ethiopia on mutual water rights was greeted as possibly setting the tone for ongoing co-operative management of the region's broader political conflicts.[11] Resource abundance can also lead to violent competition in the exploitation of those resources for the wealth that they bring. The conflict diamonds story testifies to the contribution of natural resources extraction to both the emergence and durability of armed conflict. In a number of conflict settings (Burma, Cambodia, Cote d'Ivoire, Democratic Republic of the Congo, Liberia) logging has fuelled corruption, financed weapons purchases, drawn workers into conflicts, generated militias, and helped to launder funds from other criminal activity, with the result that conflicts escalate into violent disputes over land ownership and logging concessions.[12] In the case of Sierra Leone, illicit Liberian entrepreneurs combined diamonds, timber, and arms in a trade that helped fuel the war.[13]

While natural resources are not necessarily instrumental in launching armed conflict, they can certainly serve to keep it going. Cynthia Arnson and William Zartman nicely capture the interplay of grievance, ideology, and greed in armed conflict in an essay on "need, creed, and greed."[14] In the debate over the relative importance of "grievance" and "greed" in fomenting armed conflict, the consensus seems to lean toward the view that while grievance, along with other conditions, is linked to the outbreak of armed conflict, greed frequently becomes a factor in perpetuating it, especially when a weakened state is unable to regulate activities like mining or effectively patrol its borders. In some instances "conflict is used as a strategic tool so the resources can be unlawfully extracted with impunity."[15] A number of studies document the exacerbation and extension of armed conflict through drug markets.[16] Even in conflicts that are begun in order to redress injustice, economic opportunity or greed can take over as combatants have opportunities to loot, sell valuable minerals, and trade drugs and weapons[17] – activities undertaken by government and non-government forces alike. Nevertheless, most scholars discount greed as a significant factor in the onset of wars. Most often, economic advantage is pursued as a means of advancing political objectives. When mustering the resources for war, money and the opportunities it buys are the means to an end, but over time they can become the end.[18] In a prolonged or stalemated conflict, which describes many of today's wars, there are elements for whom conflict becomes a way of life and a livelihood. A summary view is that "wars result from a complex interplay of failing state structures, a set of material grievances, hostile social identities, and political entrepreneurs who are willing and able to mobilize groups."[19]

Prominently focusing on structural conditions has a tendency to downplay the politics of conflict and understate the place of human decision making and the role of charismatic leadership in either rejecting or choosing and persisting in violence and war.[20] South Africa in the late 1980s and early 1990s had all the structural conditions associated with the onset of armed conflict: extreme grievances, deep communal suspicion fostered by a long history of politicized identity, and opportunity in the form of a mobilized and energized population with external actors ready to help. The crucial factor in the population becoming convinced that there was a non-violent alternative was not that they trusted the country's public institutions (for example, parliament and the courts) to deliver justice, rather it was because of one charismatic leader who embodied the alternative. Even while he was still in prison, Nelson Mandela embodied the sense that a just, multi-racial South Africa was still possible and could be pursued through adherence to principle and openness to compromise. The rather extreme antithesis to that model of charisma is Cambodia's Pol Pot.[21] The latter offered charismatic leadership in the 1970s that persuaded a cadre of followers not so much that there was no alternative to violence but that violence offered national cleansing and salvation. In Angola, Jonas Savimbi used his personality and cunning to keep his rebel group energized and operational for decades of persistent and destructive war, despite few prospects for success. Six weeks after his death a ceasefire was signed. Strong local personalities help to drive armed conflict in contemporary Afghanistan, Syria, and Iraq. An examination of the structural correlates of war is essential to improving war prevention strategies, but human beings shape their material and social surroundings, and they also shape "the conceptual framework and the ideas through which they understand the social order and what is possible within it."[22] As Richard Jackson puts it, the origins of intrastate conflict "are always rooted in a unique historical confluence of social, economic, and political structures – in particular, the debilitating structures of weak statehood – and a set of willing and capable *agents* – political and military elites who promote violent discourses and organize the material and human resources necessary for sustained civil violence."[23]

Forceful personalities, both in government and civil society, can also help to sustain, or undermine, the public credibility or legitimacy of public institutions, as well as social/political stability. Thomas Ohlson refers to two kinds of legitimacy: "vertical legitimacy" as public acceptance of governmental authority and the voluntary acceptance of the prevailing order, and "horizontal legitimacy" as mutual acceptance at the popular level – that is, a high degree of tolerance and acceptance across racial, cultural, ethnic, and economic lines. The two are linked. A lack of vertical legitimacy contributes to horizontal suspicions inasmuch as distrust of public institutions and governmental authority can lead to the search for stability and security through loyalty to one's own group and thus growing suspicion of "the other." The vertical "legitimacy gap" is the difference between citizen expectations of the state (i.e., protection of political and cultural freedoms, socio-economic well-being) in exchange for their taxes and loyalty, and what the state is actually willing or able to deliver. Others refer to it as the social compact. The horizontal "legitimacy gap" relates to the absence of tolerance and mutual respect between communities.[24] Loss of horizontal legitimacy heightens the role of identity in political conflict, and loss of vertical legitimacy heightens the sense that existing political mechanisms are not reliable alternatives to violence when tensions rise.

Identity

The wider these legitimacy gaps the greater the risk of intrastate violence. Government actions that contribute to both vertical and horizontal delegitimization include exclusionary and discriminatory governance arrangements, especially when the discrimination is against particular communities or classes. Political and economic inequality linked to regional or communal disparity is particularly divisive and conducive to instability. When these conditions are joined by demographic factors, like high levels of young males in the population, changing environmental conditions or other external stresses, the threat of conflict escalating to violence is intensified. On top of that, it is not uncommon for weak governments to seek to bolster their authority and hold on to power by politicizing identity and promoting group-based loyalties. Thus, as the Human Security Report Project notes, "high levels of political discrimination are a key cause of violent ethnic conflict."[25]

Identity grievances can also fester for generations and rise quickly to the fore in response to triggering events. In the clashes that engulfed Kenya in the aftermath of the 2007 election, some of the violence was linked to unresolved land and settlement issues in the Rift Valley going back to the colonial period – a longstanding horizontal "legitimacy gap." Indeed, Kenyan politicians have routinely exploited identity issues to win support from particular ethnic communities.[26] In the Middle East, history and identity are central to conflict. The journalist/writer Robert Fisk made the point about history in the context of Libya's "Arab Spring" crisis: "Their grandfathers – in some cases their fathers – fought against the Italians; thus a foundation of resistance, a real historical narrative, lies beneath their opposition to Gaddafi; hence Gaddafi's own adoption of resistance – to the mythical threat of al-Qaida's 'foreign' brutality – is supposed to maintain support for his regime."[27]

Historical grievances that become focused by one community against another foster the vilification of the "other," making that part of a community's culture and story and thus a strong mobilizing instrument. And because suspicions of the "other" have become imbedded as part of a community's "story," populations become susceptible to propaganda and mobilizing campaigns – the Rwandan radio phenomenon, the viciously anti-Tutsi Libre des Mille Colines, being a particularly grievous and tragic case in point. Grievances that are politicized along communal and geographic lines are especially conducive to long-term or extended armed confrontation because they carry the considerable emotional, political, and financial resources that are available to such communities. Recruitment to the cause, whether for groups that hold power or those that seek it, is facilitated through group loyalty appeals, and the same goes for raising financial resources. Compromise is difficult and "winning" is not necessarily associated with immediate gains but is understood to be a long-term goal, generations long perhaps, that is worth fighting for, "if not for me then for my children." When grievances over poverty and inequality parallel or are identified with particular ethnicities or regions they come to be perceived as group-based inequalities, thus increasing the potential for conflict as particular communities link their aspirations and identity to collective action in response to concrete grievances. The politicization of such grievances escalates the potential for violent confrontation, especially when communities are effectively marginalized in the national political process.

Religion and ethnicity are prominent factors in the majority of contemporary wars (e.g., Afghanistan, Algeria, India, Iraq, Israel, Kenya, Libya, Nigeria, Pakistan, the Philippines, the Caucasus in Russia, Somalia, Sudan, South Sudan, Syria, Thailand, Turkey, and Ukraine). But it is also true that religious and ethnic conflicts are as much a product as a cause of conflict. As states persistently fail to produce the security that their citizens expect and need (a failed social contract or a widened vertical legitimacy gap), pressure builds to seek other political and social units or entities, such as ethnic communities, through which to pursue individual and collective security. Ethnic or "identity" conflicts – that is, conflicts in which the rights and political/social viability of ethnic groups or religious communities are central issues – are usually reflections of a more fundamental social conflict, born of a community's experience of economic disparity, political discrimination, human rights violations, pressures generated by environmental degradation, and other factors. The resulting loss of confidence in public institutions is crucial. Identity conflicts emerge with intensity when a community loses confidence in mainstream political institutions and processes and, in response to unmet basic needs for social and economic security, resolves to strengthen its collective influence and to struggle for political/legal recognition as a community. Failure to address grievances makes sub-state group solidarity an increasingly attractive political strategy, and when easy-to-use and easy-to-get small arms are thrown into the mix (the matter of resources or capacity), the result, not surprisingly, is often persistent armed conflict.

So, conflicts that focus on identity are in fact often grounded in unmet human needs. While that obviously refers to basic requirements like food and shelter and safety and security, less tangible values like dignity, freedom, and self-esteem are also relevant and consequential.[28] To the extent that identity revolves around particular ethnic, religious, or cultural communities, the antidote is in the creation and nurture of a civic identity – essentially citizenship that is shared with a mix of communities and transcends ethnic and religious divisions. All that said, it is also painfully the case that where religion presents itself as a particular set of beliefs or a comprehensive worldview indelibly linked to particular cultures, those beliefs can be shaped into extremist views and actions. The extremism of certain Islamist movements cannot be explained simply as manifestations of economic and political grievance but has become more deeply rooted in a manufactured belief system. In the case of Nigeria's Boko Haram, researchers found ignorance of the true teachings of Islam to be a major factor in the move toward extremism. This "lack of deep knowledge of true religious teaching" was in turn influenced by three particular trends in Nigeria's northeast: the proliferation of sects in Islam and Christianity, the proliferation of independent preachers, and the prominent reliance on these preachers rather than the holy books of the religion.[29] One is inclined to see parallels in independent televangelists and the American Christian right.

Even when extremism is not present in any dramatic way, the more conflicts involve issues or questions that have become central to a party's identity and to the preservation or even survival of that identity, the less amenable those parties are to negotiation and thus the more intractable, and sometimes the more violent, such conflicts become because of the sense that there are no alternatives.[30] The "polarization of unchallengeable certainties" is a phrase used by Drew Gilpin Faust, president of Harvard, in quite another context, but it nicely describes the impossible standoff when deeply held and opposing moral convictions come to lodge at the roots of political conflict, or when competing identities hold opposing positions that both sides consider to threaten their very existence.[31] It is part of the phenomenon of intractable conflicts. Common to all such conflicts are "interests or values that the disputants regard as critical to their survival" and to their identity. "These underlying causes include parties' moral values, identities, and fundamental human needs."[32] Furthermore, such conflicts are not amenable to win-win solutions. Indeed, "those involved in moral conflict may even regard perpetuation of the conflict as virtuous or necessary. They may derive part of their identity from being warriors or opponents of their enemy and have a stake in the continuation of the conflict because it provides them with a highly desirable role."[33] Hence, their appeal to "unchallengeable certainties" strengthens them, and any move to compromise or to put "certainties" up for discussion becomes a sign of weakness.

Diaspora groups can, by becoming the focus of political mobilization in support of militants in the homeland, serve to entrench opposition to compromise.[34] They can help to frame conflicts in uncompromising and categorical ways and provide "resources and access to international media, international organisations, and powerful host governments." And this in turn "gives diaspora groups influential roles in the adoption of strategies relating to conflict." That influence means, of course, that diaspora communities can also be mobilized for peacebuilding purposes and to reduce the risks of armed conflict.

Capacity

Even in places where the political and economic conditions are ripe for the onset of armed conflict, generating the capacity for war is daunting. It is a significant challenge to assemble the financial, combat, and political/psychological resources needed to mount a sustained challenge to the demands of dissident communities or to existing authorities by means of violence. It is a challenge that is unfortunately mitigated by the abundance of small arms and weapons in most regions of prolonged conflict. The absence of effective controls on small arms and light weapons helps non-state groups, as well as states, scrape together the capability for armed conflict, even for extended periods (but, again, that doesn't mean they have the capacity to prevail). These ubiquitous small arms (from assault rifles to locally fashioned explosive devices) employ relatively simple technologies that are not only widely available but are readily usable by non-military combatants, including the children that too often are forced to become combatants.[35] In a sense, small arms facilitate the demilitarization of war – without any extensive expertise or training required to operate them, small arms and light weapons have helped to transform armed combat from the "profession of war," carried out by professional military organizations and soldiers, or even volunteer soldiers trained and commanded by professionals, to armed attacks by civilians against civilian and military targets. Many combatants, whether they are pro-government militias or anti-government forces, are civilian or citizen fighters rather than trained soldiers. Recruiters throughout today's war zones bring unemployed young men into their ranks without any knowledge of the requirements of international humanitarian law and the obligations to protect civilians in conflicts. Civilians are the primary victims of contemporary war,[36] but they have also become the primary combatants. The UN Secretary General regularly reports on the plight of civilians in combat situations, and a recent report concluded that "civilians still account for the vast majority of casualties and continue to be targeted,"[37] and at least part of what lies behind this is the fact that the distinctions between civilians and civilian combatants is blurred.

Demographic factors can also add capacity and opportunity. Half of the population of the Arab world is under thirty years of age.[38] In Egypt, with two-thirds of the population under thirty, young people – educated, urbanized, and unemployed – were key to the extraordinary revolution.[39] Sub-Sahara Africa is even younger, with some countries like Uganda with 70 per cent of the population under thirty.[40] The good news is that the advent of liberal democracies is associated with older populations, meaning that as Arab and African populations age, the prospects for less combat and more stability and accountable governance increase. In the meantime, however, a large, fighting-age, male population adds an extra layer of volatility.

In addition to basic military capabilities (arms and ammunition and the fighters to wield them), organizational capacity and governance structures within affected communities become important means of mobilizing and retaining popular consent for armed struggle. One of the reasons that political conflicts involving ethnic or religious communities are more likely to transform into armed conflict is that access to cohesive communities aids the mobilization process. Access to media, including modern social media, to influence an international constituency comes into play, as does foreign assistance (sometimes through diaspora communities).

There are other "opportunity structures" (that is, the environmental or contextual opportunities or restraints) that can also play a major role. Terrain on or from which to battle (e.g., mountains available for hideouts), opportunities to "loot" or commandeer resources, a supportive diaspora, sympathetic foreign governments or rebel groups – all of these influence capacity and can thus contribute to or restrain the military option. In advanced armed campaigns there inevitably emerge benefits that flow to actors in war that are not available in peace (employment, spoils of war).

Some analysts consider capacity to be especially important in the onset of war.[41] Grievances and communal conflicts are widely present and can always be exploited by political and civilian leaders, but those grievances and divisions tip over into armed conflict when they become feasible – when the belligerents have the capacity. When financing, arms and munitions, commitment, and the availability of young people to take up the fight are all present there are perceived opportunities to pursue otherwise unattainable objectives and to advance the interests of the aggrieved communities.

Absence of Alternatives

The capacity to mobilize a combat force creates a new option, and that becomes especially compelling when there are perceived to be no other options. A key element in developing a collective resolve to support an armed campaign is the genuinely perceived or credibly claimed absence of alternatives to violence. Societies lacking trusted institutions or mechanisms capable of managing and mediating intergroup tensions and grievances are perceived as offering no credible options to the aggrieved and thus the risk of those tensions escalating into violence increases dramatically. If the absence of alternatives is pervasively felt, then when triggering events occur, the aggrieved are likely to turn much more readily to armed options that are available, than to spend a lot of time trying to construct political alternatives in an environment and through structures that they believe have systematically excluded them. The pervasive sense or claim that there is no alternative to armed resistance in the effort to get grievances heard, and no alternative to armed confrontation in pursuing equitable solutions to intergroup competition/conflict, is at the root of transforming political conflict into armed conflict. Gerd Schönwälder of Canada's International Development Research Centre makes the point that "the prevention of political violence must include fundamental improvements to the quality of democracy as such. Creating more opportunities for political participation – including for expressing dissent – will help, especially when accompanied by institutional channels and capacities to deliver on legitimate demands."[42]

In a sense, of the four basic drivers of armed conflict discussed here, it is the lack of alternatives that is most amenable to short-term change. Grievances rooted in structural inequities obviously require long-term attention. Intergroup conflict, usually with deep historical roots, may be amenable to short-term measures and policies available to ease tensions, but such tensions are usually linked to serious and structural economic and political conditions that may require generations to shift. Similarly, cutting off access to the hardware of armed conflict requires long-term attention to things like porous borders, state capacity for law enforcement, and the political environment. What must, and can, change more readily is a group's perception that its best option is armed conflict. Changing that perception or resolve cannot, obviously, be premised on persuading an aggrieved group to accept or acquiesce to inequity. Rather, the focus needs to be on addressing the perception that there are no trusted forums or mechanisms that will take grievances and collective demands seriously. That requires the demonstration and construction, in the short term, of genuine alternatives. Such measures might include demonstrable international political solidarity with aggrieved populations and external pressures to create a seat at a credible table; external economic and political pressures on regimes; and third party mechanisms for addressing and mediating the political conflict.

The international community has been especially weak and in many cases actively counter-productive in demonstrating political solidarity with aggrieved populations. Rather than generating ideas and conditions conducive to diplomatic and non-violent remedies for vulnerable populations, too often the international community has focused on the opposite. In the decades before the Arab Spring uprisings in Egypt and Libya, the international community was in fact sending messages to the Egyptian and Libyan people that the regimes that oppressed them had the backing of the international community, served powerful international interests, and, regardless of their egregious violations of the rights of their own populations, were accepted as agents of stability. The message was that the Mubarak and Gaddafi regimes had powerful friends and backers, and the people of Egypt and Libya could expect no help from the international community in seeking peaceful change. The same goes now for Saudi Arabia, with the paragons of Western democracies happy to provide the Saudis with all the weapons oil can buy. Earlier in Africa Mobutu Sese Sako of Zaire had the unqualified support of the Western international community while the most basic of needs of Zaire's citizens were ignored and the regime was in irredeemable decline. But the examples are legion. The international community's withdrawal of support from the Mubarak and Gaddafi regimes was much too late and was done without any clear sense of what it would mean for the people of those ill-governed countries. To reverse that pattern the international community will have to find new approaches, multilaterally and locally, for challenging illegitimate regimes. Instead of dictatorial and human rights violating regimes being offered political and military support, they obviously need to be challenged by sustained efforts to delegitimize them and to generate external pressures for change that are supportive of internal, locally driven reform efforts. In short, there is a requirement for measures that build a sense that alternatives to violence can become available.

It is worth returning to the earlier question of why the rebellion in Egypt, while it involved violent episodes that reached the level of war as defined here, did not quickly descend into the kind of full-scale fighting that happened in Libya and then Syria. All three were obviously grievance-based revolts, but in Libya and Syria grievances were linked early on and more directly and emphatically to identity, with ethnic and regional cleavages playing much more important roles. In Libya and Syria, the opposition had the basic capacity for violence through access to arms, and those regimes also quickly demonstrated their political "capacity" for combat against their own people through unrestrained attacks on civilian dissidents. In Egypt, the army maintained throughout at least some channels of communication and negotiation, persuading the protestors that they genuinely had opportunities for negotiation – in other words, they saw political alternatives to violence.

Triggering War

Armed conflict is rooted in political and economic conditions that typically build up over a long time, that take a long time to alter, and that typically don't lead to violence without a significant triggering event. Such an event can be specific economic or political decisions that are perceived by a particular group or segment of the population to be particularly unjust or discriminatory toward them (e.g., sharp food price increases, infrastructure projects that threaten the livelihood or homes of a particular region or group). Triggers can also be external or unplanned events, like a drought or other natural catastrophes, adding extraordinary stress to an already fragile political/economic environment and thus also building toward a tipping point. "Trigger incidents are in a way the least important of the causes, but they are often the object of considerable contestations, as opposing sides argue over 'who started it.'"[43] The outbreak of the First World War is a famous instance of the triggering event being the least important, but most consequential, of the causes of war. The Rwandan genocide of 1994 had roots in a long and conflicted history but was triggered by the April 1994 death of the president in the downing of his aircraft. The events of September 11, 2001, certainly triggered American action in Afghanistan. The twenty-six-year-old Tunisian street vendor who committed suicide in December 2010 in protest against the Tunisian regime is widely credited with having launched the Arab Spring. In 2011, the impending attack on the city of Benghazi was the key event in launching the NATO intervention in Libya.

Mass Atrocities

It is not possible to predict whether or when an armed conflict will involve mass atrocities. While it is clear that there are governments as well as non-state groups that are prepared to engage in mass killings under certain conditions, it is not readily predictable when that point will be reached or what the triggering event will be. The primary point, however, is that they are most associated with ongoing armed conflict, which means that the best way to prevent mass atrocities is to prevent armed conflict itself. A recent Stanley Foundation Report identifies "pre-conditions of genocide and mass atrocities,"[44] noting that while certain conditions seem essential for the future commission of genocide or mass atrocities, the presence of enabling conditions does not make genocide or mass atrocities inevitable.[45]

Nevertheless, governments with an ideological commitment to radical transformation are also more likely to pursue extreme actions and mass atrocities. Mass atrocities are more likely to follow when moderates are marginalized within the elites, when "hate groups" dedicated to the vilification of the target group are well organized, when security forces purge minority groups and those thought to be disloyal, and when recruitment is expanded among radicalized groups. The establishment, arming, and training of militias with weak accountability increases the likelihood of mass atrocities, as does an escalation of unpunished human rights abuses against targeted groups along with the open publication of hate propaganda. When there are indications that civilians are intentionally targeted while the perpetrators enjoy impunity, and when there exists a significant threat to the survival of the governing regime, the potential for mass atrocities increases dramatically.

It's not easy to start a war, but it still happens with distressing regularity. These days, they start within states rather than between states, so it is individual states trying to manage internal conflicts that find themselves on the front lines of the global war prevention effort. But the context is a notably unequal international community of states, and it is the most disadvantaged members of that community, in countries where the conditions conducive to war are most concentrated, who are most directly charged with averting it. But economically weak states, the ones most vulnerable to internal disintegration and thus to political violence, are denied the resources needed to overcome the conditions that presage war. And those states that are the most advantaged regularly use their advantage, not to ameliorate but to arm conflict, not to help build conditions for sustainable peace but to consolidate their own interests at the expense of the disenfranchised and the disempowered.

3

How Civil Wars End

O NCE BEGUN, CIVIL WARS don't soon end. Of the twenty-nine wars underway in early 2015, twenty-four (83 per cent) had been underway for more than five years. More than half had been ongoing for more than twenty years, and of those, five for more than forty years.[1] Armed conflicts in which the cumulative combat death toll has reached one thousand are counted as ongoing as long as they continue to exact at least twenty-five combat deaths per year. They are regarded as ended when there is a peace or ceasefire agreement followed by a full year with the death toll below twenty-five or, without an agreement, two consecutive years of death tolls below twenty-five. According to these criteria, the longest running war is the Israel-Palestine conflict where political violence at a level to constitute armed conflict or war has been episodic but still ongoing since 1948. The sixty-five-year war holds the record, but Colombia is a close second with more than fifty years of war. The two wars in the Philippines have now been waged for well over four decades. Fighting in Afghanistan and Sudan has been a constant presence for more than three decades, and another four wars are more than two decades long and nine exceed one decade. In other words, more than three-quarters of current wars must be measured in decades rather than years.

Whatever the duration, it is rarely victory or defeat that signals war's end. Civil wars are not fought until someone wins – they are fought until the parties to the conflict can no longer ignore the hard reality that they have all lost. No matter how bitter the enmity, rarely do the protagonists fight all the way to the bitter end. No matter how deep the destruction, in the end they stop fighting not because one side has won, but because both sides, though they may agree on nothing else, agree to stop fighting. The basis of such agreement is much more likely to be mutual exhaustion than mutual accord, but it remains that all the parties to a conflict finally have to decide, and all at the same time, that continued fighting promises a worse outcome than anything they can reasonably expect to happen at a negotiating table.

Fighting to Negotiate

No matter how sophisticated or primitive the weaponry, how imbalanced the military might, the outcome of a war is only rarely conclusively decided on the battlefield. Wars carry on for years and decades because insurgencies are for the most part not amenable to military defeat and because it is very difficult for all parties to reach the shared conclusion that it is time to end the fighting. The difficulty in reaching such a conclusion is heightened by the fact it is rarely just two parties involved. Governments and insurgencies alike are rarely fully united – they represent disparate interests and constituencies and it is a challenge to produce internal accord, never mind accord with the adversary. Difficult though it may be, it is nevertheless the case that most wars end by decision, not by victory. Governments fight to win, and rarely do. Insurgents fight not to lose – and rarely expect to win. Insurgents usually gain the most because they typically fight to become contenders in a political process. So, as the well-known formula has it, insurgents win as long as they don't lose, while governments lose as long as they don't win – which is about 95 per cent of the time in contemporary warfare – and when governments don't win, they eventually negotiate.

Seventy of the ninety-nine wars in the past quarter century, of which six were interstate wars, have ended. Of the intrastate wars that ended, in only four cases did governments manage a clear military defeat over the insurgencies they were battling (a mere 6 per cent): Iraq's defeat of the Shia rebellion of 1991, Georgia's defeat of the 1993–94 rebellion, Angola's defeat of UNITA in 2002, and Sri Lanka's defeat of the Tamil Tigers in 2009. Insurgents in fact did marginally better than governments in forcing decisive outcomes, but clear insurgent wins, about 8 per cent of the time, are also hard to come by, and in some instances only with massive external support. Ethiopian rebels ousted the regime of Mengistu Haile Mariam in 1992 after decades of fighting and major international humanitarian engagement in drought and famine areas. The Rwandan Tutsis defeated the Hutu government in the extraordinary post-genocide circumstances of 1994, East Timor separatists prevailed over Indonesia in 2000, Kosovar separatists achieved independence from Serbia as a result of the 1999 NATO bombing campaign, and Panamanians ousted the Noriega regime in 1990 with major American help.

Half of the sixty-four intrastate wars that have ended since the end of the Cold War were fought to intolerably hurting stalemates on the battlefield, with the terms for stopping the fighting then worked out at the negotiating table. The remaining twenty-three civil wars gradually wound down without a formal ceasefire or peace agreement. In some of these cases government military action had gradually decimated opposition forces, leaving them with declining options, in other cases conditions and strategies changed, and in some cases governments vigorously sought to address the grievances of the rebel forces – and in those latter cases serious alternatives to fighting became available.

These overall trends are corroborated by other tabulations. Using data from the Uppsala Conflict Data Program (UCDP) at Uppsala University in Sweden,[2] the *Human Security Report* (HSR) marks the way wars end according to similar criteria – conflicts end by military victories, by negotiated settlements, or by "other" means or circumstances.[3] The HSR indicates that in the period 2000–2004 military victories accounted for only slightly more than 10 per cent of conflict terminations, negotiations for just over one-third, and a category of "other" means for just over one-half.[4] The HSR's tabulation of a higher proportion of armed conflicts as ending in these "other" ways is largely a function of definition, with the HSR counting conflicts or conflict episodes as beginning in the first year that combat deaths exceed twenty-five and ending whenever the death toll drops below that threshold in a single calendar year. Fighting in low-intensity armed conflicts tends to be sporadic, so, as the HSR points out, conflicts with intermittent violence with only a few dozen combat deaths each year are likely to hover around the threshold of twenty-five battle deaths per year, meaning that conflicts can change from active to inactive and back again fairly frequently,[5] without negotiations and without any party winning or losing – thus driving up the count of wars ending by "other" means. More new conflicts are recorded as a result of the low threshold, and more endings are recorded because they are deemed to have ended after only one year of dormancy. So it is the sporadic nature of many contemporary wars that leads to a higher incidence of wars starting and ending, and to a lower proportion ending by peace agreements in the HSR counting. The difference in counting methods also explains the relatively higher recidivism rate reported by the HSR, which notes "the trend towards small-scale armed conflict with few violent clashes that are often interrupted by months and years of tranquility."[6] Tranquility seems, however, to be an overly optimistic account of the circumstances between conflict episodes. Periods between active fighting are typically fraught with ongoing hardships, unaddressed grievances, and inevitably measures to rebuild capacity for the renewed fighting that lurks just around the corner.

The *Human Security Report* points out that since the Second World War, victories have become progressively less and less likely. In the 1950s, two-thirds of wars ended with victories by one side or the other. In the

1960s and 1970s that dropped to 50 per cent. In the 1980s, victories dropped further to 36 per cent of all war terminations. In the 1990s, it was down to 17 per cent, and in the first five years of the new millennium it was at 11 per cent. This progressive decline in victories is paralleled by an increase in negotiated settlements. And the data also show that as negotiated settlements have become more prominent they have also become more reliable – in other words, declining recidivism. [7] The *2014 Yearbook on Peace Processes* at Spain's School for a Culture of Peace looked at 108 armed conflicts since the 1970s, only 10 per cent of which ended through military victories. Just over a third went dormant but unresolved.[8]

Again, the best case for the utility of armed force belongs to opposition groups. For them, fighting wars to stalemates that lead to negotiations is an effective use of force – at least if you ignore the human and material costs incurred. The negotiating tables that emerge from violent rebellions and armed resistance campaigns were not available to opposition groups before the fighting. So what happens on the battlefield is significant, even in the absence of a clear military victory, in shaping the outcomes of wars that end in negotiations. The Sudan People's Liberation Army (SPLA) in Sudan never came close to "winning" the war or "defeating" the Khartoum forces, yet, over time and at incalculable costs, the fighting ended up in depriving Khartoum of all its options. The SPLA finally accomplished its aims, but it was not a military victory. It was a war fought to a stalemate that in turn led to negotiations. In most cases, rebel groups would never have gained a place at a negotiating table without an armed campaign, but only rarely were decisive conclusions reached on the battlefield. Instead, negotiators took over and found a political conclusion. There is thus a basic reality that governments cannot ignore: that insurgencies with significant roots in a supporting community are not readily amenable to military defeat.

The odds clearly do not ride with governments battling insurgencies, confirming Rupert Smith's recognition that no strategic objective can be achieved through military force alone. Government military forces can and usually do score tactical wins, but insurgents tend to be skilled in turning their tactical defeats into strategic gains. For governments to turn their tactical successes into strategic advances requires a much broader range of non-military measures to resolve conflict and to build conditions for a durable peace. And while insurgent military campaigns against governments produce results, insurgencies soon discover that the military tactics that brought them to negotiations and power are of little benefit when the objective is to win the peace. In other words, the question of how wars end is obviously not the same as how peace is won.

So, most civil wars are started with negotiations or some political process in mind – although in early 2015 Islamic State, at the time perhaps the most extreme of the Islamists fighting in Iraq and Syria, seemed to have no interest in negotiating or in any compromise that talks would require. But the usual strategy over the past twenty-five years has been for rebels or insurgents to fight for political recognition and legitimacy and thus for a place at a negotiating table. Governments fight back to keep dissidents from a negotiating table. But that is a contest that the insurgents almost always win – not in the sense of militarily defeating a government, but in achieving their initial objective of getting a seat at the table. That certainly doesn't mean they get everything they want in the negotiations. Not having "won," compromise is forced on them. Governments, after years and even decades of spilled human and material treasure, are usually forced to agree that their adversaries have legitimate claims and thus agree to negotiations toward ending the fighting and sometimes even co-operate in the effort to launch a new political order.

Governments Defeat Insurgencies

A clear military defeat over an insurgency is rare. In Africa, where governments have sought to retain power by meeting heightened political dissidence with military force, often to see political opposition mutate into full-fledged rebellion and prolonged insurgency, most wars have ended in the classical hurting stalemates in which governments had to turn to the political accommodations that were earlier rejected in favour of force. The Nigerian government's defeat of the Biafran uprising in the late 1960s stands out as one clear military "success" – but only if we allow the word "success" to be used in the context of millions of lives lost. Up to two million civilians died in the two-year war that followed an Ibo declaration of independence in southeast Nigeria. It was Africa's most intense and bloody civil war in which a combination of heavy military bombardment and a blockade of the region created a humanitarian disaster of extraordinary proportions, ultimately sapping Ibo resolve and crushing the secessionist rebellion.

The military defeat of the Biafran secessionists was accomplished in no small measure because the Biafrans chose to fight a conventional war against the Nigerian central government. The Biafrans even mounted a small air force but proved no match for the superior Nigerian forces. Terming Nigeria's defeat of the Biafrans a "success" also ignores the fact that, over forty years later, the roots of the Biafran War endure and the underlying political conflict is far from resolved.

There are only four instances in the past quarter century in which governments clearly defeated insurgent forces: Angola, Sri Lanka, Iraq, and Georgia. Three decades and many African wars after the Biafran war, the Angolan government's defeat of the long-running National Union for the Total Independence of Angola (UNITA) insurgency was the only instance in the past twenty-five years of a government vanquishing an insurgency in Africa. That insurgency was also rooted in ethnicity, but it was largely driven by the charisma of its leader, Jonas Savimbi. His assassination finally ended the decades of intermittent fighting. After decades of disruption, the end was quiet and anti-climactic. Even though UNITA lost the war on the battlefield, the Angolan government engaged UNITA in negotiating a final settlement that would allow it to continue as a legitimate political party. But here too it is a corruption of the term to call it victory: at least five hundred thousand people had died and many more than that were forced out of their homes and communities. The country's economy was in shambles, with no infrastructure left.[9]

The record in Asia is about the same as in Africa. Of the region's twenty-seven intrastate wars (it also had one interstate war), only one ended in a clear government victory over an armed opposition. Sri Lanka's twenty-six-year war against the separatist Tamil community ended in a series of extraordinarily bloody battles in 2009, bucking the odds against governments defeating insurgencies. Rejecting all negotiations, the Sri Lankan government defied history and launched a final assault that claimed thousands of civilian lives but brought the war to a decisive end. Estimates of the number of people killed in the final two months of fighting in April–May of 2009 range from seven thousand to forty thousand. Almost three hundred thousand civilians had been stranded and caught in the crossfire in the final combat zone. Over the war's two and a half decades close to one hundred thousand people were killed.

The war's end has not meant an end to the conflict, and it certainly hasn't produced sustainable peace. The rebel and secessionist Tamil Tigers (the Liberation Tigers of Tamil Eelam) were militarily defeated and the main successor Tamil political organization, the Tamil National Alliance (TNA), has ended Tamil secessionist demands in favour of decentralized governance under a federal structure. Nevertheless, discrimination against the ethnic Tamil minority (about 18 per cent of the population) continues, with a disproportionate share of the victims of human rights violations being Tamils. The community's grievances remain largely unaddressed.[10] While the Government of Sri Lanka did appoint a Lessons Learned and Reconciliation Commission, its report[11] was criticized by the Human Rights Council as having failed to adequately address the serious allegations of violations of international law, especially in the closing months of the war.[12] The resolution, which was supported by most Western states and India but not by Russia and China, called on the Government of Sri Lanka to take action to ensure justice, equity, accountability, and reconciliation for all Sri Lankans. Opposition forces in Sri Lanka, as well as a range of international observers, paint a picture of entrenched political/ethnic conflict, rising tensions, and fears of resumed political violence.[13] While there was a peaceful transition to a newly elected president elected in early 2015, Tamils and Muslims in the north and east were still pressing unsuccessfully for greater autonomy, and the police and military continued to enjoy immunity from prosecution.[14]

Decisive victories on the battlefield are rare in and of themselves, but they also rarely resolve the conflict. The more common outcome is a political dynamic in which a triumphalist victor marginalizes and increasingly abuses the vanquished – none of it portending political stability. As Canadian parliamentarian Bob Rae put it on his expulsion from Sri Lanka in 2009,

> there is a difference between a war ended by agreement and a war ended by death and destruction. If there is no magnanimity in victory, there is no victory. It is hard not to cry at what has been lost, how much life has been destroyed. And [at] what must still be done to bring justice to the peace that is being proclaimed so loudly.[15]

In the Middle East, the Iraqi government of Saddam Hussein engineered a brutal defeat of the Shia rebellion following the 1991 Gulf War, Desert Storm. The multilateral war saw an international coalition come to the aid of Kuwait to defeat the invading Iraqis (discussed in chapter 4), but the government defeat of the subsequent Shiite rebellion followed the same model as the end of the Sri Lankan war. The simmering Shia resistance to Saddam's vicious suppression flared into a full rebellion in the wake of Iraq's expulsion from Kuwait. At its height, the rebels had effectively wrested control of fourteen out of eighteen provinces from the Hussein regime.[16] The first President Bush encouraged Iraqis to take on Saddam, but when they did, there was no help available. Using helicopter gunships in particular, Saddam's forces attacked the Shia forces, killing an estimated one hundred thousand, including large numbers of women and children. The UNHCR estimated that, by April 1991, there were fifty thousand Iraqi refugees in Iran,[17] and Human Rights Watch said as much as 10 per cent of the population was internally displaced.[18] In Iraq and Sri

Lanka, as in Nigeria decades earlier, victory came at extraordinary cost – and in none of the cases were the underlying issues even addressed, never mind resolved.

The only other example of a government prevailing over an insurgency in an armed conflict that reached the level of warfare was in the former Soviet state of Georgia, and it was an ambiguous victory at best. The newly emerging country went into turmoil in the wake of the fall of the Soviet Union, with ethnic communities in South Ossetia and Abkhazia pursuing secession from Georgia. Failing in their ultimate goal, they nevertheless won essential autonomy and retained ongoing links to Russia. A military coup in Georgia was followed by internal fighting in the early to mid-1990s until President Eduard Shevardnadze mobilized Russian support to crush an attempted comeback by his predecessor, Zviad Gamsakhurdia. In this narrow sense, the government of the day defeated an insurgent effort, but stability did not ensue, and the territories of Abkhazia and South Ossetia remained autonomous and effectively independent of the Government of Georgia. In 2008, there was interstate fighting between Russia and Georgia. It began on August 7 when "Georgian forces launched an early-morning assault on South Ossetia." Russia responded and in the next five days drove Georgia back out of South Ossetia.[19] Internationally brokered negotiations ended the fighting with a six-point plan signed by Russia, Georgia, South Ossetia, and Abkhazia that stipulated that parties needed to withdraw to the positions they occupied before August. The Russian-Georgian "five-day war" illustrates the inadequacy in particular cases of rigid, and ultimately arbitrary, definition of war. The fighting, though fierce for several days, resulted in major destruction of property and in driving many tens of thousands temporarily from their homes, but it did not, despite some early reports of high casualties, lead to the one thousand combat deaths necessary to meet the operational definition of war.[20]

Insurgencies Defeat Governments

For the most part, insurgencies do not expect to defeat the governments they attack. Their objectives are usually limited to developing bargaining clout at a negotiating table. The victory of the Sudan People's Liberation Army (SPLA) over the Government of Sudan, which led to South Sudan's separation and becoming an independent state, is not counted as an insurgency's military defeat of a government. They fought to a hurting stalemate in which both sides had abandoned thoughts of victory. Instead, they negotiated a ceasefire and went through an extensive political process by which the SPLA's political objectives were largely achieved (but clearly the SPLA's military pressure was a key factor in its success at the negotiating table). War has remained an ongoing presence in South Sudan – tensions with the north continue, with major outstanding issues remaining, while a south-south war undermines the independence earned at incalculable costs.

The Yugoslav wars also ended for the most part in negotiations, but clearly the separatists fighting against the former Yugoslavia won, with substantial help from the international community. In Bosnia, the three-year multi-factional armed conflict ended through long negotiations leading to the Dayton Agreement, midwifed by a six-month bombing campaign by NATO. Success once again came at enormous cost, including the siege of Sarajevo, the Srebrenica massacre, and atrocities and war crimes committed heavily by Serb leaders, although the International Criminal Tribunal for the former Yugoslavia convicted Croats and Bosnians as well.

There are five other cases in which insurgent wars against governments resulted in the clear military defeat of those governments: Ethiopia, Serbia (Kosovo), Rwanda, Indonesia (East Timor), and Panama. The most clear-cut case of insurgents overthrowing a government was in Ethiopia. Rebels fought for almost two decades to finally defeat, in 1991, the extraordinarily despotic and vicious regime of Mengistu Haile Mariam. The war really began with the overthrow of Emperor Haile Selassie in the 1974 coup, with Eritrean and Ethiopian rebels then joining together in armed combat against the central government. In the 1980s, as the fighting continued, Ethiopia was visited by a series of catastrophic famines. Hundreds of thousands died due to fighting and more than a million due to famine exacerbated by the fighting, the population having been robbed of any resilience it might otherwise have had. Over the course of almost two decades of fighting, there were significant shifts among rebel groups, with the rebels rooted in the Tigray region mounting the major military role. The costs in human tragedy and deferred development are beyond counting. Eritrea and Ethiopia are now locked in stagnated conflict. Ethiopia continues to face threats to its national unity, with the government, now made up of the forces that defeated the Mengistu regime, still facing a low-level Ogadeni insurgency.

Kosovo followed up its internationally assisted fight with Belgrade with a unilateral declaration of independence. While it has not yet found full acceptance within the international community, there is little doubt that it is on the path to full statehood and ultimately acceptance into the United Nations. It is an example of an insurgent win, but it really became a multilateral war (discussed in the next chapter), and "win" in this context does not mean peace for a Kosovo still plagued by deep divisions.

In the aftermath of the 1994 Rwandan genocide, the Rwandan Patriotic Front (RPF), which had been trying to depose the Hutu-dominated government of Juvénal Habyarimana prior to a 1993 ceasefire, finally prevailed. When Habyarimana was killed in April 1994, setting off an extraordinarily violent reaction, the RPF regrouped and took control of the country during the chaos. Victory is clearly not a word that fits anywhere in that scenario either. Besides those killed in the genocide, up to half a million women and girls had been raped, some two million fled Rwanda for neighbouring countries, and thousands of those died under the extreme conditions they faced. Instability spilled over into an already fragile Zaire, helping to set the stage for another long and vicious phase of war in the newly named Democratic Republic of the Congo.

The 1980s regime change in Panama is another example of an opposition forcefully overthrowing a government, but this time with the indispensable help of the United States. General Manuel Noriega had been in control and had cultivated good relations with Washington by aiding its Contra war in Nicaragua, but he was ultimately sent to trial in the United States on drug trafficking charges. President Reagan froze Panamanian government assets and prohibited payments, including canal user fees, to the regime. Elections in 1989 overwhelmingly supported the opposition, but the regime rejected the results, and in December the US invaded and a new president was sworn in – an insurgent victory, of sorts, over a government bent on using force to prevent change and failing. While the US invasion installed an opposition by forcefully overthrowing a government, it was obviously also an interstate invasion.

East Timor represents a clear opposition "victory" over a government – namely the government of Indonesia – although it is not so clear that it was an insurgent military victory. Indonesia sought to claim East Timor following the withdrawal of Portugal in 1975. The East Timorese resisted via the Revolutionary Front for an Independent East Timor (Fretilin) and thus began an extended civil war. Indonesia received support and sympathy from many Western governments, despite the UN's declaration of the Indonesian occupation as illegal. Evidence of Indonesian atrocities in the early 1990s began to shift allegiances, as did the awarding of the 1996 Nobel Peace Prize to Bishop Carlos Filipe Ximenes Belo and the exiled Timorese political spokesman José Ramos-Horta. In 1999, Indonesian President B. J. Habibie offered East Timor a choice between political autonomy within Indonesia and independence. Pro-Indonesian militia groups sought to disrupt voting and intimidate the East Timorese, but the referendum had a high turnout, and the result was overwhelmingly for independence. However, that did not settle the matter. Militia-led violence resulted in hundreds of deaths and massive displacement of the population, which in turn led to the deployment of a UN multinational force to restore order. Indonesian security forces and militia withdrew in September 1999, leaving extensive destruction in their wake, and thus a government bent on militarily preventing a determined political movement clearly lost. Ultimately, the insurgents were helped by the UN force that restored order, and especially by the political/diplomatic campaign that shifted support away from the Government of Indonesia to the East Timorese. Chroniclers of non-violent resistance movements suggest the violent tactics were actually unsuccessful, inasmuch as the insurgents never had more than fifteen hundred active fighters and the violent campaign just strengthened the resolve of the Indonesian military against them. Erica Chenoweth and Maria J. Stephen, in their compelling book on "why civil resistance works," trace the development of "The Clandestine Front" into the key nonviolent resistance element of the pro-independence movement. Following the 1991 killing of more than two hundred protestors, public nonviolent protests became a major element of pro-independence strategies. Public demonstrations led by Indonesian students produced a shift in support among business elites and members of the security forces and created the sense that "the whole population fought for independence."[21]

Wars That Ended in Negotiations

In half of the intrastate wars that ended in the past quarter century, the final outcomes were worked out at the negotiating table, not on the battlefield. Governments found that they ended up negotiating with and coming to terms with groups they initially labelled as criminals without legitimacy and which they tried, sometimes for decades, to eliminate by military means. Analysis in the *Human Security Report* concludes that negotiated ends to conflicts become inevitable when there are no alternatives – in other words, when military victory is not available. "Where a conflict is stalemated and victory has become unattainable by either side, the only alternative to a negotiated settlement is continued warfare, perhaps interrupted by short breaks in the fighting." When war without end seems to both sides to be the only prospect, negotiation becomes a credible option. So "settlements typically stop those conflicts that are stalemated and unlikely to be resolved through any other means."[22] An interesting finding of the HSR is that while wars that end in negotiations do sometimes resume, the resumed warfare invariably has a dramatically reduced level of combat deaths. "Death tolls drop by more than 80 percent on average in conflicts that recur after a peace agreement. This is a greater reduction than for any of the other termination types."[23]

As already noted, South Sudan defeated the Government of Sudan in the sense that it achieved its objective of a separate state. It nevertheless negotiated the terms of a ceasefire and set up a process that included a referendum to decide the political future of South Sudan. The fighting had been stalemated for a long time. What the SPLA won was a credible place at the negotiating table, though at costs that will be borne by generations to come.

The decades-long violent conflict in Burundi came to a negotiated end by 2009. Negotiations led to a formal disavowal of further armed conflict, and annual combat deaths since then have remained below the twenty-five deaths per year threshold. The negotiations achieved a ceasefire but the political conflict behind the violence appears as raw as ever. Ethnic violence has plagued Burundi since independence from Belgium in 1962. The world became familiar with Hutu-Tutsi violence during the 1994 genocide in Rwanda, and the same divide dominates political life in neighbouring Burundi. The Hutu/Tutsi distinction is not a clear-cut ethnic distinction in the way that ethnic groups are typically defined. In a sense, the Hutu/Tutsi distinction is as much an economic or class distinction. Tutsis have traditionally, and with Belgian support during the colonial era, been the elites and wielded economic and political power. Coffee is at the centre of this divide. The Belgians introduced it, arranging for the rural poor, the Hutus, to grow and produce it, and for the urban elites, the Tutsis, to oversee the process and control the marketing and most of the income. Keeping this lopsided system in place has meant that violence has been endemic to political life in Burundi. The most recent phase of armed conflict, from 1988 to 2009, claimed three hundred thousand lives, warring factions carried out summary executions, rape and torture to terrorize populations, and thousands were displaced from their homes.

With the conflict unresolvable by military means, negotiations to try to end the conflict have also been a constant factor in the political life of Burundi. After many efforts and partial successes and failures, including efforts at governments of national unity with more balanced Tutsi and Hutu representation and mediation efforts led by Nelson Mandela, the African Union mounted a peacekeeping force, and a UN force of five thousand soon followed. In 2006, the government and the main rebel group, Forces Nationales de Libération (FNL), finally signed a peace agreement that included a provision to demobilize the FNL and integrate them into the national army. While violent clashes continued, it was in gradual decline and by 2010 the FNL recast itself as a political party and contested the 2010 elections.

Negotiated outcomes to entrenched civil wars invariably leave legacies of debilitating costs while still portending uncertain futures. Peace in Sierra Leone, like that in Burundi, is another case of long-term and certain costs promising a still uncertain future. The Economic Community of West African States (ECOWAS) and the UN entered into the Sierra Leone conflict with economic sanctions and military embargoes in 1997, well after fighting had begun and in the aftermath of the May 1997 military overthrow of the government. The Lomé Peace Accords were signed by the government and rebel forces in 1999, but the Revolutionary United Front (RUF) continued its operations and in May 2000 came in striking distance of the capital. That led to direct UK military intervention in support of the government. UK forces protected the airport, supported the UN forces established in the Lomé Agreement, and directly attacked RUF forces. Within four months the situation was largely stabilized in what is widely regarded as a successful foreign intervention, although the basic parameters of the peace that ensued were set out in the negotiations and agreed to in the 1999 accords.

The war drastically cut agricultural production, crippled government revenues from mining, and destroyed hundreds of schools, health clinics, and administrative facilities. Forced displacement affected more than half the population.[24] Once again, war did nothing to resolve underlying grievances – its main accomplishment being that once stability returned the means and resources available for addressing underlying conflicts were dramatically diminished. Only the war's end allowed attention to shift to issues of governance and institution building so that reconciliation could be seriously pursued and sustained.[25]

South Africa never saw the civil war many feared, and it thus becomes a major example of effective non-violent resistance supported by influential solidarity groups and economic sanctions. But according to our working definition of war, the struggle against apartheid did reach the level of armed conflict in the 1960s following the formation of Umkhonto we Sizwe ("Spear of the Nation") as the armed wing of the African National Congress (ANC), a low-level war that continued to 1990 when the ban on the ANC was lifted and Mandela was finally released from detention. Negotiations had been on the agenda since the mid-1980s, but with the precondition that the ANC first abandon military pursuits. When F. W. de Klerk became president, the pursuit of negotiations became more serious, especially in response to persistent economic crisis fed by internal instability and externally imposed sanctions. During the course of negotiations, the ANC suspended but did not renounce armed struggle. There were setbacks in the talks, including as a result of a major attack on the ANC in 1991, but the 1995 election delivered a decisive win by the ANC. In 1995, the Promotion of National Unity and Reconciliation Act was passed, which led to the establishment of the Truth and Reconciliation Commission. The serious work could finally begin on recovering from the incalculable costs of apartheid.

After a decade of armed violence in Nepal, the 2006 peace talks between the Seven Party Alliance and the Maoists led to the ousting of the country's monarchy. The Comprehensive Peace Agreement allowed the Maoists, who had been the primary rebel force during the conflict, to become part of the government. With the signing of the agreement, the number of conflict-related deaths steadily declined, and by 2010 the number of deaths linked to an explicit political agenda had fallen well below twenty-five. In this case, it was not only armed conflict that led to negotiations. Mass non-violent demonstrations also played a key role in getting the King to reinstate parliament and enter into negotiations.

The Tajikistan armed conflict ended in 2000 when the 1997 negotiated settlement appeared to take hold amid a second year of few reported conflict deaths. Following presidential and parliamentary elections, the Commission on National Reconciliation and other international peacebuilding instruments began to withdraw. Tajikistan fell back into conflict in mid-March when opposition fighters attacked government troops. A controversial election process and intermittent clashes led to an extended period of uncertainty, a reminder that negotiations and peace agreements do not necessarily lead to neat and tidy conclusions to conflict.[26]

The negotiated end to the "troubles" of Northern Ireland was a long time coming. For three decades (1965 to 1995) violence linked to the Northern Ireland conflict was at a level qualifying it as an ongoing war. The Good Friday Agreements, aided by the significant involvement of external mediators in extended negotiations, ended the violence, though with some setbacks. The one clear lesson is that superior military or police forces are most often rendered impotent by a conflict that is deeply social and historical.

El Salvador's Archbishop Óscar Romero early on characterized the country's twelve-year civil war (1979–1992) as fundamentally a struggle for human rights. The government, aided by the United States, pursued a counter-insurgency strategy of "draining the swamp" – attacks on people and communities on which insurgent operations depended.[27] A decade after the assassination of the Archbishop, negotiations produced a truce and the Chapultepec Peace Accords were signed, and "by that time more than 75,000 people (mostly noncombatants) had lost their lives, the economy was in shambles, and massive damage to the infrastructure was evident everywhere."[28] A deeply weakened and scarred El Salvador faced extraordinary challenges, but scholars assessing the accords a decade later judged them to be a genuine success, achieving

> the demilitarization of politics and an end to the left's political exclusion; reform of the armed forces and its separation from the political life of the country; improved respect for human rights; enhanced press freedoms and freedom of speech; the successful holding of presidential, legislative, and municipal elections and improved representation at the local level; and a process, albeit far from complete, of modernization and reform of key state institutions.[29]

In virtually all of these cases, and many more, negotiations were forced on governments with undeniably superior military forces – a superiority that could not insulate them from the accommodations and compromises that any negotiation must finally deliver. One conventional take on negotiations is that conflicts must first "ripen" for them to have a chance of succeeding. But ripeness is really a euphemism for a desperately hurting stalemate, that stage of an armed conflict where it has finally become impossible to deny that victory will never be available to either side, with the parties facing the possibility that their political prospects could actually weaken if they continued to pursue only armed combat. The point of conflict diplomacy is to help the parties understand much earlier in the process that combat is not serving their interests and that the accumulating costs will never be warranted by the outcome. When a hurting stalemate is obvious and undeniable, the damage has already been done. The populations affected by an armed conflict feel its destructive impact much earlier than do the elites that prosecute the war. By the time leaders left to their own devices and perceptions are willing to admit stalemate, populations have already been displaced, their economic bases destroyed, and their hopes for a better future critically undermined.

The point of diplomacy is to get to the point of negotiations long before the point of desperation. The point is not to wait for conflict to "ripen," as if that is some natural and autonomous process that permits no human intervention to alter the time line. To promote negotiation before the destructiveness of a hurting stalemate, and thus before a society's physical, human, and psychological resources have been utterly depleted by long-term war, requires especially that elite calculations about their prospects and responsibilities be changed. That in turn requires the international community, especially through the UN but supported by influential states and regions, to focus relentless attention on armed conflicts already underway and on gathering crises where violence is threatening. The objective is to generate political and diplomatic options and pressures to negotiate. The international community has available an array of measures, from the creation of forums and dialogue processes, to ensuring that leaders in conflicts will not be immune from accountability for war crimes committed in their name, to linking the legitimacy of leadership to the level of commitment to pursuing political solutions.

But the negotiations that end war are frequently not the negotiations that address the grievances and conditions that led to war in the first place. Those basic realities can remain largely unchanged when negotiations are focused on a ceasefire, except that the capacity to address those conditions is radically weakened in the wake of war. Winning the peace still requires, after a peace settlement, the long-term implementation of a credible peacebuilding agenda – also a long-term struggle, but one infused with credible hope rather than the accumulating despair of war.

Wars That Dissolved

In just over a third of the wars that ended in the past quarter century, the fighting essentially dissolved – the conflicts became dormant but without a formal resolution. In some cases, rebels concluded that they had no chance of advancing their goals by violent means and found ways of easing back into a political process. That might arguably be considered military defeat of an insurgency, but in reality it is a change in tactics in which the political opening to other options may be as much a factor as the dimmed military prospects of the insurgents. In other cases, governments actively addressed grievances with the result that gradually support for the "armed struggle" faded away. In some cases, external events dramatically changed conditions and new opportunities and perceptions emerged. To some extent, these instances of armed conflicts becoming dormant are simply a reflection of the episodic nature of much of contemporary armed conflict. Fighting waxes and wanes due to a variety of factors. For insurgents, access to ammunition is frequently uncertain – when it is available the fighting escalates, when not, the fighters tend to blend into the local population and the fighting goes dormant until such time as stocks are replenished. But more than that, conflicts that simply fade away tend to leave the basic issues unaddressed. In Rwanda, Uganda, Haiti, Turkey, and Yemen, armed conflicts that had subsided returned. Dissolved conflicts had a recidivism rate of 20 per cent compared with 14 per cent for conflicts with negotiated ends – testimony to the fact that unless the roots of the conflict are addressed and conditions for stability and peace built, the threat of returned conflict remains, regardless of whether fighting ends by agreement or for other less defined reasons.

It is notable that while on average half of all intrastate wars end in negotiations, in the Middle East only one out of the nine intrastate wars that ended in the past quarter century ended through negotiations – the civil war in Lebanon. One of the remaining eight ended in a government victory (the Iraq defeat of the Shia uprising after Desert Storm) while the other seven are all in the "dissolved" category. The tendency of Middle East conflicts to dissolve and, in some cases, resume is undoubtedly due in part to the special intractability of the conflicts rooted in religious and ethnic histories. Egypt under Hosni Mubarak, for example, experienced sustained violence at the hand of militant extremists, which in turn accelerated the regime's efforts to suppress the militants. The violence gradually declined, dissolved, and dropped below levels defined here as war without negotiations or a peace settlement or the basic or core conflict ever being resolved. The Muslim Brotherhood opted for engagement in a very limited political process which continued to keep a lid on the fundamental divides – fundamentalism and secularism, Islam and Christianity. Those divisions remained and erupted again in 2014 in violent conflict that met the criteria for a new war having begun. Further east, Kurdish communities remain in conflict with state structures in Turkey, Syria, Iraq, and Iran. The conflicts turn violent at times and then the armed element of the conflicts dissolves from time to time, with permanent political resolution of the basic divides remaining unavailable.

The Sunni/Shia divide is real and present in the Muslim world, and it too seems not to be amenable to a durable solution. Unlike the Israel/Palestine divide, for which the basic outlines of a negotiated, political, two-state settlement have been well known for a long time, there are no obvious or currently realistic political accommodations available to resolve the Islamist/secular, Sunni/Shia, or Kurdish divides. There are few prospects for negotiated settlements, certainly not without extraordinary levels of political energy and engagement assisted by the international community. But it is even clearer that there are no military solutions available, and that's not for lack of trying. So armed conflicts regularly flare up, but then they dissolve, only to return in new forms.

In Africa, conflicts also regularly dissolve, though proportionally fewer than in the Middle East. In Guinea, for example, fighting by the Revolutionary United Front depended heavily on support from neighbours, and when conflicts in both Liberia and Sierra Leone subsided so did support for the rebels, leading to a gradual decline until the conflict went dormant. The Government of Guinea chose to pursue measures other than an escalation of military operations against the rebels. While the rebels did not participate directly in official negotiations with the government, there were some discreet attempts, but the main focus was to engage neighbouring countries. In 2001, foreign ministers of Guinea, Sierra Leone, and Liberia met and agreed to re-activate a Joint Security Committee. The following year a summit held in Morocco led to an accord on border security. Co-operative implementation of this agreement led to de-escalation even though there were no direct talks between the rebels and government. Isolated incidents of violence along the Liberian border occurred, but gradually the armed conflict went dormant.

While it was an extraordinary achievement for South Africa to avoid black versus white violence on a national scale in the transition from apartheid to democracy, it would also have been surprising had that transition been accomplished without any severe tensions within the black population and without black on black violence. Enough of that did occur to meet the definition of war, but South Africa's real miracle is that internecine conflict in a society in which tribal differences and nationalisms had been formally promoted for generations did not become more widespread. The black on black conflict that did occur involved the historically prominent Zulu community, which appealed to a rich history of conquest and dominance to seek an identifiable and prominent national role. In Mangosuthu Buthelezi, they had a national leader of international stature, ability, and charisma. Inevitably, a power struggle between supporters of the pan-South African ANC, led by Nelson Mandela, and the Zulu nationalist Inkatha Freedom Party (IFP) emerged. Tension and violence escalated in late 1990 when the ANC initiated recruiting drives in various townships in the Zulu heartland of Natal province. IFP supporters attacked ANC supporters in response, and many were killed. Soon the political rivalry and violence were in full swing. While there were police actions in response to the violence, the breakthrough in 1996 was political. Municipal elections in KwaZulu-Natal featured candidates from both parties, there were no casualties, and both main parties had victories. In December 1996, President Mandela signed into law a new constitution, which also received the endorsement of the IFP. During 1997, the KwaZulu-Natal provincial legislature extended peace initiatives through a special bilateral IFP-ANC Peace Committee and a Portfolio Committee on Safety and Security. Relations between the ANC and the IFP improved, but the tension in KwaZulu Natal flared again in 1998 with waves of killings in Richmond. The bloodshed was blamed on the United Democratic Movement (UDM), a new party whose leaders were expelled from the ruling ANC, and the tension was between the UDM and the ANC rather than the IFP and ANC. But then things just seemed to die down. There were no formal negotiations, no party "won." Conditions had changed to undercut the conditions for violence, and the conditions for stability gradually built.

Sectarian and geographically contained wars within Indonesia (reflecting secessionist causes, Christian-Muslim clashes, ethnic rivalries, oppressed minorities, and so on) were prominent in the latter years of the twentieth century. In East Timor, as already noted, secessionists ultimately prevailed through a combination of negotiations, external assistance, and a persistent diplomatic campaign by the Timorese. In Aceh, the devastation of the tsunami changed everything. As the WorldWatch Institute describes it, "the humanitarian emergency triggered by the tsunami provided a critical opportunity for change in Aceh – prying open the province, which was under martial law, to international scrutiny, promising an end to the security forces' human rights violations and freedom from prosecution, and offering an avenue for ending the conflict."[30] In part, the military/police control system was physically destroyed by the tsunami. The repressive infrastructure was largely erased – buildings, documents, and identity cards were lost. Then massive international intervention followed. Not armies, but relief and reconstruction workers. In Maluku, West Papua, Kalimantan, and Sulawesi, the violence gradually dissipated. All had been significant armed conflicts that produced more than one thousand combat deaths each. In some cases the reversal included aggressive Indonesian police and judicial responses to acts of violence, in others Indonesian authorities engaged communities. Support for violence in the various conflicts, most of which were based on local communal differences rather than conflicts with the government, declined. The Maluku Islands conflict was notable for the sectarian violence between Christians and Muslims over some three decades. In June 2000, the government declared a state of emergency, which allowed for a military intervention and curfews and imposed military police authority. This led to a reduction in violence. In February 2002, a number of Muslim and Christian groups signed an agreement with the government. Had the violence ended then, this would have more properly been recorded as a conflict ended by negotiation. However, violence persisted over the next few years with more than twenty-five deaths each year; thus the war had not in fact ended. The fighting did, however, gradually decline and thus dissolved. In West Papua, in a long-term conflict extending back to the 1960s and focused on independence aspirations of many Papuans, the fighting also gradually dissipated, but the conflict remains unresolved and is still a source of sporadic violence.[31]

West Papua is an example of an ongoing armed conflict that the adopted definition of war fails to recognize, a reminder, as is Indonesia's Kalimantan, that low levels of violence can persist and reflect the absence of either justice or harmony even if there is also an absence of war. Western Kalimantan erupted in deeply sectarian conflict at the turn of the millennium between the minority Madurese, migrants originally from the island of Madura, and the combined majority of Malays and Dayaks. The latter two groups had been traditionally marginalized and the forests they depended on were progressively taken over by the Indonesian government and its business partners. The conflict dissolved after widespread evacuations of Madurese communities in deliberate ethnic cleansing strategies to permanently change the ethnic make-up of the region.[32] The UCDP notes that only a few thousand Madurese (out of a previous population of 150,000) were left in Central Kalimantan by 2002.

In Sulawesi, sectarian violence between Christians and Muslims first erupted in 2000. A brawl triggered Muslim attacks on Christians, which were followed by retaliatory violence. By mid-2001, members of Laskar Jihad arrived (they had been fighting in the Maluku Islands), and violence escalated in November. The Red Force, a Christian paramilitary group, emerged in response. Sporadic clashes continued. Violence led to over one thousand deaths and fifty thousand displaced. In December 2001, leaders of Muslim and Christian communities participated in government-sponsored peace talks, which led to a declaration (Malino) and an apparent end to violence. However, in August 2002, violence erupted again. The government sent in security forces as part of a larger crackdown on Laskar Jihad. In 2002, despite continued violence, some Christian and Muslim leaders met to reaffirm support for the peace agreement. In 2003, the government withdrew one thousand troops, but more attacks followed, this time linked to Jemaah Islamiyah, a regional and more extremist organization that changed the conflict's dynamics. More soldiers and police were deployed. Violence has mostly subsided in the years since though sporadic attacks have continued. There was military involvement and a peace agreement, but neither was decisive (and not all groups involved in the conflict were included in the negotiations).[33]

Peru's long-standing conflict triggered by the 1980 attempt by the

Sendero Luminoso, or Shining Path, to overthrow the Peruvian government, also ended through a gradual decline in fighting. The movement was undermined by the government's focused attacks on its leaders. By 2000, the conflict had become dormant – two successive years with deaths below twenty-five – but the issues didn't go away and less than a decade later rebel group actions under Comrade Artemio were re-ignited. The threshold of one thousand deaths was not crossed, but there were more than twenty-five deaths in each of those years. In December 2011 the Sendero Luminoso announced that its military struggle was over and that they wanted to negotiate with the government. The Sendero Luminoso, they said, would continue its struggle for political goals, but without arms. Some clashes continued, but at low levels of less than twenty-five deaths per year, and in 2012 Artemio was captured. Again, conflict escalated somewhat but not to the level of twenty-five deaths.

Wars begin in a wide variety of circumstances and conditions, and they end in similarly multiple ways. Decisive military conclusions are rare, negotiations are the norm, and some do fade away, at least for a time. In Europe, where most wars were relatively brief, most ended through negotiations. Diplomatic interest and concern for European wars was intense, and the tolerance for chaos and uncertainty so close to central Europe was low. In the Middle East, where diplomacy is reluctant, and the tolerance for disorder seemingly high, less than 20 per cent were negotiated. Instead, most conflicts that ended dissolved – the issues being intractable, but the futility of fighting also increasingly obvious.

The way intrastate wars ended is significantly influenced by the nature or type of civil war. Sixty per cent of state control and state formation intrastate wars – generally conflicts in which the issues were sharply delineated – ended in stalemates that led to negotiations (this is slightly above the average of 50 per cent ending in negotiations). In state control and state formation wars, the stakes are high and it is rare that either side is willing to give up the fight. The entities involved and issues being contested are relatively clear, and the commitment to them, whether on the battlefield or at the negotiating table, persistent. But neither can they indefinitely avoid the reality that they are not and will never be in a position to win their objective by military means. That leads them to negotiating tables to see how much of what they have been fighting and sacrificing for can be salvaged. The parties to such conflicts tend to be well defined and organized and thus able to mount serious negotiations. When issues remain intractable, in a minority of conflicts (some 20–25 per cent), there is a tendency for the fighting to subside. Sometimes these are temporary retreats by opposition forces, as was the case at particular points for Kurdish aspirations in Iran, Iraq, and Turkey, but Kurdish aspirations were certainly not abandoned.

The fate of state failure wars is very different. In only one case (Bangladesh) was the fighting ended by negotiations. In almost 90 per cent of cases of failed state wars ending, they essentially faded away. The issues in failed state wars are much less defined than in state control and state formation wars, meaning that the negotiating points are much harder to find. Leadership of the parties or factions is also much more diverse, meaning that it is much more of a challenge to find the right people with whom to deal. The fighting factions tend to be less organized and therefore less able to mount serious negotiations. Battlefield superiority is of little consequence. So neither combat nor negotiations are particularly effective. Instead, the way to end failed state wars is not to defeat or negotiate with an adversary, but to provide disaffected citizens with the conditions of stability and basic government services that have to that point been denied them.

Overall, the central point is confirmed – namely, governments that choose to respond to dissidence with armed force rather than political engagement and accommodation are fighting against very high odds. They rarely win.

4

How International Wars End

OR A GROUP OF KABUL HIGH SCHOOL BOYS in a crowded dormitory, there was nothing new in the notion that contemporary wars – whether intrastate, interstate, or multilateral – fail to deliver promised political outcomes. Their temporary home had all the scattered laundry, books, soccer balls, electronic music players, and general messiness you would expect to find in any room crowded with a dozen double bunks and twenty-four active young men. From homes in many parts of Afghanistan and representing a diverse range of ethnic communities, they were high school seniors who had been given the opportunity to come to Kabul to study English in the hope of earning scholarships to universities in India. On this particular day in April 2008, they had all agreed to take a break before the evening meal to meet a foreign visitor and talk about their experiences of the then seven-year war. They were unfailingly polite and welcoming, but they saw no need to hide their feelings of thorough contempt for the rich and powerful of the international community who were obviously no match for what they called the tribal fighters resisting the foreign occupiers of their country. Some hinted that they supported the Taliban, others clearly did not, but they all shared in the bewilderment that led to one question above all others: "If forty of the world's richest and most powerful countries [by which they meant the countries in the International Security Assistance Force (ISAF)] have come to tiny Afghanistan to change things and help Afghans, why can't we see any change for the better?" There was little anger or frustration in the question. It was asked more out of an overwhelming sense of weariness – the kind usually found in their more jaded elders. These young men made it very clear that they weren't expecting a credible answer from their visitor. Indeed, they had little appetite for ideological debates or discussions of extremism or terrorism. Their own experiences told them that the conflicts tearing at their country were all about regional, political, economic, and social divides that were not amenable to military bridging. They were drawn repeatedly and movingly to descriptions of the growing poverty in their home communities. "It was not like this under the Taliban," said one. "The people are poor and they are getting poorer under this corrupt American-backed government, and that is why they are fighting," said another. They had seen first-hand that superior military force was no guarantor of the rule of law in deeply troubled societies and that it has no capacity to set the foundations for durable social and political stability in the face of chronic, politically driven violence. As their teacher said later, without relief from the rising food prices and dashed commerce that left millions of Afghans struggling and in urgent need of assistance, "there won't ever be enough tanks and bomber aircraft to make Afghanistan safe." The events of the ensuing years have done little to challenge his insight.

It is not only intrastate or civil wars that fail to resolve the political divides that spawned them or that fail to advance human security. Interstate wars and multilateral wars like the one in Afghanistan from 2002–14 are also bent on the futile aim of mobilizing enough tanks and bombers and young fighters to deliver the safety and security for which the young students of Kabul longed, but the results much more often than not look a lot like the Afghanistan they were experiencing first hand.

Interstate Wars

If ever there was a war for which the costs were unwarranted by the outcome, it was the eight-year Iran-Iraq war. Whether it was born out of Sunni-Shia rivalry and mistrust, Arab-Persian strategic competition, personal rivalry between the countries' respective leaders, border disputes, Iraqi President Saddam Hussein's miscalculation, or all of the above, when the war finally ended in a ceasefire brokered by the UN Security Council, all of the rivalries and disputes that predated the war remained. While Iraq gained a huge military advantage over Iran as a result of the war, it was squandered in 1991 because war could clearly not end the megalomania and miscalculation of Saddam Hussein. Invading Kuwait in 1990, Saddam triggered a major US-led multilateral response that, besides overturning Iraq's capture of Kuwait, trashed the Iraqi military and wiped out any advantage it had gained over Iran. The result was two dramatically weakened states. GlobalSecurity.Org summed it up this way: "At the end, virtually none of the issues which are usually blamed for the war had been resolved. When it was over, the conditions which existed at the beginning of the war remained virtually unchanged."

Indeed, that is a theme that extends well beyond the Iran-Iraq War. While the military advantage was with Iraq when the war ended, and before Saddam's invasion of Kuwait, it certainly did not "win" in any meaningful sense. The two states fought to a prolonged and acutely hurting stalemate and then finally turned to UN-brokered negotiations and settlement. The human casualty figures, while they don't come close to European losses in World War II, nevertheless reached devastating levels that remain central to the psyches of both states. Iran may have suffered a million casualties – more than three hundred thousand killed and more than five hundred thousand injured. Iraqi casualties approached four hundred thousand. Children were led into slaughter. Chemical weapons were used.[1]

If it is possible to extract anything positive from this avoidable and pointless human-made disaster, it has to be the recognition that in the second half of the twentieth century and the first decade of this one, wars like the Iran-Iraq War have become increasingly rare. It cannot yet be said that states no longer go to war against other states to settle conflicts between them, but in early 2015 there was no interstate war – that is, there was no instance of two countries directly at war with each other. By 2015 there hadn't been a straightforward state-to-state war for well over a decade. It's obviously true that in 2015 an international coalition of states was launching attacks on Iraq and Syria, but whatever the political justifications mustered for the attacks, these are interventions in intrastate wars – hence they are characterized as multilateral wars of the kind discussed below. Even though all wars in a globalized world are internationalized, very few of the wars of the last quarter century were between states. Contemporary wars, as we've seen, are overwhelmingly within states and fought over conflicts that are essentially internal to those states. Globalization complicates efforts to make strict distinctions between interstate, multilateral, and intrastate wars, but fewer than one in ten wars in the past twenty-five years was an armed conflict between two states in an effort to settle disputes between them.

Two of the six interstate wars of the past quarter century – Iran-Iraq and Iraq-Kuwait – involved Saddam Hussein. Of Africa's many wars during that period, only one was unambiguously interstate – namely, the series of border clashes between Eritrea and Ethiopia at the turn of the millennium. In 1998, Eritrea and Ethiopia went to war with each other in the old style of tank and artillery battles supported by bomber aircraft for cover. There was European-style trench warfare in long lines of trenches carved out of the rocky terrain of the disputed border region that only a few years later had the deceptive look of a tranquil countryside decorated with neatly constructed stone walls. In three brief spurts of battle, in 1998, 1999 and 2000, those two former friends went to war to settle the disputed border in a largely barren region of little geographic or economic consequence. Of course, the real estate in question was neither the core of the dispute nor worth the cost of defending it. The intermittent warring was in fact a proxy for the growing economic competition and the kinds of deep suspicions and recriminations that bedevil close friend-ships gone bad. Less than a decade earlier, the two had been the closest of partners in the overthrow of the Ethiopian regime of the dictator Mengistu Haile Mariam.

Some seventy thousand people, mostly combatants, were killed in the fighting between the erstwhile friends and perhaps a million people left homeless in those three bursts of interstate warfare. Nasty, brutish, and short, the war solved nothing, serving only to further the impoverish-ment of both countries. There is no more persuasive sign of the futility of the Eritrea-Ethiopia war of 1998–2000 than the fact that more than a decade later Ethiopia was once again raiding Eritrean military bases and fears of renewed conflict were in the wind. A replay of the all-out battles of 1998–2000 was still unlikely, partly because the two countries had done the math. Regardless of the price paid and the costs incurred, the war clearly could not produce anything approaching commensurate ben-efits. Despite continuing enmity and suspicion, both Eritrea and Ethiopia seem to have absorbed the sober truth that another war could promise only what the earlier one delivered – extraordinary human and financial pain on both sides, leaving the political dispute only more deeply entrenched. Unfortunately, it's not possible to report that the two sides have finally given over their dispute to diplomacy and mediation in search of a durable peace between them (they did so at one point, but then ignored the results). Instead both have now taken up mutually destructive destabilization tactics – each supporting and arming dissi-dents within the other's borders, while at the same time spending scarce billions of dollars to replenish their weapons stocks (and to keep their trenches and stone barricades neatly groomed).

Negotiations were integral to transitioning Eritrea and Ethiopia from the hot war to their current and ongoing cold war. The Organisation of African Unity (OAU) established a mediation committee and negotiations were based on proposals by Rwanda and the US in June 1998. That attempt failed, but indirect talks were taken up again the following year. They too failed when the parties were unable to agree on a ceasefire in advance of negotiating a full peace accord. Following a major Ethiopian offensive, Eritrea withdrew troops from certain disputed areas, and in December 2000 new peace talks were held. When a ceasefire agreement was finally signed, it entrenched the military positions at that time, an arrangement that was generally thought to favour Ethiopia, and estab-lished a 25 km-wide de-militarized security zone to which peacekeeping forces were deployed. Despite the cessation of hostilities, tensions have remained high, with periodic military build-ups and posturing between the two states. The UN peacekeepers pulled out in 2008, and though there was fear that conflict would re-ignite, it has thus far remained inactive.

On the surface, and to a considerable degree in reality, Vietnam's 1978 attack on Cambodia was a success – and an exception to the futility that marks most contemporary warfare. It was a war that Vietnam largely won and that substantially met Vietnam's political/strategic objective – namely, the removal of the Pol Pot regime in Cambodia and an end to the Cambodian attacks on Vietnamese territory that had been a major thorn in its side since the 1975 defeat of the Americans and reunification of Vietnam. Vietnam defeated Pol Pot's Khmer Rouge government and a new Cambodian government dominated by Vietnam was established, which lasted for another ten years. While the international community and Cambodians never really accepted Vietnam's occupation of Cambodia, and the pressure on Vietnam to withdraw was considerable, it was nevertheless effectively tolerated. After all, the viciousness of the Khmer Rouge when in power (the 1975 to 1979 genocide that was not formally called genocide in order to bring remnants of the Khmer Rouge into a final settlement) was beyond extraordinary. But Vietnam's intervention was costly in lives, with estimates of the number of Vietnamese soldiers killed ranging from fifteen thousand to thirty thousand, and it was only "largely" successful because it could not defeat the Khmer Rouge insurgency. That continued even after the withdrawal of Vietnam and the establishment of a provisional UN-administered government supported by more than twenty thousand UN-mandated peace support troops. UN forces withdrew in November 1993 following elections and the launch of a new constitutional monarchy, but the Khmer Rouge continued to resist and foment internal upheaval until new elections finally set a path toward recovery and greater regional stability.

The 1990s war between the two newly independent states of Armenia and Azerbaijan ended in a ceasefire, again with the central question – the status of Nagorno-Karabakh – as unresolved as it was at the start of the war. Two decades later, border clashes once again threatened another round of war. In a sense, this conflict could be classified as internal to Azerbaijan. Armenia did go to war against Azerbaijan for control of Nagorno-Karabakh, but once Azerbaijan and Armenia became fully independent countries, the conflict took on greater domestic prominence within Azerbaijan. Nagorno-Karabakh sought independence from Azerbaijan (in the mode of a state formation intrastate conflict), but with active support from Armenia. The relationship between the two states remains tense. In 2005 and 2012, levels of violence surpassed the twenty-five-death threshold – though not meeting the criteria for considering it a resumed war. But it is clear that the conflict is far from resolved. The earlier Armenia-Azerbaijan War was extraordinarily costly. Some 100,000 lives were lost and 2.2 million were displaced, its one lasting achievement being ongoing tension.[2]

The 2006 Israeli attack on Lebanon was in one sense simply one more skirmish in the never-ending Middle East crisis, but the war counting criteria could qualify it as a distinct, though brief, interstate war in which both Hezbollah and Israel pursued political aims through military attacks. However defined, the 2006 Israel-Lebanon war followed the pattern of most wars of the past quarter century – that is to say, the political objectives for which the war was fought were hardly closer to being realized after the war than they were at its start. Hezbollah was neither politically nor militarily diminished (at least not for long – two years later Ehud Barak, as Defense Minister, told a Knesset committee that Hezbollah had grown three times stronger than it was after the war[3]), and its close links with Iran continued. In mid-2006, Israel responded to a cross-border raid by Hezbollah forces based in Lebanon. It had killed eight Israeli soldiers and, even more provocatively, two Israeli soldiers had been kidnapped. The subsequent thirty-four-day war resulted in the deaths of over 1,110 Lebanese and 156 Israelis and the displacement of more than 500,000 Lebanese civilians. A UN-brokered ceasefire included provisions to deploy UN forces to southern Lebanon under the existing UN force in Lebanon. Israel was widely criticized in the international community for using cluster bombs and for a particular attack that killed "at least 34 children and 22 adults as they slept in this village [Qana] believed by the Israelis to be the source of terrorist missiles fired at Israel."[4] Other civilians were killed in Israeli attacks on Beirut's international airport. Both sides claimed victory, but in reality a shaky ceasefire agreement is all the war produced.

Ethiopia's 2006 invasion of Somalia was in one sense simply a continuation of Addis Ababa's long-standing meddling in Somali affairs and civil war. Ethiopia had and has good reason to be attentive to developments in Somalia. The two states fought a war in the 1970s that featured Somalia's irredentist designs on the Ethiopian Ogaden. Ethiopia had also been trying, without much success, to influence developments throughout Somalia's decades-long civil war, and in 2006 Ethiopia invaded Somalia with the intention of dealing a fatal blow to the rising Islamist forces and stabilizing the provisional government. It didn't turn out to Ethiopia's, or Somalia's, advantage.

Categories of warfare don't always apply with crystal clarity, this war being a case in point. Ethiopia's invasion of Somalia was in one sense an interstate war, but in another sense it was just a significant episode in Somalia's ongoing civil war. After the initial cross-border attack, Ethiopia essentially got caught up on one side of Somalia's civil war (similar to the American-led attacks on Afghanistan and Iraq, which were blatant attacks by one country, primarily, against another, landing the attacker in the midst of a civil war). The Ethiopian invasion came with the support of the Transitional Federal Government of Somalia (TFG) and the encouragement of the United States. But given Ethiopia's long-standing quarrels with Somalia and notoriously persistent meddling in Somali affairs, the invaders were met with almost universal suspicion and hostility, exacerbating the wariness that Somalis already felt toward the transitional government. The invasion was an initial success, with the first attacks securing Baidoa, where the transitional government was battling Islamist forces. The Ethiopians then moved on to Mogadishu to capture the capital from the Islamic Courts Union. While Ethiopia pledged an early withdrawal, it stayed for two full years, long enough to generate an energized opposition to the foreign occupation and a more militant and entrenched opposition to the TFG – a familiar pattern.

Ethiopia was in fact borrowing from two US war adventures – and neither is a worthy model. The US attacks on Afghanistan and Iraq were obviously intended to change the course of events in both countries in directions more favourable to US strategic security interests and the interests of Afghans. In the early days of each war the US too found success, but it also didn't last. While the Afghan and Iraqi regimes were quickly dispatched, what followed was closer to events in Somalia in the wake of Ethiopia's intervention. Opposition to the foreign occupiers was galvanized and active insurgencies soon followed.

Interstate wars are typically wars of "choice" – making prevention the seemingly simple matter of making a different choice, the choice against war. While armed conflicts don't usually come down to "simple" choices, as we've already noted, states are in fact increasingly choosing against war in state-to-state political conflicts.

Multilateral Wars

The end of the Cold War ushered in a new kind of war – the multilateral wars by coalitions of the willing. These are not peacekeeping or peace support operations, which are military operations in the context of peace agreements and involve related political and humanitarian measures (chapter 9). Instead, multilateral wars are military interventions by coalitions of multiple states intended to force particular outcomes by dint of force. They are wars intended to override political and diplomatic process and impose security. Multilateral interventions have been and are pursued in the context of both inter- and intrastate armed conflicts. Such interventions are usually formalized as multilateral, which is not the same as being legal or politically legitimized, by means of agreements among the intervening states themselves, or by action of the United Nations Security Council.

Multilateral interventions by coalitions of the willing were briefly given a good name by the UN-mandated and US-led expulsion of Iraq from Kuwait in 1991, following Saddam Hussein's invasion and attempt to conquer or control the small oil sheikdom. The Iraq-Kuwait War is the only instance in the past twenty-five years of an interstate war being multilateralized. The Iraq invasion of Kuwait stands, of course, as a prime example of the failure of interstate war to yield benefits that would remotely warrant the human and material costs. Iraq got an early victory and a nineteenth province. The billions of dollars of debt that Iraq owed Kuwait as a result of borrowing for the Iraq-Iran War was meant to be wiped out by the invasion, and Iraq thought it would henceforth control (as it turned out, rather temporarily) Kuwaiti oil production and the generous revenues that flowed from it. But, in the face of worldwide condemnation, sanctions, and, ultimately, military action, the occupation lasted a mere seven months. Attacks on the Iraqi occupiers restored Kuwait to the Kuwaitis and the UN Charter's prohibition against aggression was honoured, making this multilateral war a genuine success in meeting its objectives. But whether Desert Storm offers a compelling model remains an open question. The Iraqis killed perhaps one thousand people in Kuwait and caused another three hundred thousand to flee. The US-led international forces killed at least thirty thousand Iraqis in order to return Kuwait to dictatorial rule – confirming that when constructive nation building is not the objective, force can be very effective.

However, reversing blatant aggression was what the UN and the international community were supposed to be able to do – collective security arrangements were to build respect for international law and challenge state impunity, as well as reverse aggression. Under the UN Charter, the world is called to rally round and defend the rule of law and restrain those regimes in unequivocal violation of the norms and standards of international behaviour. This success in the early years of the post–Cold War era inspired other coalitions of the willing to force desired political outcomes – but none has matched the success of the Kuwaiti action.

Interventions, as we'll see, largely produced the sought outcomes in Bosnia and Kosovo and even Haiti, but not without leaving some complicated legacies. The US invasions of Afghanistan and Iraq, both briefly interstate wars when the initial attacks took place, produced early successes inasmuch as they led to the rapid defeat of governments in the invaded states. Then both of these wars in turn spawned drawn out multilateral wars fought by international coalitions of the willing. While the international community intervened militarily to reverse the Iraqi takeover in the case of Kuwait, in Afghanistan and Iraq the international community intervened militarily to consolidate and legitimize the newly installed regimes. The Afghan and Iraqi civil wars are among the six instances of intrastate wars becoming multilateralized (the other four being Haiti, Kosovo, Bosnia, and Libya). In only half of the six did the interventions end the war (Haiti, Bosnia, and Kosovo). In the other three cases, intense wars continue.

The 1992 US intervention in Somalia is a special case. The UN-authorized intervention met with early success in the sense that the combat forces were able to push through to the beleaguered city of Baidoa to save many thousands from starvation, without a shot being fired. Somalia had by then been reduced to a humanitarian disaster relief zone by the civil war that began in 1986 and heavily escalated in 1989. Relief efforts were underway throughout this period, but on-the-ground distribution had run afoul of a proliferation of local militias who seized food shipments and redeployed them to their own regions or sold items at markets, leaving millions of Somalis in desperate straits. In the fall of 1992 President George H. W. Bush launched operation "Restore Hope" by which American forces entered the country, famously met by television cameras and journalists rather than any armed resistance, to establish secure corridors for aid distribution. At its peak, the operation included thirty-eight thousand troops from twenty-three countries and almost fifty international humanitarian organizations. Many thousands of lives were saved from famine, but the conflicts and dysfunction at the root of the crisis were not addressed, and gradually, Somali hostility towards foreign forces grew. At the same time American forces were drawn into the civil war, especially in Mogadishu. The Americans identified Somali faction leader General Mohammed Farah Aideed as the chief villain and set out to get him. But not all agreed, and General Aideed had plenty of friends who helped him stay a step ahead of his American pursuers. It was a conflict that America's eminently superior force could not control. The famous "Black Hawk Down" episode, in which American helicopters were shot down and soldiers killed and dragged through the streets of

Mogadishu, galvanized opposition to the American presence and per-suaded the Americans to leave just as soon as they could manage it.[5] The Somali operation was not conceived as a military intervention to end or influence the course of the civil war, but the availability of impressive fire-power can cloud judgment and fuel hubris, and so the Americans couldn't keep themselves out of the fight they thought they could settle. They got involved, but they certainly couldn't settle it. They soon left and Somalis have continued varying levels of fighting ever since.

While success has spectacularly eluded the international community in Afghanistan, Iraq, and Libya, in each of these cases a new kind of inter-nationalized civil war was launched with the intention of shaping, by col-lective force, the course of events within a single state. After the initial destruction of the former regimes, civil wars either continued or re-emerged. In Afghanistan and Iraq, they were fought largely by foreign international forces against indigenous rebel forces, with the latter in effect bent on doing what the international community did in Kuwait, namely, reverse the invasions. The international forces were there to sup-port weak replacement regimes that the American invasions had spawned – setting up the phenomenon of multilateralized civil wars by interna-tional coalitions of the willing. Over the past twenty-five years, there were six particular instances of foreign forces intervening in intrastate armed conflicts with a view to ending those wars or at least coming to the pro-tection of vulnerable people.

Afghanistan

The multilateral war in Afghanistan, which sought to entrench the new government after the Taliban were deposed, has been persistently char-acterized as the necessary or good war, primarily to distinguish it from the optional and bad war in Iraq. But one moniker that the war in Afghanistan has not earned is the "successful war." If Kuwait gave multi-lateral interventions a good name, Afghanistan is the counterpoint.

The war in Afghanistan – the "good war" that initially breathed life into NATO's aspirations for a global mission – has gone through two dis-tinct phases. The first was the interstate war that saw US forces spear-head an attack that successfully defeated the then Government of Afghanistan. The second phase was the extended multilateral war that also met with early success, and, as we'll see in chapter 9, followed basic peace support principles in its early stages in 2002 and 2003.

For the early defeat of the Taliban regime, local forces provided the boots on the ground to gain territory in the wake of American air strikes, and together they produced the kind of tactical "win" that is readily accomplished by superior military force. The second phase, the formally multilateralized phase of the Afghan war, began immediately with the ambitious strategic objective of establishing a stable social/political order. And Afghans now know better than most that military forces, no matter how powerful or sophisticated, cannot force or forge predetermined political and social outcomes and are incapable of reshaping reality to fit those predetermined objectives. The presence and actions of international forces obviously influence political outcomes, including peace negotiations, and they clearly achieve tactical objectives. In Kuwait, the only objective pursued was the removal of the Saddam Hussein regime. After that, strategic objectives and outcomes would depend on the local actors, sensibly so since long-term stability and peace are well beyond the competence of military forces to deliver. That objective requires reliable local entities. In Kuwait, the ruling family was available to consolidate the military gains of the international forces and to resume its authority over the state. In Afghanistan, Iraq, and Libya no credible authorities were available to establish effective governance.

Iraq (US Invasion)

Iraq, like Afghanistan, was already steeped in chronic armed conflict, at war by the definition applied here, at the time of the US invasion. The American attack essentially transitioned the Iraqi conflict into a new multilateralized war. By some definitions, the war may have started and ended in 2003 with a definitive victory for the coalition forces, who were swiftly successful in achieving their goal of ousting Saddam Hussein. But the ousting of Hussein did not come close to meeting the declared objectives and international forces continued heavy fighting in an effort to achieve the ends that were eluding them – a stable, democratized Iraq that would not be a haven or base for terrorist operations, against either the Government of Iraq or other states or targets. The US declared an end to the war on May 1, 2003, and the beginning of a "stabilization" mission, but it was a distinction without a difference. The war obviously continued, even if in a somewhat different form. The ouster of Saddam is more properly understood as one campaign within a much longer-term civil war.

The withdrawal of American combat forces during continuing high levels of violence was a de facto admission that, in the circumstances, military force was not going to resolve anything. The annual combat death rate had increased dramatically – it was at a consistent level of about four thousand annually from 2009 through 2012, but then jumped to ten thousand in 2013 and seventeen thousand in 2014.[6] Amid declarations that Iraqis would now have to look after their own security while working to establish a functioning civil-political order, the custodians of the world's largest and most significant military coalition came face-to-face, again, with the sobering reality that it could not deliver what it advertised. The guardian of global freedom cannot deliver it to even one small corner of the globe where its military challengers are laughably weak by comparison, but where the absence of a basic national consensus and minimally trusted national institutions has rendered foreign military forces at best irrelevant and, in truth, a major part of the problem. Strategic consent – from a national population that welcomes local authorities and institutions and the international forces sent to support them – has throughout been totally absent, and it could not be won militarily. Superior military force can win wars bent on destruction, Iraq tells us again, but it can't win peace – the latter has to be built out of other kinds of political and economic realities.

Libya

The multilateral war on Libya made that same point abundantly clear. The multilateral phase of that war was brief, and while it may well have prevented mass atrocities in Benghazi, the threat of which was key to the UN authorizing the international coalition, the aggressive move to help topple the Gaddafi regime was undertaken without any credible idea, let alone plan, for what would follow. The NATO intervention ended, but as in the interventions in Afghanistan and Iraq, the multilateral war did not end the civil war. In the latter half of 2014 and early 2015 the fighting had escalated dramatically, and two hundred to four hundred people were being killed monthly.[7]

Bosnia

The war in Bosnia began as a classic internal identity conflict that ended in negotiations, but with one phase including the major intervention of a multilateral coalition of the willing. The 1992–95 war was part of the breakup of Yugoslavia. Economic stresses added to the tensions among the key Bosnian communities, the Bosniaks, Croats, and Serbs, with the central contention being on the future of the state. The Bosniaks and Croats preferred to follow the independence route already taken by Slovenia and Croatia. The fighting among the three communities broke out following the referendum that led to independence in 1992. It was then a civil war, but outside forces, especially those of Serbia, exacerbated the fighting. Serbian regions fought to break away, aided by Serbia's national army, and the UN force, UNPROFOR, was sent to protect "safe areas." The siege of Sarajevo and the Srebrenica massacre led to NATO bombing attacks on Serb forces. About one hundred thousand people were killed[8] and more than a million displaced[9] in the overall conflict. Developments on the battlefield, enormously influenced by NATO, certainly had a key impact on how the conflict ended, but diplomatic efforts also played a role. The peace agreement negotiated in Dayton (the Dayton Agreement) led to the recognition of Bosnian, Croatian, and Serbian sovereignty and borders, and Bosnia-Herzegovina itself was divided into two republics, one Bosniak-Croat, the other mainly Serb. In 2004, the European Union took over peace support operations from NATO and continues to assist in policing and in the training of security forces in what is still a fragile political context. The office of the High Representative, a key international presence in the country, continues to oversee the implementation of the Dayton Agreement.

Kosovo

NATO's 78-day bombardment of Serbia in 1999, to end Serbian attacks on the region of Kosovo in response to an armed independence movement, is routinely hailed as a successful multinational war in which the international community supported a beleaguered and vulnerable population. It is true that the Kosovars were under brutal attack by Serbia, dead set against allowing Kosovo's ethnic Albanians to follow the example of the Croatians and Bosnians in withdrawing from what remained of Yugoslavia to become an independent state. At the same time, it was a deeply entrenched political dispute, and the NATO intervention did not come anywhere near to resolving the conflict that started the war in the first place. Nor was the intervention an unmitigated success in protecting the Albanians of Kosovo. A province of Serbia, Kosovo was 90 per cent Albanian with an advanced independence movement. But the Serbs felt a special link to Kosovo as the historical birthplace of the Serb state. After the fall of the Iron Curtain in 1989 Albanian Kosovars pursued independence through a largely nonviolent movement. The Serbian leadership responded with harsh repressive measures. The Kosovo Liberation Army (KLA), with roots in the 1980s, had been carrying out low-level attacks since the early 1990s but came to prominence when it stepped up its activities in 1996. The Serbian attacks on the increasingly popular KLA became more severe and when peace talks failed, NATO, without seeking or receiving UN authorization (the assumption was that Russia would veto any proposed action through the Security Council) launched a bombing campaign against targets in Serbia and Kosovo that lasted seventy-eight days. That led to Kosovo being administered by the United Nations Mission in Kosovo (UNMIK), supported by a thirty thousand-member NATO-led peace enforcement mission. Over two hundred thousand Serbs fled Kosovo in order to avoid reprisal killings undertaken by Albanian armed groups. The return and reintegration of these Serbs into Kosovar society alongside the ethnic Albanian population remains a major challenge. In 2013 the European Union facilitated the Brussels Agreement through which Bosnia and Serbia agreed to a fifteen-point plan to, among other things, integrate northern Kosovo into the Kosovo state recognized by Serbia. The population of the northern region remains ambivalent over the agreement and a UN protection force remains in place to assure security, public safety, and freedom of movement. NATO has remained in Kosovo since 1999.

Haiti

Haiti's ongoing domestic turmoil has been accompanied by multiple, and controversial, international military and nonmilitary interventions since the early 1990s. Jean-Bertrand Aristide was elected in 1991 and months later was ousted in a coup and sent into exile in the US. From 1991 to 1994, the UN and OAS (Organization of American States) imposed sanctions in an effort to restore civilian government and in 1994 the UN authorized a multinational force. The military government was forced out and US troops occupied the country. Aristide was returned to power by the US after he agreed to serve a shortened term and to implement IMF-backed economic policies. UN peacekeepers formally took over from the US in 1995 and Aristide was again replaced in 1996 by the election of René Préval. Aristide's influence continued. In 2000, the opposition boycotted disputed elections, which Aristide won, and in 2001 an attempted coup failed to remove him. The UN withdrew from Haiti in 2001, while a US-led economic embargo devastated the economy. The US also began financing opposition parties and civil society organizations led by Haiti's economic elite. Popular support for Aristide began to erode and his administration turned increasingly authoritarian, arming urban gangs that were used to violently suppress dissent and guard against potential coup attempts. In February 2004, insurgents led by former military and paramilitary personnel launched an armed uprising, quickly taking over much of the country.

On February 27, 2004, with the capital Port-au-Prince surrounded by the rebels, Aristide was flown out of the country by the US military. The exact circumstances of Aristide's departure remain disputed, the US military claiming Aristide left voluntarily while Aristide claimed he was forced to leave. In March 2004, a transitional government led by Gérard Latortue, a former United Nations economist and a US resident for fifteen years, was created and began governing with the assistance of the UN-mandated Multinational Interim Force (led by the US, France, Canada, and Chile), later replaced by the United Nations Stabilization Mission in Haiti (MINUSTAH). The collapse of state authority allowed powerful, armed urban gangs and criminal organizations to emerge, further escalating violence. Haiti met the criteria for war, according to the definition used here, in 1993–1994, when US forces were present, and in 2005–2007. The 2005–2007 fighting involved MINUSTAH and Haitian police operations against local groups. After that MINUSTAH returned to state-building and humanitarian efforts, which included policing and stabilization efforts following the 2010 earthquake.[10] The 2014 UN Security Council resolution renewing the UN mission to Haiti recognized "the interconnected nature of the challenges in Haiti," citing simultaneous action on "security, rule of law and institutional reform, national reconciliation and development, including the combat against unemployment and poverty." But Haitians and a range of international observers have heavily criticized the international presence, which is understood to have brought cholera to Haiti.[11]

Given the outcomes of the wars of the past quarter century, states in serious political disputes with other states are clearly not justified in considering the resort to war a likely way out. Whether it is a last resort or the early resort to combat, state-to-state war in the past twenty-five years has an almost unblemished record of coming to a disastrous end for all parties. Iran-Iraq, Iraq-Kuwait, Eritrea-Ethiopia, and Israel-Lebanon – none of these advanced the interests of any of the parties in any desirable way, all inflicted costs that will take generations to recover, and all left fully intact the political disputes that gave way to war. Only the Vietnam-Cambodia War can lay any claim to actually mitigating, if not finally settling, a dispute and furthering stability. In all five cases, war was chosen in the context of chronic instability and only in one could the war be viewed as having been instrumental in recovering stability.

Multilateral wars also take place, by definition, in contexts of chronic instability and always in some of the world's most intractable trouble spots. Without exception, multilateral military coalitions of the willing are launched into contexts of advanced conflict, including levels of violence that meet the definition of an ongoing war. Afghanistan, Bosnia, Haiti, Iraq, Kosovo, Libya, and Syria were all, when attacked or invaded by multilateral coalitions, in advanced stages of disarray. They were all places of extreme human rights violations, among the world's primary producers of IDPs (internally displaced persons) and refugees, and largely devoid of signs that political stability might soon take hold. Multilateral coalitions enter into scenes of advanced disorder, but that doesn't guarantee that they bring order to the chaos. Of the six multilateral wars of the past quarter century, half of the states at the centres of those wars (Afghanistan, Iraq, and Libya) were in much greater disarray following the multilateral interventions and not one of those shows signs of recovering any time soon. In the other three (Bosnia, Haiti, and Kosovo), active warfare ended following the interventions, even though in each case political fragility remains. The difference is that in the absence of war, the pursuit of stability and a durable peace can move higher up the political/economic agenda. The first three fit Rupert Smith's definition of "spectacular failures," while the latter three cannot yet be hailed as durable successes.

Neither interstate nor multilateral wars of the past quarter century build a compelling case for relying on military force in pursuit of sustained political stability.

5

The Limits of Force

THE IDP (INTERNALLY DISPLACED PERSONS) CAMP was new when our small observer group arrived. It was in the late 1990s and the north-south war in Sudan was in one of its more intense phases. Some seventy-five thousand South Sudanese villagers were once again on the move – this time they were fleeing their former IDP camp *en masse*, travelling for days in a desperate trek to escape the raids of Khartoum's Antonov bombers. The whole point of Khartoum's bombing was to set southern Sudanese on the run, to disrupt and demoralize local communities and their traditional governance structures, and to rob the southern fighters of their base of support. The fleeing civilians had crossed the border into Uganda only three days earlier, so now they were refugees. They had ended up in a bush area and the bishop fleeing with them said the people now fashioning makeshift shelters out of the small trees and twigs of their new surroundings, the only building materials available, didn't really know whether they would be there for ten days or ten years.

As we toured this teeming instant bush city struggling to build some order out of the relentless chaos of life in war-torn southern Sudan, we came upon a clearing of heightened commotion and noise. It turned out to be an ever-expanding field designated as the burial ground. Already there were several rows of small crosses made of twigs and sticks marking the mounded graves. At the edge of a row of graves there was more digging – constant digging, we learned, to accommodate the steady stream of arrivals. We approached and then held back when we saw the excavation still being done. Waiting alongside were three wrapped corpses surrounded by family survivors wailing in animated mourning. The previous day they had buried seventeen, and there was no letting up.

We should not have been surprised; we could all do the math. If war in Sudan was claiming an average of more than one hundred thousand per year, as it was at the time – some two thousand per week and three hundred a day – scenes like the one we now saw were being repeated over and over again every day around the country. These were not combat deaths, but they were unmistakably war deaths – premature deaths owing to the extraordinary hardships and deprivations imposed by the decades-long war.

After September 11, 2001, the *New York Times* ran personal accounts of all the victims of those attacks, at least momentarily rescuing from anonymity all those who had died, putting a face to the statistic, giving public acknowledgement to loss and personal tragedy. For the victims of Sudan's wars to be similarly acknowledged it would take three hundred photos and brief biographies each and every day for several decades. And that would do it only if the killing were finally stopped – but it hasn't. In fact, to remember all those who are dying in today's wars around the world (deaths due indirectly to war, i.e., deaths due to the deprivations of war, as well as the direct deaths by violence in combat) would require upwards of one thousand photos and brief biographies each and every day, year in and year out. Most victims of contemporary wars will never be featured in any newspaper. Their loss will be felt by those closest to them, but they will never be publicly acknowledged and counted, either in the name of public accountability or simply to honour the dead. The 2011 "Charter for the Recognition of Every Casualty of Armed Violence," a project of an international group of civil society organizations, affirms the principle that "no person should die unrecorded, and calls on states to uphold this principle for the victims of armed violence."[1]

War is costly. Immeasurably so. And if we admit the wars of the past quarter century into evidence, the costs are not warranted by their outcomes. Contemporary wars don't produce winners, but they are certainly effective in spreading loss. Measured against even the most minimal of expectations of restored political stability, they predictably fail. They don't settle the political conflicts that spawn them, but they do deplete the human, material, and psychological resources, and the political good will, required after the war to address those very same conflicts and to rebuild.

To acknowledge the futility of war is not to deny that police and military forces play important roles in domestic law enforcement, in boosting confidence in the re-emergence of the rule of law in post-conflict settings, and in restoring public order and stability through peacekeeping and peace support operations, including combat, in troubled states and regions. The challenge, in a world in which the rule of law and public safety are relentlessly undermined, is to be realistic about the roles they can perform and the limits of the force they are asked to wield. What are the most effective means of supporting the rule of law and political stability where these are severely challenged? How do security forces bring protection to the most vulnerable when they are threatened, without exacerbating war and adding to its debilitating costs?

The Costs of War

Statistically, the frequency and direct human costs of contemporary war are declining. The number of wars has been in modest decline since the mid-1990s, as has the number of direct combat deaths. That is to be welcomed but not relied upon to continue. By late 2014, the Arab Spring, the Syrian war in particular, and Ukraine had reversed that decline.

Because the fighting is often intermittent, it is easy to understate the costs of contemporary warfare. In some cases, like Syria and Iraq, the fighting is extensive and constant, but much of modern warfare is episodic and rarely involves massed armies or air forces engaged in blanket bombing. More typically, it involves small militia groups or government military units in hit and run operations. But like terrorism, armed conflict requires only minimal operations to inject major disruption into the social order – putting uncertainty and thus fear into the hearts and actions of people, disrupting economic activity, and driving underdevelopment and mal-development with consequences that stretch into generations. For those who study war and its effects closely, the modest post–Cold War declines in warfare are not persuasive evidence of measurably reduced suffering. One survey concludes simply that "contemporary intra-state war is an enormous social evil and the cause of immense human suffering,"[2] and the fact that there are now twenty-nine of them, compared with the thirty-five at the close of the Cold War, suggests that it is not yet a significantly declining social evil. Besides those killed in war, millions are driven from their homes, and rape, torture, extreme human rights abuses, and mass atrocities all flourish in the fog of war.

Counting the dead is one concrete way of calculating the costs of war, but it is ultimately an incalculable cost. It is not measurable in two senses – in the sense that the value of human life is obviously immeasurable, and in the practical sense that it is impossible to know fully and accurately the number of people killed in combat, never mind the number of people who die due to the conditions imposed by war. In Afghanistan, for example, the United Nations has to its credit worked hard to track the number of civilians killed in military or combat operations. It is part of the UN's commitment, initiated by Security Council resolutions, to monitor and reduce the civilian victims of war. The International Security Assistance Force counted force members that were killed, but there were no officially reported counts of the number of insurgent deaths. Bodies can be counted, even if not with total accuracy, and we are all indebted to those who persist in trying to count the victims in Afghanistan, Iraq, Syria, and the two dozen-plus other wars and thereby seek to offer at least some minimal public recognition of loss. Any consistent count of

war dead also offers a clearer indication of the changing pace and conduct of a war. In Afghanistan, for example, UN reports on civilian deaths
revealed a doubling of the death toll from 1,523 in 2007 to 3,021 in 2011,
belying official assurances that the Taliban were increasingly on the
defensive. In his 2010 report, the UN Secretary-General indicated that
"civilians continued to bear the brunt of intensified armed conflict." In
2012 the death count was down from the previous year for the first time
since 2005,[3] but in 2013 the civilian death toll began to climb again and
in 2014 the direct civilian deaths were once again at the highest level in
the post 9/11 phase of Afghanistan's war.[4] Besides acknowledging loss,
the death toll served as a grim reality check on the conduct and progress
of the war. Some estimated that civilian deaths made up almost 50 per
cent of all Afghan combat deaths, but there is no way of knowing that
with any certainty.[5]

In Iraq, reports of the numbers of accumulated deaths vary from
200,000 violent civilian deaths (an average of more than 15,000 per year)
recorded at *Iraq Body Count*[6] to as high as 800,000 reported in a study
undertaken for the British medical journal *The Lancet* in October 2006.[7]
Iraq Body Count reported a huge increase in Iraqi civilian war deaths in
2014–17,049, up from 9,743 in 2013 and about 4,000 in 2012.[8] In Syria, the
war's death toll had reached about 200,000 by the end of November 2014,
according to the British-based Syrian Observatory for Human rights,
about 30 per cent of which were civilians. The organization also noted
that it considered it likely that combatant deaths could be underreported by as much as 80,000.[9]

Counting the war dead remains an imprecise enterprise. Most studies
of direct combat or violent deaths rely on public reports of violent incidents, which is generally assumed to result in under-reporting, in Syria by
as much as 40 per cent. As already noted, the 2009 tabulations of casualties
in the fighting that climaxed in Sri Lanka ranged from 7,000 to 40,000 combat deaths that year. It is at least intuitively obvious that many clashes and
deaths that occur in remote places are never reported. Epidemiological
surveys do not count individual deaths through incident reports but measure excess deaths as a result of war by using pre-conflict mortality rates to
compare projected population growth with actual growth or decline. The
Center for Systemic Peace reports that civilian noncombatants accounted
for 62 per cent of combat deaths in wars from 1946 to 1991. For wars from
1991 to 2011, the Centre estimates that the civilian death toll was as high
as 84 per cent of all combat deaths.[10] The organization Every Casualty
Worldwide is working to encourage comprehensive reporting and challenging governments to "ensure that all lives lost to armed violence, any-

where in the world, are properly recorded." It has developed a "casualty recorder network" and casualty recording standards.[11]

The *Global Burden of Armed Violence* (GBAV)[12] puts the average annual death toll from armed combat, actual combat deaths (combatants and civilians), at 55,000, or just over 1,000 per week (that figure is roughly confirmed by the informal count maintained by Project Ploughshares[13]), but those are pre-Syria counts. In the last three years, the combat death toll has been at least 50,000 per year in Syria alone. And if extraordinary events like the genocide in Rwanda and the invasion of Iraq are taken into annual averages, the numbers are pushed even higher. Even at that, combat deaths represent only about one-quarter of the total annual death toll due to war. That estimate is also at the conservative end of the scale. The 2008 GBAV report, while indicating that some 200,000 people die annually due to the extraordinarily harsh conditions of war, also notes that surveys in the Democratic Republic of the Congo (DRC), where people in the fighting zones are subjected to the most heinous of conditions, estimate that it is more likely that about 400,000 were dying each year in recent times due to war. The Canadian *Human Security Report* disputes the latter figure. It doesn't dispute the high mortality rates in the DRC, but it says that the pre-conflict mortality rate was already high so it is not possible to say that the current abnormally high mortality rate is war-related.[14] Figures on deaths indirectly attributable to war are not available for other major war zones like Somalia or most of today's war zones. The only certainty is that the numbers are high and the tragedy of those deaths unmitigated inasmuch as those wars do not produce any discernable public good in return for the sacrifice.

Reports on the global burden of armed violence also make the point that despite these extraordinary human costs exacted by politically rooted (and therefore avoidable) armed conflict, war is still not the primary source of death by armed violence. The GBAV 2011 report estimates that from 2004 to 2009 the annual death toll by homicide was about 450,000. It will surprise some that worldwide homicides far exceed war combat deaths each year, but that ought not to obscure the significant difference in the impacts of murders and armed conflict deaths. While the impact of a murder goes well beyond the particular life lost, affecting families and communal well-being, the social and political impacts of war combat deaths are undeniably much more far-reaching. Even a small number of combat deaths can paralyze communities, cause flight, and displace large numbers of people. In one incident of fighting in Jonglei state in South Sudan, just over 200 people were killed – a terrible loss of life by itself, but the clashes also led to 20,000 people being displaced.[15] By 2014, the renewed fighting in South Sudan had forced 900,000 to flee their homes, many to neighbouring countries, and all of them into extraordinarily harsh conditions that will leave many more people dead.[16] Similarly, fierce factional fighting in Somalia near the border with Kenya has typically killed relatively few directly, but in one incident in 2010 the fighting forced an estimated 60,000 people from their homes in a matter of a few days.[17] Those killed by the dire conditions forced on them by war will far exceed the number killed in actual combat. And the impacts on survivors are life-long. Large numbers are injured, and many of those suffer permanent physical disabilities and psychological scars. Families are left without income earners, there is community-wide economic stagnation, and public health costs expand.

The relatively low levels of direct combat deaths (compared to the high levels of indirect deaths) reflect the nature of most contemporary wars. The objective of insurgents, with the obvious and tragic exception of Rwanda, is not to maximize the number of deaths but to render a state ungovernable by the existing regime. That can be accomplished through relatively low levels of combat and the displacement of people that attends it. Well over 20,000 persons per day worldwide are forced to leave their homes due to conflict, violence, and human rights violations.[18] At the end of 2013 51.2 million people had been forcibly displaced, as refugees (16.7 million) and IDPs (33.3 million) – the highest number since the 1990s. An estimated 8.6 million people (1.2 million refugees and 7.4 million IDPs) were newly displaced in 2013, the highest annual number in ten years. The five top source countries for refugees are also the scenes of the world's most prominent wars: Afghanistan, Syria, Somalia, Sudan, and DRC. And the top five locations for IDPs in 2013 were Syria, Colombia, DRC, Sudan, and Somalia.[19]

And then there is sexual violence as a deliberate tool of warfare. In one grisly weekend in 2011, between July 30 and August 4, fighters of the Democratic Forces for the Liberation of Rwanda and elements of the Mai Mai, a local militia, entered Luvungi and surrounding villages in the DRC and raped 150 to 200 women and children, including a number of baby boys. They then looted the area and moved on.[20] When the UN investigated, it established that the actual number of rapes in that incident was 242. However, investigators also learned of another 267 previously unreported rapes in the district.[21] The context was the ongoing civil war in the DRC, but somehow the term "war" doesn't come close to capturing the scale of horror of Luvungi. The rapes are beyond extreme by any measure, but as part of the chaos and fighting that have engulfed the DRC since 1990, the Luvungi victims represent but the tiniest fraction of the war's human toll. Hundreds of thousands have been victims of a broad range of sexual assaults, inflicting on them the special brand of stigma that produces life-long consequences and is fundamentally life altering. Such crimes are widely acknowledged to be underreported. And adding to the absolute horror of war-centred sexual violence is the fact the perpetrators are rarely held accountable but rather are granted de facto impunity. UNICEF reports there are more than four million orphaned children in the DRC.[22]

A 2012 book on *Sex and World Peace*[23] shows a link between the well-being and security of women in a society and the security of the state and the incidence of war. One of the book's authors, Valerie Hudson, writes in *Foreign Affairs* that there is "robust empirical evidence" in a large database on the status of women which suggests that the "best predictor of a state's peacefulness is not its level of wealth, its level of democracy, or its ethno-religious identity; the best predictor of a state's peacefulness is how well its women are treated."[24] She says that "the larger the gender gap between the treatment of men and women in a society, the more likely a country is to be involved in intrastate and interstate conflict, to be the first to resort to force in such conflicts, and to resort to higher levels of violence." The way women are treated thus becomes a reliable indicator of national security. "What happens to women affects the security, stability, prosperity, bellicosity, corruption, health, regime type, and (yes) the power of the state." Since 2009 there has been a Special Representative of the UN Secretary-General on Sexual Violence in Conflict. Priorities include addressing the problem of impunity, protection of civilians in conflict, increased recognition of rape as a tactic and consequence of war, and co-ordination of action by UN agencies and promoting action by national governments. There are currently eight priority countries, including the DRC.[25]

To the direct human costs – the human tragedy – of war must be added the economic costs. Specific numbers are hard to come by and usually focus on costs incurred by Western states. We know that the wars in Afghanistan and Iraq had by 2013 already cost the US $2 trillion dollars. A Harvard study indicates the legacy costs will be at least as much and could be as high as $4 trillion – meaning a total cost of the two wars of $4–6 trillion.[26] The single highest legacy cost will be ongoing medical and disability costs related to the veterans of those wars. The Harvard study points out that disability compensation for First World War veterans in the US did not peak until 1969, and for the Second World War it was the late 1980s. Such legacy costs for the Vietnam War and the first Gulf War are still climbing. So the costs to the US and coalition partners for Afghanistan and Iraq will continue for generations. To those costs are added a variety of others, including the replacement of spent military equipment and charges on the escalated debt imposed on those economies by those wars. Less quantifiable but no less debilitating are the social costs – the diminished quality of life for those scarred by the wars, the families put into enduring stress, the careers destroyed or undermined. The Costs of War project, documenting a wide range of human, social, and economic costs, puts a similar price – $4.4 trillion – on the costs to date and estimates of legacy costs incurred by the US in wars in Iraq, Afghanistan, and Pakistan.[27] And that is only the US. All of the coalition partner countries also incurred the same kinds of costs. The dozens of other countries involved spent public funds that would therefore not be available for other purposes. They suffered casualties, combat deaths, and serious injuries, placing extraordinary burdens on their societies and families.

Coalition partner countries certainly have a better capacity to shoulder those burdens, heavy as they are, than do the countries where the fighting takes place, but for none do the returns justify the investment (read sacrifice). For the host countries of these wars, the costs get truly incalculable. Armed conflict is development in reverse. One study of the "development consequences of armed conflict,"[28] not surprisingly, finds armed conflict to have a negative impact on a range of development indicators, notably poverty and hunger, primary education, child mortality, and access to water. In one poignant statistic, states can reliably expect that for every combatant killed an infant dies that would otherwise have survived. After five years of sustained war, and the overwhelming majority of intrastate wars extend well beyond five years, some 3–4 per cent of the population will have been pushed into undernourishment. But studies also show that when war finally ends, recovering states, with the benefit of international assistance, can experience above average rates of economic recovery. As long as conflicts persist, the social and economic burdens are devastating, but when wars end, recovery is possible – the key requirement is for the fighting to end. And to make that happen, the record also shows, what is required is not accelerated combat but accelerated diplomacy and attendance at the negotiating table.

The $1.7 trillion the world spends annually on military forces is said to be the price of security, but we're not getting good bang for the dollar. The inimitable US Congressman Barney Frank had it about right when he allowed that he "would be very happy if there was some way to make it a misdemeanor for people to talk about reducing the budget without including a recommendation that we substantially cut military spending."[29] The Massachusetts Congressman's wishful thinking is consistent with economic studies that regularly demonstrate that spending on social public goods – health care, education, mass transit, infrastructure repairs and energy conservation – creates more and better jobs"[30] than military spending. Spending on environmental clean-up and combatting global warming, like military spending, is a drain on any economy, except that environmental spending, in addition to creating more jobs than the equivalent in military spending, is also an economic investment. If increased insulation, for example, reduces future demand for energy, the economy saves, freeing up resources for other purposes.[31] As Nobel Peace Laureate Óscar Arias argues, no comparable economic dividend springs from military spending. "If we continue to focus on weapons and soldiers at the expense of basic human needs," he argues, "no real security will ever be possible."[32]

The 2.5 per cent of global GDP spent on militaries around the world and the labours of the 33 million soldiers and 54 million reservists are not delivering the results promised. Armies win few wars, aren't designed to build peace, and the consequences of the wars they prosecute are both incalculable and vividly apparent in the fate of the people who endure them.

Respecting the Limits of Force

For the overwhelming majority of states, the capacity for and the overt resort to military force has severely limited national utility. The vast majority of states cannot rely on it for ensuring their territorial integrity, basic sovereignty, or durable internal security. Few states, from Australia to Zambia, have the means to "defend" their borders, let alone their entire territory. Instead, they rely on an international order that respects the sovereignty and territorial integrity of individual states, no matter how small or powerless, and allows them to benefit socially, politically, and economically from peaceful and lawful engagement in that global order. Of course, that order functions in reality well short of perfection, but force is not the final arbiter of status and well-being. Individual states rely not on military prowess but on the UN Charter's explicit prohibition on aggression by individual states[33] and its promise of assistance from the international community (through a range of collective measures set out in Chapters VI and VII, ranging from peaceful, consent-based assistance to nonmilitary and military coercion) when their sovereignty and territorial integrity are violated. When the Security Council concludes that there exists a serious threat to international peace and security, or that a breach of the peace has occurred, or that an act of aggression has taken place, multilateral intervention becomes an option available to the international community. At the 2005 UN Summit – an extraordinary meeting of the UN General Assembly attended by heads of state and government, focusing on development, security, and human rights – the international community also agreed that intervention, military and nonmilitary, should be available when groups of people are vulnerable to crimes against humanity (more on this in chapter 9).[34]

There has been a post–Cold War trend of significantly increased collective military intervention by the international community to reverse aggression, to mitigate extraordinary human suffering, and to respond to advanced state failure. Some 250,000 security personnel are at any one time deployed worldwide in collective security operations. At the end of 2012, some 97,000 security personnel (roughly 82,000 troops, 2,000 military observers, and 14,000 police) were serving in 19 UN missions in peace support operations, that is, operations intended to support the implementation or pursuit of peace agreements and peacebuilding efforts. In addition, regional and other governmental organizations such as the African Union, NATO, the European Union, and ad hoc coalitions had deployed just over 132,000 troops and police in 15 non-UN missions.[35] Roughly another 50 civilian-only, multilateral, non-UN missions were engaged in a variety of monitoring and advisory missions. Non-UN missions range from peace support missions to multilateral warfighting operations, with most in the latter category producing the mixed results already discussed. The numbers deployed in multilateral wars were much higher prior to the American withdrawal from Iraq and Afghanistan.[36] These two distinctly different styles of military intervention – peace support and warfighting – raise a fundamental and consequential question for states in collective security operations, namely, when and how is the resort to collective force likely to be most effective? Under what circumstances is collective force likely to advance stability of the kind that facilitates long-term peacebuilding, and when is military intervention most likely to escalate into the kind of war that recent history shows rarely resolves the conflict at hand?

Warfighting or Peace Support Operations?

Enforcement by national forces responding to threats to the national order or by collective external military forces intervening in local conflicts is recognized as an important element, but only one element, of restoring and consolidating the institutions and practices that deliver human security. Indeed, the prevailing lesson of post–Cold War peacebuilding is that the durable safety of people cannot be achieved militarily but rather depends in large measure on the presence of, and trust in, public institutions capable of peacefully mediating the conflicts that are an inevitable part of any modern society. In some circumstances, such institutions require the protection of security forces from determined spoilers. However, winning the peace in troubled societies is primarily a political, social, and economic enterprise – an enterprise made even more difficult in the digital age, owing to its use in recruitment, fundraising, propaganda, and all the instant messaging that cannot be silenced.

Law enforcement, including collective external military force, is recognized as an important but largely subsidiary element of restoring and consolidating the institutions and practices of accountable governance. Military force can achieve tactical objectives, but unless these serve a strategic plan that engages a much broader range of nonmilitary measures to resolve conflict and to build conditions for a durable peace, tactical wins regularly deliver strategic setbacks.[37] When threats to national institutions go beyond isolated spoilers to reflect a more fundamental loss of consensus and breakdown of national cohesion, even obviously superior military force is incapable of restoring stability without determined political efforts to restore political coherence. The UN has well over four decades of learning about what works and what doesn't work in military operations in contexts of chronic conflict. The lessons have been written down, and they point to the importance of recognizing a basic distinction between "peace support" operations and "warfighting."

Peace support operations range from traditional monitoring and blue helmet peacekeeping to "robust" peacekeeping that engages armed spoilers in tactical combat. Peace support operations now can include explicit combat missions – for example, in the DRC, Mali, and Somalia. In the DRC, the UN Security Council has authorized an "Intervention Brigade" to combat key groups engaged in violence against civilians, including sexual violence. The mandate includes "targeted offensive" operations.[38] Similarly, the UN's "Stabilization Mission" in Mali is mandated to carry out combat operations in support of stabilization and the protection of civilians.[39] And in Somalia, the African Union mission engages in direct combat with al Shabaab militants. Its Security Council mandate includes authorization "to take all necessary measures ... to reduce the threat posed by Al Shabaab and other armed opposition groups."[40] A key element of these particular offensive operations is that they are carried out against spoilers in the context of much broader missions involving support for democratic processes, law enforcement, human rights monitoring, security sector reform, humanitarian support, and other measures.

The UN Department of Peacekeeping Operations' Principles and Guidelines Document describes peacekeeping as "a technique designed to *preserve* the peace, however fragile, where fighting has been halted" and where, in some instances, "robust" peacekeeping involves tactical combat against spoilers.[41] Enforcement is described as "the application, with the authorization of the Security Council, of a range of coercive measures, including the use of military force" at the strategic (non-consent) level to *restore* peace and security (essentially multilateral warfighting operations which in practice are not always authorized by the UN). "Peace support operations" is used here as a generic term for multilaterally conducted and authorized interventions designed to support the political settlement of conflict and, in some instances, to challenge spoilers directly in tactical combat operations. The key is for peace support operations not to become alternatives to a political process, and that points to the primary way in which peace support operations differ from "warfighting." Rather than being designed to facilitate or support the political resolution of conflict, warfighting is designed to override politics by dint of force and to impose, rather than negotiate, an outcome.

The point here is not that warfighting operations are without exception illegitimate; rather it is that warfighting operations are fundamentally different from peace support operations, and are rarely decisive. An exception was the international community's action under UN authority to force Iraq out of Kuwait in 1991, which was unambiguously a warfighting operation.[42] That is, it clearly set aside a political process – it eschewed negotiation and ongoing Security Council diplomacy in favour of war. In the process, it must be said, it upheld a key principle of international law and produced the primary desired outcome (the restoration of sovereignty to Kuwait). Furthermore, it is a result that has proven to be sustainable. Whether intensified diplomacy and sanctions could have produced the same result at less human and material cost can be debated, but as a warfighting operation it is broadly judged a success – one of very few such successes. So the distinction is explicit: "warfighting" operations over-ride political processes, while "peace support" operations aid them.

The global norm for effective multilateral military intervention in complex conflicts has come to be heavily oriented toward peace support operations that support a political process (those nineteen multilateral peace support operations referred to above), rather than warfighting operations that seek to override a political process. This change in orientation has multiple roots. In part it is due to growing deference to basic principles of international law, not least the UN Charter; in part it is due to considerations of the vital collective interests of the global community, that is, to the idea of a global public good that UN-authorized operations should support; and, as is argued here, it is due, as it should be, to the very real limits to the utility of military force in trying to impose sustainable peace and security outcomes in contexts of severe political dysfunction.

Military force can achieve tactical advantages but it relies on a favourable strategic context to consolidate those wins within a stabilizing political structure. It cannot therefore ever be self-sufficient in advancing security and stability. Military force relies on a supportive political climate and social institutions to sustain its gains, and its effectiveness is constrained by the environment in which it functions, just as the effectiveness of peacebuilding depends on the environment in which it is pursued. In other words, there are limits to the effectiveness of force that cannot be overcome simply by the application of greater force. For national and collective military force to contribute constructively to the strategic objective of sustainable human safety and well-being, it must be accompanied by certain social, political, and economic conditions or measures that can integrate tactical military advances into a gradually maturing political and economic order. These measures can be gathered under five basic themes.

Political Consensus

A primary requirement for the effective use of military force in restoring peace and stability is the active pursuit of a basic political consensus in support of the political/economic order that the military interveners are sent to protect. As we've seen, civil wars are rarely settled on the battlefield because, ultimately, political consensus cannot be coerced. Certain voices can be silenced for a time, but increasingly for only a short time. Effective action against spoilers depends on generating and preserving support for the proposed or prevailing order. In the absence of strategic consent or support for the prevailing order, dissidents have options in readily available small arms and light weapons, which circulate widely, especially in regions of multiple conflicts such as the Horn of Africa and the Middle East. Governments, on the other hand, are confident of their superior military force and thus are typically reluctant to engage politically with dissidents. But in the overwhelming majority of cases, they end up doing just that. The point is to start the process sooner rather than later. When multilateral forces intervene, the absence of an active peace process puts them squarely on one side of a civil war – in other words, on one side of a war that, experience suggests, they are unlikely to win.

If there is no effort to bring significant stakeholders into a national consensus, and if dissidents believe that acquiescence to the prevailing or proposed political/economic order will leave them marginalized indefinitely, they will prefer war to peace and insurgencies will continue to thrive. When a disaffected population regards political institutions as unrepresentative and antithetical to the interests of their community, they experience deployment of military force to protect those institutions as an assault on their interests. Thus, when consensus is absent, it is not military coercion but a renewed political process that is most likely to bring dissident communities and regions into the political and governance process. Negotiations between adversaries are the rule, not the exception, in the successful termination of armed conflict.

Legitimacy

The legitimacy of those in charge of a governance system and its public institutions depends not only on how they are chosen, but also on them being accountable to and guided by public, rather than private, interest. Force in support of governmental authorities that are widely regarded as illegitimate is necessarily regarded as a hostile effort to give power to leaders that are not trusted. An International Peace Academy report makes the point that "where external donors [and one could add external military forces] provide resources to corrupt, predatory central governments in the name of strengthening their institutions (think of Zaire during the Cold War), then State-building only advances abusive authority and fuels resentment and armed resistance."[43] And the intervening forces also lose legitimacy when military operations lack full respect for international humanitarian law and fail to take all the necessary precautions to protect civilians in conflict. Legitimacy is not a one-time accomplishment or acquisition through an election. It requires daily renewal by acts that gradually build trust. Dissident military forces fighting for their particular brand or promise of leadership are similarly forced to build and nurture the loyalties of their constituencies. When loyalty and trust erode, they are unlikely to be restored by force. Restoring loyalty depends not only on a political process, but also on a governance process and style that wins the confidence of people.

Military Restraint

Military force, including collective international military force, that abandons restraint and fails to respect the safety of civilians caught in the crossfire undermines support for domestic and foreign security forces and, in turn, for the leadership and institutions that those forces are there to uphold. Skilled and accountable domestic police action offers the model for the restrained resort to force. In effective policing there is a presumption of care and restraint that privileges the safety of innocent bystanders over the safety of police personnel and even the objective of capturing suspects. The report of the International Commission on Intervention and State Sovereignty, which pioneered the "responsibility to protect" doctrine and possible collective military action to that end, emphasized the importance of conducting military protection operations with such restraint: "This means accepting limitations and demonstrating through the use of restraint that the operation is not a war to defeat a State but an operation to protect populations in that State from being harassed, persecuted or killed."[44] British analyst Mary Kaldor similarly argues that the job of protection forces "is not to defeat an enemy but to protect civilians and stabilize war situations so that non-extremist tolerant politics has space to develop. The task is thus more like policing than warfighting although it involves military forces."[45] It is a model that applies equally to national forces fighting armed challenges to the government in power and to multilateral forces in the interests of restoring peace and stability.

Multilateral peace support forces that become combatants on one side of a counterinsurgency war immediately get caught up in an escalating spiral. The temptation is to accelerate military operations in the interests of winning an early and decisive victory against insurgents, but it's the kind of victory that has proven more than elusive. Accelerated military operations inevitably accelerate collateral damages – in Afghanistan, when security assistance forces were sharply increasing their attacks on the re-emerging Taliban in 2007, they killed almost as many civilian bystanders as did the Taliban, a major factor in the decline of Afghans' trust and confidence in them. There have thus been significant explorations, such as a US study on "Just Policing, Not War," of the potential for more deliberate efforts to adopt policing methodology in counter-insurgency operations.[46] Multilateral military forces face extraordinary challenges in today's high-intensity conflict zones. The conflicts themselves are unequivocally inimical to military resolution, yet the international community cannot ignore marauding forces like the Islamic State and Boko Haram in the face of the extraordinary harm they do to civilian populations and civic order. Thus in October 2014 the UN Secretary-General, mindful of these challenges, appointed Nobel Laureate José Ramos-Horta of Timor-Leste to lead an independent panel to review peace operations in the context of the changing nature of armed conflict and the evolving mandates of such operations.

Regional Support

Collective military engagement against spoiler elements in the context of an intrastate peace support operation faces major trouble when the spoilers enjoy the co-operation and support of neighbours. Neither political nor materiel intrusions from neighbours can realistically be blocked by military force, so those neighbours need to be influenced, accommodated, and somehow brought on side, especially when conflicts span decades and are in regions of entrenched patterns of interaction. That really means the development of some semblance of a regional security community. A minimal feature of such a community is the reliable expectation that states within the region will not resort to war to prosecute any disputes among them.[47] That expectation is made more credible if it is matched by "the absence of a competitive military build-up or arms race involving [its] members."[48] In the context of intrastate political conflict, states in a regional security community should also be assured that neighbours will not employ destabilization tactics against each other or provide safe haven to rebels from neighbouring states. Without that assurance, as the international force in Afghanistan soon learned, efforts to resolve a conflict internal to one of the states in the region will, to say the least, founder. Regional stability and co-operation are thus critical, not only for the sake of regional co-operation itself, but also for the internal harmony of states in the region.

Peacebuilding

The ongoing resort to force in the absence of measurable improvement in the daily lives of people amounts to just one more adversity for residents already overwhelmed by trial and hardship. If national or foreign security forces are to make an effective contribution to reversing state failure they must, above all, ensure that the everyday lives of people are improving. A primary lesson of efforts to end and prevent armed conflict and thereby set the stage for sustainable peace is that security operations and peacebuilding need to be pursued simultaneously. This is generally not feasible in situations of all-out war, a reminder of the two earlier points that such wars do not usually end in military victory and that peace negotiations toward national consensus must be a component of collective military intervention in support of human security.

In complex conflict situations, each of these factors – the pursuit of political consensus, legitimate governance, the restrained and lawful application of force, regional co-operation, and energetic peacebuilding – will by definition be a work in progress, but the absence of discernable action on any of them jeopardizes the entire peace support effort. Without attention to these nonmilitary components, a peace support operation risks being converted into warfighting with all the attendant limitations. But done the right way, heeding the lessons learned from several decades of peacekeeping and peace support experience, multilateral interventions, as analysis for the Stockholm International Peace Research Institute put it, need not be "a fool's errand."[49]

6

Disarming Security

Preventing War

HEADLINES DOMINATED BY BEHEADINGS, an international coalition trying to reverse dramatic territorial gains by jihadists in Iraq and Syria, and village massacres and kidnappings in Northern Nigeria are not a promising context for claiming that war prevention is actually working in this first quarter of the twenty-first century. Mass rape and disorder remain the perpetual and debilitating reality in large swaths of the Democratic Republic of Congo (DRC), there is no end in sight for American drone strikes from Pakistan to Somalia, and the Israel-Palestine war is in its seventh decade and still regularly produces deadly attacks and clashes, so the claim that we are living in the most peaceful era in human history needs an explanation. You won't find it reported on cable television that ours may be the generation that witnesses the fulfilment of the vision of the ancient Hebrew prophets that swords would one day be beaten into ploughshares and that nation would no longer take up sword against nation. Evidence of swords being beaten into ploughshares is still hard to come by – a 50 per cent jump in global military spending over the past decade to today's $1.7 trillion suggests ploughshares are still being beaten into swords at a pretty steady pace. But in the past fifty years something extraordinary has happened. Some seventy-plus years after the most determined human slaughter of the modern era, we can now actually observe, rather than just dream about, the fulfilment of the latter part of that ancient vision, the part about nation not going to war against nation.

In the latter years of the twentieth century and the first decade and a half of this one it has become increasingly rare, as we've already seen, for states to go to war against other states to settle conflicts between them. Given the energetic public commemorations of two extraordinary twentieth-century wars in which multiple nations took up all manner of swords against each other, it is hard to absorb the remarkable fact that of the more than two dozen wars now active around the world, not one is an interstate war. That doesn't mean we've reached the end of that particular element of history. There have regularly been twenty-first-century interstate attacks by international coalitions on countries like Afghanistan and Iraq, but they are really international interventions in intrastate conflicts rather than interstate wars. The still prominent urgings to attack Iran to stop its support of extremist groups or if the nuclear negotiations falter remind us just how dangerously available the state-to-state war option remains, and just how fragile the current absence of such wars actually is. But that should not detract from the reality that, in early 2015, the world is free of state-to-state war. In contemporary relations between independent nation states, it is the exception for two states locked in serious conflict to choose to settle their dispute through direct confrontation on a battlefield. And that is a genuine achievement, even if sustaining it is far from guaranteed and other forms of warfare remain endemic.

War Prevention is Working

Recent accounts have documented the decline in human violence and warfare throughout the ages.[1] The best known of these is the ambitious tome *The Better Angels of Our Nature* by the American academic and psychologist Steven Pinker, who persuasively claims that we are living in the most peaceful time in our species' existence. He cites six trends contributing to this steady progress towards less violence in human society. First came a millennia-long transition from hunters and gatherers to agricultural societies with emerging systems of governance. Second, beginning in Europe in the later Middle Ages, was a process of evolution from feudal societies to larger kingdoms with more centralized authority and organized commerce. The third trend Pinker calls a "humanitarian revolution" that led to the radical decline of certain forms of hitherto socially sanctioned violence like despotism, slavery, torture, and public executions – although abolition of these is obviously not yet accomplished. Fourth, Pinker describes "the long peace": the contemporary decline in wars between states and largely the end of war between highly developed states. The "new peace" is his fifth trend, namely the post–Cold War decline in wars or armed conflicts of all kinds. Finally, he uses the term "the rights revolution" to mark the universal declaration of human rights and advances in civil rights, gender and sexual orientation rights, animal rights, and so on. The fact that despotism, slavery, torture, and intrastate war are still very much with us doesn't negate his basic point that we are the beneficiaries of major progress against these enduring plagues.

These six positive trends are matched by five "inner demons," which

Pinker says still drive humans to be violent toward one another and account for those diabolical behaviours not being fully conquered. Humans still seek, he says, advantage from violence that seemingly advances their interests. We still turn to violence to dominate others. We seek revenge and moralistic retribution through violence. Sadism continues to be part of human nature and violence is deployed to such an end, and we are still susceptible to ideologies and the resort to violence in righteous anger. But he argues we also are served by better angels that restrain our inclinations toward violence: empathy, self-control, morality, and reason. These are buttressed by five historical forces: the Leviathan or social contract speaks to governance and a monopoly on the use of force; commerce allows for the exchange of goods and service to everyone's potential benefit; feminization increasingly respects the interests and values of women; cosmopolitanism refers to literacy, mobility, and the role of the mass media; and finally there is the rise of reason and an openness to be guided by knowledge and rationality.

Ian Morris provocatively argues that war itself is the source of peace, which is not exactly a new claim. The US Strategic Air Command, the group tasked in the Cold War with launching a US nuclear attack if called upon, had as its motto: "War is our Profession – Peace is our Product." It was later changed to the more simple formulation, "Peace is our Profession." Morris, like Pinker, goes back to the earliest days of human society to argue that "what has made the world so much safer is war itself." The emergence of organized society, governed societies, required leaders to develop the means of suppressing dissent and violence and fending off challenges – "war made governments and governments made peace." And while the obvious counterpoint is that it has actually been governments, not war, that have made the world safer, Morris points out that while war may be the very worst way to create governments and more peaceful societies, "it is pretty much the only way humans have found." So the argument is that conflict and competition are endemic to the human condition, and only force can keep control – only the defeat of those who challenge ordered society can finally achieve order.

For much of human history that may in fact be a persuasive narrative, but very recent history tells another story. War no longer delivers that kind of defeat. Massively superior military forces cannot defeat al Qaeda or the Islamic State, and especially, they can't defeat the ideologies or pathologies or xenophobia that drive extremism and challenge contemporary states. Furthermore, while Morris insists that war created governments (or is it simply that governments followed wars?) and governments then went on to create the peace that created prosperity, he does agree, or admit, that war has become so destructive that it can no longer serve the role that he claims for it. In our own age, "humanity has gotten so good at fighting – our weapons so destructive, our organizations so efficient – that war is beginning to make further war of this kind impossible." Indeed. Not all will agree that it is the extraordinary efficiency of military organizations that has rendered war obsolete – the inefficiency and debilitating costs of war being well documented in the daily news – but it is undeniable that modern war is now a means of destroying the conditions for durable peace rather than creating them. The destructiveness of nuclear weapons is but the most extreme example of war's inability to create peace. Wars in Afghanistan, Iraq, the DRC, Sudan, Libya, Syria, Somalia, Nigeria – and the list could go on – have been means of destroying, not producing, accountable governance and the conditions for sustainable stability and durable peace.

In the present era, to the extent that war is declining, it is due not to the effectiveness and efficiency of past wars but rather to the ineffectiveness of today's wars. To go back again to the words of Rupert Smith, today's wars are invariably "spectacular failures." The good news is that war is being shown not to work and, gradually, the human community is starting to turn away from it. In Pinker's words, humankind has been doing something right in now being more inclined to resist the resort to war, and that in turn makes it possible to redouble those efforts:

> We enjoy the peace we find today because people in past generations were appalled by the violence in their time and worked to reduce it, and so we should work to reduce the violence that remains in our time. Indeed, it is a recognition of the decline of violence that best affirms that such efforts are worthwhile.[2]

That's about as good a case for vigorous war prevention efforts as we're likely to find. There is persuasive evidence for the utility of war prevention in the multi-era decline in human on human violence, and there is opportunity in these opening decades of the twenty-first century to reinforce that trend and reach new levels of peaceableness.

There are obviously myriad reasons for this decline in warfare – including the decline in interstate wars, even while the daily news continues to report war's deadly toll in multiple locations. If humankind truly is, at least in its better moments, guided by rationality, it is probably safe to say that one reason for the decline in warfare is the unavoidable truth about its declining utility. States rarely win wars, so the benefits tend not to warrant the costs, and the incentive structures favour avoiding war if at all possible. Most states can't resort to war to expand their territory or to grab resources or control ocean areas beyond their legal limits. Advanced industrial states and even many less developed states are in possession of such deadly military firepower that they can lay to waste lives and physical infrastructure at a rate that makes it inconceivable that there could be any advantage in drawing these hi-tech swords. Increasingly, states have had to come to the conclusion that there are few national objectives worth the human costs and physical destruction that would result from war between militarily advanced states. Wars fought with an abundance of state-of-the-art military equipment promise extraordinary destruction. In the accumulations made possible by the hundreds of billions spent on it each year, conventional weaponry is capable of reversing decades of development and destroying infrastructure in mere weeks of bombardment. And any benefits, whether in territorial conquest, political domination, or strategic advantage, are short-lived and politically discredited. National aggrandizement and the pursuit of national advantage are as prominent as ever, but the resort to overt military conflict with other advanced states toward those ends is now shown to be unambiguously counter-productive. States certainly continue to prepare for all-out military confrontation with well armed adversaries, but those large and highly sophisticated forces tend to be used against only those states that have little capacity to resist (but even then, ironically, with little long-term success). The resort to major military force can "efficiently" destroy regimes, but winning the peace under the replacement regimes proves to be well beyond the capacity of the major military powers.

The United Nations' war prevention efforts, international diplomacy more broadly, and peacekeeping all offer alternatives for addressing intense conflicts.[3] States are increasingly bound together through mutual economic, social, and cultural interests. Relations between states are increasingly governed by international law, with economic, environmental, and other areas of international regulation usually supported by elaborate dispute settlement arrangements. Though interstate war remains a readily available option inasmuch as most states, even economically fragile ones, maintain military establishments and standing armies, it is not the option states now tend to choose when confronting other states in bilateral disputes.

The point is not to claim that interstate wars have ceased for all time, but that it is demonstrably possible to prevent such wars and to do so to impressive levels. Humanity is not condemned to a world of never-ending war. It really has become unthinkable that the United States and Russia or the United States and China would turn to direct military attacks on each other in order to settle a political dispute between them. That doesn't guarantee it won't happen, and it is a case of self-destructive folly that they still spend vast sums to prepare for just such suicidal wars and hurl threats and counter-threats at each other (e.g., over Ukraine), but it is true that the likelihood of such a war is receding rather than mounting. It is not that we have reached a golden age and can thus relax and stop fretting. Rather, because positive change is demonstrably possible, it is well worthwhile to redouble war prevention efforts. We are not condemned to repeat the patterns of wanton destruction and inhumanity that characterized so much of the twentieth century. To work ceaselessly to prevent war is to be rooted, not in a world of fantasy, but in a world of both urgency and realism.

The US analyst and academic Michael Mandelbaum optimistically makes the point that the mandate of states has shifted "from warfare to welfare." In Europe and North America at least there exists a popular "conviction that war [within those regions] is both abnormal and undesirable, and that it is usually illegitimate to fight for the goals on behalf of which wars have been waged in the past: wealth, territory, glory."[4] But Gareth Evans, the former Australian Foreign Minister and former head of the International Crisis Group, says the best explanation for declining interstate armed conflict

> is the one that stares us in the face, even if a great many do not want to acknowledge it. This is the huge increase in the level of international preventive diplomacy, diplomatic peacemaking, peacekeeping and peacebuilding operations, for the most part authorized by and mounted by the United Nations that has occurred since the end of the Cold War.[5]

He speaks of "a six-fold increase in UN preventive diplomacy missions (to stop wars starting); a four-fold increase in UN peace operations (both to end ongoing conflicts and reduce the risk of wars restarting); and an eleven-fold increase in the number of states subject to UN sanctions (which can help pressure warring parties into peace negotiations)."[6]

Evans' comments are also relevant to the declines in intrastate wars. Just as wars between states are preventable, so too are wars within states. Improved economic and social conditions reduce the likelihood of war. Representative and accountable government and the rule of law reduce the likelihood of war. The availability of national institutions to manage conflict and promote reconciliation reduces the likelihood of war. The international community has made significant strides in creating diplomatic alternatives to fighting between states; the current challenge is to create the same kinds of alternatives to fighting within states.

A 2014 Security Council session on conflict prevention highlighted the possibilities, even if the discussions sometimes seemed more aspirational than brutally frank.[7] As an example of interventions that work, the UN High Commissioner for Human Rights noted that the armed conflict in Nepal was abated especially through institution building, including a constituent assembly, through security sector reforms, and by measures to address caste-based discrimination. Preventive diplomacy came ahead of the 2013 election in Maldives when, in response to heightened tensions, the UN's Assistant Secretary-General and Council defused the situation through visits and calls for restraint, leading to a peaceful election and the orderly transfer of power. In Guinea, massacres in 2007 were followed by immediate development of a civil society capacity to investigate and document human rights violations. The Security Council established a commission of inquiry, and there is continued support for justice institutions and efforts toward transitional justice and reconciliation.

Also in Guinea, the Special Representative of the Secretary-General and head of the UN Office for West Africa successfully mediated between conflict groups in response to signs of conflict ahead of the 2013 legislative election. In Colombia the Office of the UN High Commissioner for Human Rights (OHCHR) helped to create a climate for respectful dialogue by promoting human rights and democratic culture through such measures as compensating victims, a truth commission, encouraging governmental recognition of indigenous authorities, mediation in local disputes, and developing an early warning system to detect and prevent violations of human rights. In Kyrgyzstan conflict between Kyrgyz and Uzbek communities claimed four hundred lives and drove eighty thousand people from their homes in 2010 (a devastating set of events that nevertheless is not included in the list of conflicts used here since it did not reach the one thousand deaths threshold). Subsequently, however, when disputes over water supply broke down along ethnic lines and threatened to spill over once again into violent conflict, intervention from the UN Development Programme engaged both communities in repairing irrigation canals, avoiding the outbreak of violent conflict and promoting better relations between estranged communities.[8]

When Gareth Evans says the decline in warfare is explained in part by the increases in diplomacy, diplomatic peacemaking, and peacebuilding, this is what he is talking about, and it's important to get a sense of how widespread this kind of activity is and why it makes a difference. The same Security Council report refers to mediation and conflict management interventions in Burundi (supporting national dialogue to prevent a labour dispute from escalating to violence), Madagascar (local level dispute mediation and assistance to develop the government's violence prevention efforts), Kenya (engaging sports stars in advocating for peaceful elections to avoid a repeat of the 2007 descent into widespread violence), and the Philippines (support for the peace accord between the government and the Moro Island Liberation Front). In Guyana in 2006 the United Nations Development Programme (UNDP) supported a national dialogue and a network of local mediators to ease tensions during the country's first violence-free election. In Ghana, the 2008 election was held in a climate of tension and suspicion, but even though the results were very close, the National Peace Council led the way toward a violence-free transition. Also in 2008, Bolivia was on the verge of political violence when the UN country team offered low-key support for negotiations toward a new constitution. Kenya's 2010 constitutional referendum was violence free; to avoid the kind of violence linked to the 2007 election, the UNDP supported a combined governmental and civil society early warning and response system that defused some 250 incidents that could have turned to violence. In Timor-Leste conflicts over land that escalated in the context of returning internally displaced persons were managed without violence, and that experience led to work on a Department of Peacebuilding. Sierra Leone's first election after the end of the civil war had huge potential for a return to violence but UNDP support to the Political Parties Registration Commission and the deployment of local-level mediators kept the process peaceful. In Lesotho tension and political deadlock threatened to break out in violence, as it had a decade earlier, but a church-led and UN-supported effort mediated conflicts among the major actors. Such reports focus on the successes, not the failures, but UN staff are also familiar with the latter. And when prevention efforts fail, as they obviously do, the consequences are tragic. The important successes, however, demonstrate not only that war prevention is possible but also that it takes every bit as much preparation and commitment as it takes to fight a war.

When Prevention Still Fails

All wars are in fact preventable, but if that is so, why does prevention fail with such regularity? The presence of the four primary conditions identified earlier as broadly indicative of armed conflict (grievance, competing identities, capacity for armed action, and the absence of credible alternatives) represent a major breach of the social compact. That social contract holds sway and militates against armed conflict when the majority of citizens voluntarily conform to state legal and political conventions in exchange for benefits the state has to offer in return. As one study puts it, "typically, the state acts to reduce people's risks – through law and order, services and infrastructure – in return for their commitment to the state (including a willingness to finance it through taxation)."[9] When this social compact is weak and there are not trusted national institutions through which to settle disputes, stability is compromised, the risk to people's well-being increases, and the risks of confrontation and violence climb. A viable social contract – what the study calls "a set of mutual obligations between the citizen and their state" – is thus central to conflict prevention. Elements of a social contract include an effective and accountable system of public finance (including revenue generation), along with governmental credibility (confidence in public institutions, governance). Governmental credibility in turn depends in large measure on its commitment to state policies and practices that reduce people's risks (advance human security), through the rule of law and the provision of services. Thus, a fragile state is one that either has no capacity or simply refuses to reduce individual risk. Indeed, "in the worst cases, the state is violently predatory – dramatically increasing people's risks, and impoverishing them" (e.g., Zimbabwe).[10] In a sense, the opposite of a fragile state is one that embodies a governmental commitment to measures that reduce individual risk. The economic system is of course central to mitigating personal risk (e.g., employment, education, and the kind of social safety net that many cannot afford, health services for the poor, health insurance for others, and so on).

So it is useful to think about a state's function as "reducing individual risk," a term that is more inclusive and more oriented to human security than is suggested in the language of state capacity. A strong state, one that can readily implement government policy and intentions, may simply be a more efficient predator that actually increases the risks to people. The international "responsibility to protect" also fits this paradigm in that it reflects an obligation to protect and reduce the risk to individuals in extreme cases when national governments can't or are themselves the source of risk. When states fail in reducing the risks to individual safety and well-being, they by default encourage people who feel at risk to "turn to non-state actors for their risk reduction." Some of these are certainly legitimate (e.g., NGOs, religious communities), while others may not be (e.g., ethnic militias and warlords).[11]

In support of the idea that all armed conflicts are preventable, the UN's High Commissioner for Human Rights (HCHR) lists a number of current serious conflicts (Afghanistan, Central African Republic, DRC, Iraq, Libya, Mali, Palestine, Somalia, South Sudan, Sudan, Syria, and

Ukraine) with the reminder that none of those crises erupted without warning. Each "built up over years – and sometimes decades – of human rights grievances; deficient or corrupt governance and judicial institutions; discrimination and exclusion; inequities in development; exploitation and denial of economic and social rights; and repression of civil society and public freedoms."[12] And, as the commissioner told the Council, "although the specifics of each crisis could not necessarily be predicted, many of the human rights violations that were at their core were known. They could have been addressed." But instead of these violations being seriously addressed, first by each of the states and then, when they failed, by the international community, "short-term geopolitical considerations and national interests, narrowly defined, have repeatedly taken precedence over intolerable human suffering and grave breaches of and long-term threats to international peace and security."

While wars emerge out of various and complex factors and circumstances, the broad strokes of conflict prevention are clear enough: being responsive to grievances, alleviating poverty, building community-to-community engagement and trust, promoting economic equity, employment, education, and building national institutions that have the demonstrated capacity to mediate conflict and thus earn people's confidence. That is essentially the broad, traditional, peacebuilding agenda, or, put another way, measures to reduce personal risk and restore the social contract. And, it bears repeating that at the core of armed conflict prevention is the construction of genuine political alternatives to armed conflict. These alternatives are sometimes referred to as "infrastructures for peace."[13] These infrastructures are best assembled with a variety of official and unofficial mechanisms and resources. The UNDP and the UN Department of Political Affairs have been working to build such infrastructures in some thirty countries. Chetan Kumar and Jos De la Haye, UNDP officials, report on the UNDP's work on conflict prevention measures: local and national observatories that serve early warning efforts to detect potential outbreaks of violence and monitor recurring violence; dispute management and resolution; training local and national mediators; ensuring participation of the marginalized, including women, young people, and ex-combatants in conflict prevention activities; and community dialogue opportunities on specific conflicts. Greater reliance on national and local actors, they argue, is both possible and cost effective.[14]

Rethinking Security

Some environments are obviously much more conducive to sustainable security than are others, and the Institute for Economics and Peace identifies the three core elements as good governance, economic equity, and a reliable business environment.[15] Bolstering these are other conditions like transparency and a free flow of information, low levels of corruption, acceptance of the rights of others, high levels of education, and good relations with neighbours. Sound security strategy focuses on nurturing those conditions and structures and on reducing risks to individuals. The most immediate experiences of insecurity come in the form of weak economies incapable of meeting basic needs, political exclusion, the denial of basic rights, social and political disintegration, and the related escalation of criminal and political violence that inevitably attends such conditions.

This focus on "human security" measures that advance the safety and well-being of people redresses the imbalance in security discourse that has paid disproportionate attention to the security of the state. While state security and behaviour are obviously central to the security of persons, the inordinate focus on military capacity to protect sovereignty and to defend territory, and, in too many cases, straightforward regime survival, frequently comes at the expense of, and with little regard for, the security, welfare, or safety of persons. It is not that the doctrine of human security emphasizes personal security over state security; rather it makes human safety the measure of state security. The extent to which the people of a particular state live in freedom and safety, under just laws, and with their essential needs met, is the extent to which that state is secure. And so primary threats to security defined as the safety and welfare of people rarely come from external military forces bent on attacking the territorial integrity of a state or on undermining its sovereignty. Thus, if insecurity is most manifest in conditions of economic failure, the violation of basic rights, and political marginalization, it follows that the primary guarantor of the security of people is less likely to be a formidable military equipped to keep foreign powers at bay than favourable social, political, and economic conditions. The promotion of human development, basic rights, and political participation is, in the long run, more important to advancing human security, and thus national and international security, than the development of effective military forces.

Ultimately, the foundations of security are not enforcement mechanisms but the policies and practices that address the ways in which insecurity is most directly experienced – what can be thought of as the five Ds of security:

1. **Development** – measures to create the kinds of economic, social, and environmental conditions that are conducive to sustainable peace and stability.
2. **Democracy** – measures to promote good governance that emphasize political inclusiveness and participation, as well as respect for human rights.
3. **Disarmament** – measures to prevent excessive and destabilizing accumulations of arms and to prohibit weapons of mass destruction.
4. **Diplomacy** – engagement in multilateral efforts toward the prevention of armed conflict, the peaceful management of political conflict, the development of a rules-based international order, and the promotion of development, democracy and disarmament.
5. **Defence** – the capacity to resort to the use of force in extraordinary circumstances in support of the full range of peace and security efforts.[16]

Development is clearly a long-term enterprise of meeting basic economic and social needs – the promotion of economic growth and employment generation, poverty alleviation, the reduction of economic disparities, and the provision of public services, notably education and basic health care. The *Human Security Reports* document the relationship between higher levels of state capacity and war prevention inasmuch as most civil wars take place in the poorest countries, which means states with the least capacity: "one of the strongest findings from econometric research on the causes of war is that the risk of civil wars declines as national incomes – and hence governance and other capacities – increase."[17]

Democracy is far from a guaranteed product of growing economic capacity, but improved economic well-being most certainly makes more effective governance available. Building national institutions that earn the support and confidence of the people is a primary structural response to the perception of a lack of alternatives to violence when grievances are not being acknowledged and addressed. It is a painstaking process, but improved economic performance helps to make that possible, and the absence of mediating institutions is most certainly a primary factor in the descent into war. Institutions that bridge economic, ethnic, and religious divides, and facilitate trusted power sharing are at the core of any effective national security infrastructure. The decline in civil wars worldwide correlates to the expansion of democracy worldwide. The Human Security Report Project cites declines in ethnic discrimination and the recognition of minority rights, both a product of more democratic institutions, as key to declining armed conflict.[18] Respect for human rights, another key expression of democratic governance, is similarly central to armed conflict prevention. Inasmuch as gross and persistent violations of human rights are a primary measure of corrupt governance and a prominent indicator of impending violent conflict, monitoring and reporting human rights violations is critically important on two counts. First, it helps to generate action in support of the victims of abuse, and second, in providing early warning of violent conflict, it can be a spur to preventive action. Through its Resolution 2171, the Security Council "acknowledges that serious abuses and violations of international human rights or humanitarian law, including sexual and gender-based violence, can be an early indication of a descent into conflict or escalation of conflict.[19]

Diplomacy is all about creating alternatives to armed conflict. Diplomacy can refer to national mediation and consensus building as well as to the more traditional pursuits of international diplomacy. While there are regular calls for early diplomatic engagement in emerging conflicts in order to defuse tensions and create forums for dialogue, early intervention is especially difficult to justify in the face of charges of interference in the domestic affairs of states. Under Article 99 of the UN Charter, the Secretary-General has a broad mandate to bring onto the Security Council agenda any situation he or she considers a threat to international peace and security. The Secretary-General is regularly encouraged to exercise this mandate more often, and earlier, but concerns about interference in internal affairs and violations of sovereignty undermine *early* action. As the Russian ambassador told, or warned, the Security Council: "Unfortunately, we have often heard proposals in the Security Council that border on attempts to manage the internal affairs of States or to interfere in their constitutional processes."[20] On the other hand, at the same Security Council meeting, the UN High Commissioner for Human Rights argued that sovereignty is also undermined when some of those internal affairs are unaddressed, leading to internal divisions that threaten the authority of the state and erode confidence in its institutions. Early intervention, with co-operation from the host state, can actually strengthen state sovereignty. And the Security Council, charged with ensuring that disputes do not become threats to international peace and security, certainly has the authority to engage early. The Department of Political Affairs has a standby Team of Mediation Experts, and the demand for their services has increased every year since its inception. The UN system has a presence in well over one hundred countries, including peacekeeping missions and special envoys.

Disarmament is key to rebalancing resources within the five Ds security envelope. High spending on military forces with limited utility in preventing or ending wars reduces resources available for nonmilitary initiatives in development, democracy, and diplomacy. War prevention requires eminently more attention to these four Ds of security. The fifth D, defence, also warrants further development and reinvention as a restrained constabulary response to crisis that promotes other avenues of intervention and steers military engagement away from replacing rather than supporting political processes. In extraordinary, though not infrequent, circumstances (often when vulnerabilities are not addressed early enough with appropriate measures), conditions of human insecurity translate into military challenges. The spreading disorder that accompanies chronic human insecurity and direct military threats arising from armed groups trying to advance their own interests in the context of state failure challenge the international community to develop effective responses to armed threats to people in peril. In early 2015 few populations were as imperilled as those at the mercy of the violent operatives in Iraq and Syria, including the Islamic State, or Boko Haram in northeast Nigeria. And it is clear that the international community has no clear military or other mechanism available to provide protection. Multinational military forces may manage to interrupt the likes of Islamic State and Boko Haram, but they are unlikely to stop or reform them.

What all this means is that there is a need for a major overhaul of the practices and programs that are intended to deliver reliable security in conflicted and troubled societies. The objective is to "disarm security" by reshaping the security envelope. While it is by now understood in theory that equitable economic development, democracy (good governance and human rights), diplomacy, and disarmament all contribute, along with security forces (defence), to establishing greater stability and security, the extent to which there must be a shift of resources within these "five Ds of security" is less widely appreciated. The roots of contemporary armed conflict are concentrated in adverse economic, social, and political conditions. Hence, the central message here is that the resort to military force must be approached with far greater caution and scepticism and that significant proportions of the vast sums spent on the capacity for force must now be shifted to war prevention and peacebuilding efforts that address the roots of conflict. These five Ds are essentially a familiar list of what most states will claim they already pursue, but the main point is the urgent need to reallocate resources among them. The current overwhelming focus on funding military capacity amounts to what the former Canadian Prime Minister Lester Pearson and Nobel peace laureate described as a "grim fact"[21] – namely that the world spends with seeming abandon on war preparations, but with miserly caution on preparing the conditions for peace. UN Secretary-General Ban Ki-moon regularly points out that the national priorities of the major powers "have left the world over-armed and peace under-funded."[22] We still follow the old paradigm of preparing for war while hoping for peace. Mobilizing military capability will obviously always be more expensive than mobilizing diplomatic capability, but investment in economic development is costly and the present imbalance in the funding of the five Ds of security represents a dangerous strategic weakness.

Institutionalizing War Prevention

As the power and sovereignty of states erode in the face of economic, cultural, environmental, and security conditions that transcend national boundaries (globalization), it is those same increasingly dependent and essentially weakened states that bear the primary responsibility for maintaining local and thus ultimately global security. Inasmuch as the main contemporary threat to global security is not the threat of war between states but within states, it is national governments even more than international systems that find themselves on the front lines of war prevention. To meet that responsibility, according to the OECD *Guidelines on Conflict, Peace and Development Cooperation*, each state needs "institutions capable of managing socio-political tensions and avoiding their escalation into violence."[23] But, of course, states that are failing, where the threat of disintegration into armed violence threatens directly, are the states that also have the weakest political institutions and are the least likely to find means of effectively mediating national conflict.

The concentration of war in weak states is entirely predictable in the sense that armed conflict is heavily correlated with underdevelopment, especially institutional underdevelopment that results in the absence of conflict management capacity. However, the international community has been very slow to recognize that the promotion of human development and good governance – not only moving states into higher rates of national income, but also building trusted mediating institutions – needs to become a strategic security objective. The threats are well understood, especially the fact that threats are globalized. Well before 9/11 Jean-Marie Guéhenno, the former French diplomat and UN official who is now president of the International Crisis Group, warned it had become "clear that isolating chaos with a *cordon sanitaire* was not a realistic option in a world in which the movement not only of people, but also that of information could not be stopped."[24] Global strategic stability cannot be separated from the promotion of stability and accountability within particular states, which means that armed conflict mitigation actions need to be focused much more prominently at the state level and the absence of political alternatives to violence in getting grievances addressed.

Conflict resolution capacity at sub-national levels is also a key to preventing the build-up of suspicion and enmities between ethnic communities or sub-regions within a state. The more grievances are linked to ethnic or regional or religious identities the more likely it is that a conflict will turn to violence, making the bridging of those divides, nationally and locally, an essential element of war prevention. War prevention literature calls for governmental support for domestic processes that are committed to developing local mechanisms that respect international standards but focus on improving everyday life for individuals and local communities. Peaceful and legitimate states emerge out of an "everyday consensus," and it is peaceful states that anchor international stability.[25]

Major powers specifically and the international community generally have been slow to recognize that the advancement of human security along multiple tracks is a vital strategic interest. Instead, they still prefer to think of the components of human security as general, even optional, humanitarian goals. The failure to understand human security as a vital strategic interest and thus an international security priority produces two prominent consequences. In the first instance, conditions of human insecurity tend to be ignored until they produce overt violence that threatens the stability or credibility of particular states or regimes. Second, the military option continues to be the most generously funded and thus the most available. When violence does break out, the primary response is a military one, because by then it is deemed too late for the other four "Ds" – the preventive action of diplomacy and the longer-term efforts in development, democracy, and disarmament – to meet a dire situation. The military option is always on standby, well equipped and ready, once again feeding that mythology of force as a decisive last resort.

Shifting resources within the security envelope to reduce the heavy focus on the military and to upgrade capacity in the other four Ds is part of changing the security ethos. A primary element of that change needs to be to focus attention on conflicts before they erupt into a full crisis. Governments that give prominence and enhanced capacity to development, democracy promotion, regional disarmament, and diplomacy as conflict prevention and crisis response mechanisms will also see them as the "go to" mechanisms for addressing conflicts. For most states, especially middle powers within the UN system, mounting major military operations will not be in their purview without the leadership of a major power. But middle powers do have the wherewithal to mobilize alternatives to force. As the great Canadian academic James Eayrs once said in the context of Canadian options:

> Force is the monopoly of the Great Powers, for all the good it does them. But Great Powers enjoy no monopoly over ideas. The foreign minister of a small state may not be able to summon a gunboat in aid of his diplomacy, to carry a big stick let alone to brandish it. But he can carry a briefcase well enough, and stock it with proposals.[26]

7

Disarming Conflict

A Treaty to Control the Arms Trade

I T WAS OCTOBER 24, 1974, and Independence Day in Zambia. The country, then our home for a two-year period, was celebrating the tenth anniversary of the founding of the new state out of what had been Northern Rhodesia. Similar scenes were being played out across Africa throughout the 1970s. Some thirty-two African states had won their independence in the 1960s, and a decade later elaborate ceremonies and festivities were being held to celebrate what in most cases were very hard won freedoms. Inevitably there was controversy – the promises of independence were far from realized, and weren't these impoverished countries spending far too lavishly on fleeting extravaganzas? But most of all it was a time of great optimism. Promise still drove hope and populations were energized.

It turned out to be a busy African decade for the North Koreans as well. They were then the choreographers of choice for mounting national pageantry, and especially for training the throngs of young people who performed complicated stadium animations by manipulating large color coded cards in the stands to render patriotic slogans, images of national leaders, and various portrayals of hardworking citizens building a brighter future. As our young family settled into the stadium seats in Lusaka, the enthusiasm was infectious. In the stands across from us, along the entire length of the playing field, the animated slogans and images unfolded. The dual themes were the celebration of freedom and reminders that the nation's and the continent's struggles were far from over. The campaign against apartheid in South Africa figured prominently, as did the ongoing effort to forge a durable unity (One Zambia! One Nation!) out of the dynamic mix of tribes and languages and disparate geography of this emerging country. Then came the long speeches and the march-pasts of young people from an array of regions, clubs, and athletic pursuits, all representative of a diverse society trying hard to become a single whole.

And, of course, there were the inevitable marching soldiers and

parades of military equipment. The latter displays were modest by contemporary standards, but there were enough trucks, tanks, artillery
pieces, and transport aircraft, and that special sign of independence and
statehood, a fly-past of fighter aircraft, to offer a convincing image of
nascent nationhood – and to claim a significant and unaffordable share
of the new state's scarce resources. Newly independent countries like
Zambia, Tanzania, Kenya, Zaire (now the Democratic Republic of the
Congo or DRC) and many others were bent on assembling all the trap-
pings of statehood, and that meant importing all the military parapher-
nalia that foreign loans and military credit schemes could make
available. In the Africa of that time, most of the demand for military
hardware was actually not homegrown. Few if any of the newly independent countries were facing hostile neighbours with designs on their territories, but a confluence of pressures and assumptions produced a climate
of extraordinary willingness to commit large sums of money the governments of the day clearly did not have to build up significant military
establishments.

It was the height of the Cold War, and the Russians and Americans
and their respective allies were desperate to solidify spheres of influence
in the emerging Africa. The supply of arms was a key element of their
strategy. It was a way of creating ties of economic, political, and security
dependence. When an African country acquired a major weapons system, it was tied to the supplier country for training in its use, for repairs
and spare parts, for a steady supply of munitions, and for meeting the
payment schemes throughout the decades-long life of the system. All of
that meant a long-term political relationship, expressed in supportive
voting at the United Nations but particularly in being inhospitable to the
superpower rival. And, of course, the weapons suppliers were eager participants – state suppliers in the case of the Soviet Union and largely
commercial firms in the case of the United States. International sales
complemented their production for national purposes, keeping workers
employed and profits high, and accordingly there was a major surge in
the international arms trade in the 1970s and 1980s. There was also a
prominent, though certainly contested, view that military establishments
in newly independent countries would be agents of modernization. Military force structures, the argument went, would model modern organizational and bureaucratic structures and systems. Military technology
would build practical technical know-how that would fuel civilian
advancement. And modern armed forces would be symbols of national
pride and prowess and thus aid political cohesion and confidence.

But from the vantage of that Lusaka stadium, it was a vision of statehood that even then spelled looming disaster. It could not have been clearer that the long-term viability of Zambia and the many other states like it would not depend on the protection of national armed forces. It would depend on those cheering and dancing young people around us, and the millions beyond the capital that had yet to see much of anything that was being celebrated, having access to education, to health care, to jobs. Their security had nothing to do with fighter aircraft, but everything to do with their families having the means to meet the most elementary daily needs of food and shelter. The tanks and jet fighters would deliver none of that, but worse, those military showpieces were rapidly becoming major, and obvious, obstacles to meeting the minimal goals of human security.

The ploughshares that would till the soil and spur the development on which Zambia's future would be built were being methodically beaten into swords, not to fend off threatening armies but to serve the interests of competing superpowers and arms factories far beyond Africa's borders. Far from disarming conflict, the international arms trade that soared throughout the 1970s and 1980s hijacked development and militarized political conflict. Right on cue, sub-Saharan Africa went to war. Wars of decolonization had no sooner ended than the civil wars began. Namibia, Angola, Mozambique, Zaire (now DRC), Uganda, Burundi, and Nigeria – the list goes on of countries that found themselves in long-running, externally enabled, debilitating wars. And when the Cold War finally ended, and when many of the superpower proxy wars also ended, militarization remained sufficiently entrenched, and development sufficiently stunted, to ensure that the continent was primed for ongoing violent conflict. Zambia, to its great credit, never did fall into that cycle of warfare, although it was heavily affected by the wars around it in Rhodesia/Zimbabwe, Angola, Zaire/DRC, and Mozambique.

The arming of Africa and much of the rest of the world via an unmonitored and uncontrolled arms trade was not what the founders of the United Nations had in mind only a few decades earlier. They were looking for a commitment to disarm conflict and even embedded that idea directly in the UN Charter itself. Article 26 instructs the Security Council to establish "a system for the regulation of armaments" as part of a larger effort to "promote the establishment and maintenance of international peace and security with the least diversion for armaments of the world's human and economic resources." It is an instruction that the Security Council has steadfastly ignored. Governments have been less than zealous or entrepreneurial in support of that vision, and instead have generally lavished, some obviously more than others, material and human resources on armaments and the hope that they will deliver both national advantage and security.

There is no denying the advantages reaped by the militarily powerful, but nor can it be denied that those advantages have substantially eroded, to be replaced, rather ironically, by a heightened sense of insecurity. In the US, the world's most heavily armed state, with extraordinary military advantages over all others, the prevailing security discourse is nevertheless dominated by powerfully felt perceptions of national decline, acute vulnerability, insecurity, and advancing threat. Huge arsenals cannot actually be assembled without generating the demand for them – that is, without generating a pervasive sense of threat and vulnerability. The sense of vulnerability that justifies weapons accumulations is in turn reinforced rather than mitigated by the military build-up. Peace and security are seen to be in growing peril, even in the most powerful of countries, and in weaker and impoverished states the same dynamic takes hold with even greater conviction.

In conflicts between states or blocs of states, the greater the armaments and armaments competition, the more the focus shifts away from the political and economic substance of the conflicts to concentrate instead on the competitive accumulation of arms and fighting forces and the political distortions that accompany them. It is a process of dynamic militarization that both relies on and generates a climate of intense suspicion, distrust, hostility, and confrontation, all of which are deeply inimical to rational attention to the substantive political conflicts that visit an interactive world. The arms race itself becomes a primary point of contention while the political issues at stake are lost first to the drum beat and then the fog of war.

The vision of a world in which fewer resources are wasted on arms, and on armies that are less and less capable of delivering security, nevertheless survives. The point of arms control and disarmament – the point of Article 26 – is to both ease tensions and allow political energy to refocus on substantive questions. Were the mandate to disarm political conflict seriously heeded, conflict and vulnerability would not magically vanish, but the capacity to start and sustain wars would be sharply curtailed, and the capacity to advance development, democracy, and diplomacy, the primary means by which political conflicts are ultimately managed and resolved, would be dramatically enhanced.

But the capacity to wage conflict by military means, between and within states, continues to enjoy disproportionate attention and funding. Political and business acumen has been employed to the fullest to exploit the lack of controls and the pervasive secrecy that characterizes the arms industry in order to promote universal access to the tools of war – arms and ammunition – along with maximum profit. President Eisenhower's famous warning about the military-industrial complex is certainly no less salient today than it was when he raised it in his January 1961 farewell address. It continues to drive an insatiable appetite for military aggrandizement that can never admit to reaching a point of sufficiency. The perceived threat seems always to exceed the accumulated military might to counter it. And so a relentless culture of vulnerability is promoted by the military-industrial-congressional-scientific-think tank complex (one could keep adding to the list of the component elements). It seeks to keep military funding on track, it helps to shape the political culture and national psyche, and it turns Article 26 on its head – to promote the establishment and maintenance of international peace and security with as much diversion of the world's human and economic resources as can be got away with. Military Keynesianism, the idea that military spending can be a driver of economic growth, is certainly a factor. Support for public spending increases in some political settings is inexplicably more palatable if it is for "national security," whereas social and civilian infrastructure spending that actually advances the well-being and security of populations arouses suspicions. Transparency International notes the particular susceptibility of military spending to corruption, estimating that $20 billion is lost annually to corruption in the defence sector – with the weapons trade a particular avenue for bribery and pay-offs.[1]

Trends in the Global Arms Trade

The means by which military capacity is distributed to the far corners of the world is primarily the international arms trade, which includes all transfers of arms, including through military aid.[2] One implication is that the arms trade helps to equalize or at least redistribute some military capacity and thus undermine military monopolies within particular regions. Without any overall reductions in military spending, some importing states argue, sharp restrictions on international transfers of military commodities would concentrate military power even more than it already is and could result in much more concentration in particular regions. Exporting states don't see externally defined restraint as in their interests, so the international community has never found the consensus to severely restrict the arms trade or even regulate it. Until now. The new Arms Trade Treaty (ATT), which came into force on December 24, 2014, moves gingerly in that direction through principles and regulations that include the UN Charter's Article 26 objective of "the least diversion for armaments of the world's human and economic resources" (thus acknowledging restraint as a principal objective). The nod toward restraint is mitigated by the acknowledgment of the right of each state to self-defence and to acquire arms, and other military capabilities to contribute to collective security efforts are also included. However, a key achievement of the ATT is also to recognize the security, social, economic, and humanitarian costs of the failure to regulate the arms trade at all.

The pace and volume of that trade are closely linked to trends in global military spending. The post–Cold War quarter century has seen both declines and increases in military spending, and thus declines and increases in the international arms trade. By 2015, the levels on both counts had stabilized on the high side, near the heights that prevailed at the end of the Cold War. After the immediate post–Cold War military spending declines of the 1990s, the next decade, from 2000 to 2010, saw spending increase by about a third. Since then it has levelled off, showing modest declines in 2012 and 2013, but current global military spending of $1.7 trillion per year remains near the all-time global high. Post-2000 increases were due substantially to major increases in US spending, which included funding for the wars in Afghanistan and Iraq, but in recent years NATO spending, including American, has declined while some other regions have increased considerably. The Stockholm International Peace Research Institute (SIPRI) reports that in 2013, US spending dropped by almost 8 per cent (in real terms), due in large measure to reduced overseas operations and to American budgetary constraints and the sequestration mechanism that cut spending in the wake of the financial crisis of late 2008. A decade earlier the US accounted for roughly 50 per cent of global military spending, but by 2013 its share was down to just over one-third. Even so, US military spending was still equal to that of the combined spending of the next nine of the world's leading spenders.

Outside North America and Western Europe, the annual rates of spending increased in all regions. China's grew by more than 7 per cent and Russia's by almost 5 per cent, driven by an ambitious plan to replace 70 per cent of its equipment by 2020. North African increases were the highest of any region at almost 9 per cent, with sub-Sahara Africa next with an increase of about 7 per cent. In East Asia and South East Asia increases were over 4 per cent, while Central and South Asia had a more modest 1 per cent increase. In Eastern Europe spending went up over 5 per cent. In Latin America the increase was at 2 per cent per year. Notably, in twenty-three countries[3] military spending has doubled or more over the past decade.[4] Just over half of those countries were significant oil producers, which, after oil's decline in 2014–15, could yet produce future military spending declines.

Of this annual $1.7 trillion outlay (2013), an estimated 20 per cent, or roughly $350 billion, goes toward arms procurement – that is, toward the acquisition of the weapons and related military equipment that make up national military arsenals.[5] The vast majority of this procurement is for the arsenals of advanced industrial states and comes largely from their domestic production. Only one-fifth to one-quarter of world military procurement is acquired from foreign sources through the arms trade.[6] The US Congressional Research Service (CRS), which for many years produced an annual report on global arms transfers, set the value of international arms deliveries in 2011 (the last year for which its figures are available) at $44 billion. SIPRI, which measures trends in international transfers of major weapons only, puts the 2013 level of transfers at just under $30 billion and just slightly below the levels of the closing years of the Cold War. Both military spending and the arms trade declined following the end of the Cold War (military spending by about one-quarter and the arms trade by about a third). When military spending began to rise again about a decade later, the arms trade also grew. The $44 billion trade in 2011 reflects the value of arms actually delivered that year, but the CRS also tracked annual sales for future delivery, and those registered a major jump in 2011 when sales agreements reached a record $85 billion. Arms sales agreements always trend significantly higher than deliveries, by about one-third, because not all agreements reach the delivery stage, but the huge 2011 increase in sales, heavily influenced by a US deal with Saudi Arabia that year, portends significantly higher deliveries in the coming years.

About two-thirds of the global arms trade is to non-OECD (Organisation for Economic Co-operation and Development) buyers, that is developing countries. While some countries defined by the CRS as developing countries, such as India, possess significant military production capabilities and many others have some niche capacities, most of the developing world relies entirely on foreign sources to equip its military and police forces, and sales to these countries have registered a steady increase since 2007. While Africa accounts for only 9 per cent of sales to non-OECD countries, it has shown the greatest increase in recent years. Asia is the main recipient of transfers worldwide, at 47 per cent, followed by the Middle East (19 per cent), Europe (14 per cent), the Americas (10 per cent), and Africa (9 per cent).

Implementing effective controls confronts major challenges. The supply "chain" for conventional weapons and ammunition is more a complex web than it is a straight chain. Take, for example, the Brazilian-built Super Tucano, a versatile small single-engine aircraft, available in single- or two-seat models. The Tucano is a multi-role aircraft, including for training. The manufacturer's ad copy lauds the aircraft's "small visual and radar signatures combined with high speed and agility," which, it explains, "gives the aircraft high survivability." When a country – Colombia, or Ghana, or Angola, for example – bought the Tucano from Brazil it had to satisfy only Brazil's export control system, even though a worldwide network of military and civilian manufacturers collectively built it. The Tucano engine, a 1,600 horsepower PT6A-68 turboprop, was built at Pratt and Whitney Canada. The machine guns were built by FN Herstal of Belgium, and the targeting for the bombs and missiles that were fired when it entered Colombia's counter-insurgency campaign was provided by laser rangefinders from FLIR Systems of the United States. The pilot's navigation avionics were supplied by Elbit Systems of Haifa, Israel. Cockpit breathing is aided by an onboard oxygen generation system provided by Northrop Grumman Corporation of the United States. The pilot keeps in touch with headquarters via a jam-resistant voice and data advanced software radio provided by Rhode and Schwarz of Germany and, should things go horribly wrong, bail-out is available by means of the lightweight ejection seat supplied by Martin-Baker Escape Systems of the United Kingdom. All of these elements, plus other components from other companies and countries, were assembled in Brazil by Embraer, the aircraft's primary manufacturer. Embraer is one of the world's larger aircraft manufacturers and as such is a major exporter, but it is also one of Brazil's large importers, since many of the machine guns, engines, avionics, and other subsystems and components are purchased abroad. Even major manufacturing countries rely on this global network of designers, developers, and builders of the components and subsystems they assemble into functioning weapons systems. But only the country of final assembly, not the entire group of countries that collectively built the product, is involved in regulating the product's final destination. Under the new Arms Trade Treaty, all the suppliers, once they join the treaty, should have similar standards, but for the suppliers of components and subsystems those standards will be applied to transfers to the country of final assembly. Only the country of final assembly will make assessments and decisions regarding transfers of the finished system to the military end users.

In the contemporary globalized arms factory, there has also been a gradual erosion of the sharp distinctions between military and civilian production. During the Cold War military technology tended to be ahead of civilian technology. In the Soviet Union and the West, governments invested heavily to upgrade military systems continuously and to pursue technological advantage, but after the Cold War with technological innovation refocused on civilian markets, emerging civilian technologies were increasingly applied to weapon systems. SIPRI notes that, instead of hyping the civilian spin-offs of military technology, military manufacturers now focus on "spinning in" civilian technologies, especially electronics. Cost-conscious military forces are also increasingly buying civilian aircraft and vehicles for military end uses. The practice is sufficiently common to have earned its own acronym, COTS for commercial-off-the-shelf.

This internationalized production, along with the "spin-in" of civil technologies and increased military acquisition of civilian equipment for military end use, has created not only a new kind of global industry, but also a new set of challenges for arms transfer control efforts. While many countries were and still are involved in producing the Super Tucano, only one, Brazil, had any say over its sale. The component suppliers control the destination of their products only to the point at which they are used in manufacturing, not to their ultimate military use. So, if a country that manufactures a particular component has more restrictive export standards than the country of final assembly, it is nevertheless only the latter that determines to where exports are approved. Uneven standards also create incentives for companies in more restrictive states to license production or set up subsidiaries in more permissive states in order to expand the market for their products. And because traditional transfer control practices have made a sharp distinction between civilian and military technology, with controls focused on commodities predefined as military goods, there is now no systematic control of goods that start life as civilian commodities but get spun into military systems, or of complete systems like aircraft or vehicles that are designated civilian but sold as is to military users.

The Arms Trade Treaty

Controlling access to the tools of war is not a primary war prevention strategy. It may be far too simple to allow a variation on the trope that weapons don't cause wars, people do, but there is truth in it in the obvious sense that many countries have been well armed for generations and have at the same time avoided war. On the other hand, there really is such a thing as the destabilizing accumulation of arms in a particular region, and when that happens weapons can and do raise tensions, which in turn can lead to miscalculations and war. Whatever the causal dynamics, controlling the arms trade is a key element of disarming conflict, particularly when it is part of a larger strategy of reducing tension and easing military confrontation in order to shift resources to other more effective means of managing and resolving political conflict. Hence, the ATT is long overdue. Years of study, advocacy, resistance, and ultimately a lot of compromise produced what such global processes representing a broad range of diverse interests normally produce – a less than perfect outcome. Less than perfect, but more than worthwhile. It won't fill all the regulatory gaps, and it certainly won't have much immediate effect on current warfare, but being the first sustained attempt at a comprehensive response to the need to address the unrestrained arms trade, it is a significant achievement. It optimistically declares the objective of establishing "the highest possible common international standards for regulating or improving the regulation of the international trade in conventional arms" (Article 1), which it says will in turn contribute to international peace and security.

Indeed, the formal commitments undertaken by states signing on to the ATT are impressive.[7] The foundational commitment is to establish within each state party an effective national arms transfer control system (the term transfers includes exports, imports, transit, trans-shipment, and brokering). National control systems are to apply at least to the eight categories of conventional arms covered by the ATT, as well as to related ammunition, parts, and components. The relevant categories of arms are battle tanks, armoured combat vehicles, large-calibre artillery systems, combat aircraft, attack helicopters, warships, missiles and missile launchers, and small arms and light weapons. The inclusion of small arms is key. Small arms remain the primary weapons of war, no matter how "sophisticated" some military systems have become. Fighters with automatic rifles, grenades, landmines, light rockets, and anti-aircraft guns are still the key to gaining and occupying territory, and that applies equally to pro- and anti-government forces.[8]

The ATT mandates particular prohibitions on arms transfers: those that violate a Security Council measure (particularly an arms embargo); those that would violate any other international obligation or agreement (particularly as might relate to illicit trafficking); and those that would be "used in the commission of genocide, crimes against humanity, grave breaches of the Geneva Conventions of 1949, attacks directed against civilian objects or civilians protected as such, or other war crimes as defined by international agreements to which it is a Party." The formulation here is similar to the UN's doctrine on the responsibility to protect, which calls on the international community to intervene to protect populations in states when "national authorities are manifestly failing to protect their populations from genocide, war crimes, ethnic cleansing and crimes against humanity."[9]

For exports that are not expressly prohibited, states commit to taking the following factors into account when deciding whether or not to authorize a transfer: will the proposed transfer contribute to or undermine peace and security; could the item to be transferred be used to commit or facilitate serious violations of either international humanitarian law or international human rights law; would the transfer violate obligations regarding the combat of terrorism; or would it contribute to serious acts of gender-based violence or acts of violence against women and children? The international development community lobbied hard to have the transfer's impact on economic development included, but some importing states in the global south were particularly wary of that provision, concerned that individual developing states could be targeted with unofficial embargoes with claims that the importing country's economy could be adversely affected by imports – it undoubtedly being the case that any military imports represent an additional economic burden. The assessment of whether a particular transfer is likely to undermine peace and security or any of the other factors is to be undertaken solely by the exporting party and the ultimate decision on authorization remains solely that of the exporting state. That is the central but unavoidable weakness of the ATT. It is unavoidable because no state is about to cede its export discretion to another authority. But the weakness is also mitigated at least somewhat by transparency requirements related to record keeping and reporting annually to the treaty secretariat on "authorized or actual exports and imports of conventional arms" covered by the treaty.

While there is lots of room for interpretation regarding the imminence or severity of the risks considered in the formally mandated assessment process, the treaty does firmly say that "if, after conducting this assessment ... the exporting State Party determines that there is an overriding risk of any of the negative consequences ... the exporting State Party *shall not* authorize the export" (Article 7.3, emphasis added). But there is in reality no enforcement mechanism. The treaty article entitled "Enforcement" says simply, "each State Party shall take appropriate measures to enforce national laws and regulations that implement the provisions of this Treaty." That is the entire enforcement regime. There are no penalties for failure to implement. States make their own assessments and decisions. Asked how the treaty would affect the potential for arms transfers to Syrian rebels in the context of the civil war there, the US negotiator would only say the treaty would "require a careful study by a national government on making that decision."[10] In fact, the negotiator encouraged the US Senate to ratify it on the grounds that "becoming a party to the Treaty would not require any additional export or import controls for the United States."[11] The United States does have an elaborate export control system, but one could be forgiven for finding it strange to model a global arms trade control treaty on the standards and behaviour of the world's most profligate exporter of arms.

Saudi Arabia will be another key test of the effectiveness of the ATT. It is perennially in the top five of weapons importers worldwide, and it is of course within one of the most volatile regions of the world. The International Institute of Strategic Studies sees no let-up in Riyadh's continuing "substantial" purchases,[12] and it remains to be seen whether it will have any trouble finding suppliers, but it should. In this region of chronic conflict, where the danger of destabilizing accumulations is real, exporters are exhorted by the ATT to consider whether the arms to be transferred "would contribute to or undermine peace and security." The ATT is also meant to ensure that human rights violations in a potential recipient state will introduce caution into the decision making of the exporting state, and such violations in Saudi Arabia ought to induce extreme caution. Human Rights Watch reports that "girls and women are forbidden from traveling, conducting official business, or undergoing certain medical procedures without the permission of their male guardian."[13] While there is some easing of regulations and restrictions, strict clothing requirements are enforced, and severe violence against women receives only the lightest reprimands when a case is taken up at all.

Human Rights Watch further describes the treatment of migrant workers as approaching the conditions of slavery. Detainees under the criminal justice system, who often include children, "commonly face violations of due process and fair trial rights, including arbitrary arrest and torture and ill-treatment in detention." Sentences of thousands of lashes are routinely applied. Just as Canada was in 2015 proclaiming the employment benefits of its new long-term contract to supply $15 billion worth of armoured vehicles to Saudi Arabia, the Saudi justice system was publicly flogging (fifty lashes per week, or as soon as the wounds from the previous lashing healed, to a total of one thousand lashes – suspended after the first week) a man whose family had been granted refuge in Canada. The UN Commissioner for Human Rights voiced alarm over the use of the death penalty and cruel sentences such as "cross amputation," whereby both the right hand and the left foot are chopped off. Nor is the long-term stability of Saudi Arabia assured. Leadership transitions, say some analysts, could expose serious internecine conflicts.[14] The potential for violence is real and made more so by the fact that, in addition to its heavily armed military and National Guard, Saudi Arabia boasts the world's seventh highest rate of gun ownership among the civilian population.[15] Saudi Arabia's main weapons suppliers, such as the United States and the United Kingdom (with Canada having become a major supplier of armoured vehicles), do not make a habit of expressing public outrage over human rights abuses in the Saudi Kingdom or speculating on its future stability, but when the Arms Trade Treaty meeting of state parties next occurs, they may have to break their silence.

So the Arms Trade Treaty is both very important – where else are states required to justify their arms sales to gross and systematic abusers of citizens' rights? – and seriously flawed. Its primary failing is that, while it establishes global standards, it vests all decision power in individual states, where it always has been. But a key achievement of the treaty is its consultation provisions in the form of regular conferences of the state parties to the treaty which are intended to review the treaty's implementation, and where presumably exporters will have to face questions about how they justify the sales made. At the same time, the remedies are largely political rather than legal.

But it never was going to be any different. There was no prospect of a treaty or export control system in which arms transfer decisions would be taken even partly out of the hands of individual states. States engaged in a lucrative industry worth billions of dollars and inextricably linked to their own self-perceived economic and security interests (as perverse as those perceptions might frequently be) were not going to do anything to challenge all that. That's not how states act. So the relevant question isn't whether the treaty is adequate to deal now with a destructive arms trade. It isn't. The relevant question is whether it articulates basic principles of state responsibility and introduces the kinds of mechanisms and processes that can be employed over time to help shift perceptions of self-interest and to modify behaviour – in other words, does it point to a shifting global norm in favour of restraint? The treaty does that, and while that may be a modest achievement, it is nevertheless an achievement on which to build.

Some critics argue that the treaty not only falls well short of perfection but also has the effect of legitimizing the arms trade and especially of uncritically deferring to the interests of arms exporters. That is a fair criticism of the arms trade control system, even with the treaty in full force, but legitimation of arms transfers did not arrive with the ATT – that all happened at least a century ago. The arms trade has long been legitimized by prevailing political assumptions, and arms exporters most certainly pursue the trade in the belief that it advances their interests. What the treaty does do is begin a serious political process to challenge those assumptions and to shift perceptions of self-interest.

A good model for how this treaty might be expected to work is found in other flawed treaties, notably the Nuclear Non-Proliferation Treaty (NPT) and the landmines and cluster munitions treaties. Through the NPT (negotiated in 1968 with entry into force in 1970) the nuclear weapon states pledged, in paragraph VI, to stop the nuclear arms race. In the decade and a half following that solemn pledge, those same states engaged in the most extravagant and irresponsible arms race, the nuclear arms race, the planet has ever known. So much for the treaty – except, that isn't the full story. The NPT certainly didn't persuade states to begin acting immediately against what they perceived their interests to be. That they were perverse perceptions of self-interest (the obscene notion that the world could be made secure by accumulating arsenals capable of reducing it to radiation-contaminated rubble within minutes) didn't make them any less appealing to those states, but the still heavily flawed NPT turned out to be a key instrument for challenging the actions and logic of the nuclear weapon states. Over the decades it has changed perceptions of self-interest and has reinforced and consolidated nuclear reductions when they have finally occurred. The NPT review process gradually clarified and reinforced disarmament obligations, and now all parties to the treaty have agreed that they are under a legal obligation to disarm and to achieve a world without nuclear weapons. It was the international conversation and consultative process mandated by the NPT that helped to reshape perceptions and commitments. The conversation mandated by the ATT's transparency and review provisions will, if states are diligent and persistent, initiate reconsiderations of what constitutes legitimacy and legality in arms production and exports, and the treaty articulates key principles to guide that normative, behaviour-changing conversation. It will also be possible to further develop the treaty through new protocols – new provisions, including its application to a wider range of commodities going to military end users, and clarifications or enhancements of conditions governing transfers.

If perfection had been available, that would certainly have been the obvious choice, but failing that, international mechanisms like treaties that encourage more responsible behaviour and introduce mechanisms to enhance accountability represent real progress – and the flawed ATT does both of those things. Thus, it promises to become an essential though insufficient tool in the long and difficult effort toward greater controls and restraints on the international transfers of arms.

The challenge at the moment is to get all the major exporters to become part of the ATT. The United States has signed, which indicates its commitment to the principles and intent of the treaty, but other major arms suppliers like Russia and China have yet to sign. As Malcolm Chalmers, research director at the Royal United Services Institute, points out,

> So far many of the signatories are Western states (who believe they already meet ATT criteria for export regulation).... If it is to make a real difference, however, states like Russia, China, India, Pakistan, Iran and Saudi Arabia will also need to join. Until at least some of these states take part, it will be a job only half done.[16]

Canada is one of few Western states that has not yet signed, let alone ratified the treaty.

A particular focus for advocates of the Arms Trade Treaty has been on the need to limit the spread and availability of small arms and light weapons. Small arms actually kill more people outside of war zones than within wars, but their contribution to increasing the frequency, duration, and intensity of intrastate or civil wars is also undeniable. Africa has been particularly affected and thus African states were generally advocates of the ATT, but in 2014 they still seemed to be slow to sign and ratify it. At a spring meeting in Dar es Salaam of the Regional Centre on Small Arms of east and central Africa, the Tanzanian vice-president, Mohamed Gharib Bilal, urged states from the region to sign and ratify the treaty. "We need to strengthen our joint and concerted efforts and focus on harmonizing legislation, mounting more joint cross border and simultaneous operations in the region and marking all small arms and light weapons for easy tracing."[17] The point has frequently been made that small arms and light weapons, the primary weapons in most contemporary wars, are in fact weapons of mass destruction one victim at a time. More effective controls are central to preventing political conflict from transforming into armed conflict.

Transparency and Demand Reduction

International control agreements and arrangements, of which the ATT is one element, are gradually pulling together an infrastructure on which to build a more effective control system for conventional arms. As long as countries maintain military and police forces, there will necessarily be an international trade in arms. The challenge is to restrain that trade, and especially to ensure that it does not lead to excessive and destabilizing accumulations or undermine human security by supporting human rights violations and organized crime, exacerbating or prolonging conflict, or undermining development.

The political context for arms control implementation is key. Even the most ubiquitous substances can be effectively controlled if there is political will to do it. For example, trade in materials or technology for use in chemical and biological weapons is prohibited, even though materials that are potentially useful in the production of chemical or biological weapons may be widely traded for non-weapon uses. The focus of regulations cannot therefore be a simple ban on all such materials, but must be on preventing the diversion of otherwise legal materials to weapons purposes. That becomes possible only because such prohibitions and regulations are supported by a broad international consensus against the use or acquisition of chemical and biological weapons. Commercial enterprises that engage in diversion for weapons purposes are subject to deep public moral opprobrium. There is a broad international sense of disgust linked to chemical and biological weapons. Simple human decency is understood to be incompatible with their use, and that disgust has allowed the emergence of an international control regime, including transfer controls. The Australia Group is a group of states (currently thirty-nine) that has developed and maintains a set of voluntary arrangements to prevent the diversion of chemical and biological materials for weapons purposes.[18] The group focuses on national export licensing arrangements that are designed to implement obligations under the Chemical Weapons Convention and the Biological and Toxin Weapons Convention. Similarly, the Nuclear Suppliers Group produces voluntary guidelines to regulate the trade in nuclear materials for peaceful purposes, again in an effort to ensure that such materials are not diverted for weapons purposes.[19] Its exposure of clandestine transfers of nuclear technologies from Pakistan, for example, reinforced the overall effectiveness of the regime and NSG controls – and especially confirms the strength of normative support for prohibitions of unconventional weapons (weapons of mass destruction). In other words, even voluntary controls can be effective if supported by a pervasive political climate of support.

While there are prohibitions on some conventional weapons such as anti-personnel landmines and cluster bombs, general restraint on conventional arms enjoys only a modest level of political support. Economic interests promote sales, and while foreign policy objectives sometimes favour restraint, at other times they promote the abundant supply of arms. The momentum is however probably shifting towards greater control. The Wassenaar Arrangement on Export Controls on Conventional Arms and Dual-Use Goods and Technology,[20] the primary instrument for voluntary co-operation in transfer constraint measures, maintains a set of voluntary guidelines for a group of thirty-nine participating states, and recently managed to agree to limits on the spread of man portable air defence systems (MANPADS). Because of MANPADS' threat to civilian aviation and the strong global consensus in support of measures to address non-state extremist threats, the international community was able to act. It was political support, rather than strict enforcement capacity, that produced the MANPADS initiative.

It is the relevance of public attitudes to effective arms control that makes the transparency measures in the ATT so important. They are, to be sure, inadequate, but they are also to be welcomed, especially because governments, both democratic and autocratic, usually resist transparency in security policy. And there is a special set of sensitivities linked to security. Military officials and security professionals are frequently reluctant to allow engagement – seeing it as interference – by an interested public or even members of parliament. The consequences of a lack of transparency are not difficult to discern. Chief among them is the growing disparity between regime security and the security of the population. The more security policy making is confined to the domain of security professionals the less the requirements of human security figure into the national equation. Security requirements are exaggerated, spending escalates, and regional accumulations become destabilizing as neighbours and adversaries see new threats and in turn exaggerate their security requirements. The absence of transparency undermines civilian and parliamentary review and assessment of military spending budgets and arms purchases or arms exports. And, of course, the greater the secrecy, the greater the susceptibility to corruption.

Transparency, the disclosure of information on defence and security policy and security assessments to citizens, other states, and the international system, and disclosure of military procurement, including imports, obviously enhances confidence and stability among states. Or if it raises security concerns, it does so openly and more accurately and brings resulting security concerns to political and diplomatic attention. A primary test of the adequacy of disclosure is the degree to which information on military budgets and procurement and actual spending allows the public and policy experts to fully examine and debate policy and the decision-making process itself. Transparency is the means by which the public develops the capacity to assess the degree to which security and procurement decisions are carried out as proposed and within mandated funding limits. Transparency challenges are particularly evident in some developing countries with emerging democratic institutions. As SIPRI reports, developing countries with minimal resources tend to have limited capacity for overseeing security operations, including procurement. The security sector promotes itself as too specialized for monitoring from nonspecialist politicians. Secrecy prevails, and parliaments are excluded.[21]

The ATT's provision for record keeping requires states to maintain records of exports authorized and actually carried out and then "encourages" states to maintain records on trans-shipments. States are also "encouraged" to include in those records the quantity, value, and model/ type of equipment exported or authorized for export, as well as details on the end user. For states to maintain and make public such records would be a major improvement over current practice in many instances. States are required, within a year of the treaty's entry into force, to report on measures taken to implement it, and subsequently to report on any new measures taken. The regular conferences of the states party to the treaty are to receive reports on "authorized or actual exports and imports of conventional arms." The fact that commercially sensitive or national security information may be excluded, or that reporting may be of authorizations or actual exports, not both, represents a huge set of transparency loopholes. That said, the principle of full disclosure is established. The review conferences will address, and potentially change, such disclosure details. As in the NPT, this review process promises to be slow and frustrating, but it also holds the promise of promoting accountability and restraint and consolidating changes in norms and behaviour as they occur.

The transparency objectives of the Arms Trade Treaty are an explicit acknowledgement that the way individual states pursue security, including the acquisition of weapons, has implications well beyond those particular states. National security is by definition not exclusively within a national domain. When national security is defined in terms of relations with other states, those other states are by definition involved. The international community is involved by virtue of its essential interest in the stability of the international system and in promoting harmony or at least laws-based stability among states. When national security is defined in terms of domestic stability and domestic concerns, the international community still has a direct interest inasmuch as the stability of the international system and the well-being of all people depends on adherence to basic standards of human rights and the peaceful settlement of disputes.

As a rule, secrecy escalates demand while transparency reduces it, and it is clear that effective and durable restraint in the arms trade will require significant and enduring reductions in demand. Beyond transparency, measures to reduce demand include social, political, and economic measures designed to create conditions for durable peace and stability, as well as mutual security arrangements within regions and subregions.

Patriotic celebrations on national anniversaries are not about to quit featuring marching armies and fighter aircraft fly-pasts. And we would do well to remember that the soldiers and pilots are also the ones who respond to their countries' calls, prepared to meet whatever dangers may come their way, when authorities on our behalf press their armed forces into service. They are to be honoured for their commitment to duty and willingness to sacrifice, but they are not the sole or even the primary guardians of freedom and democracy. Those are values that require a much broader commitment and are preserved day by day by all citizens who live by them. No less for us in the world of 2015 than it was for Zambia on Independence Day in 1974, it is the institutions and services of human security, the physical and social well-being of people, that secure a future of stability free from war. And no less today than in the Africa of the 1970s, the world is too heavily invested in the institutions, mechanics, technologies, and strategies of military coercion and too little committed to the institutions, technologies, and strategies of peacebuilding – all the five Ds of security. The UN Secretary-General was right – we've a world that is grossly over-armed, in which peace is woefully under-funded. National stability and security are finally not rooted in enforcement but in a national consensus, political cohesion, and the conditions of human security. The Arms Trade Treaty is but one of the flawed but critically important instruments for reining in the appeal to force and promoting its abundant alternatives.

8

Disarming the Bomb

Nuclear Disarmament

WERE ANY STATE TO THREATEN to carry out by conventional weapons even a fraction of the deliberately indiscriminate destruction threatened by nuclear weapon states in the name of deterrence, the international community would rightly recoil in horror at the brazen and unconscionable willingness to commit mass murder. Deterrence threatens to use nuclear weapons and the impact of their actual use is not in doubt, with the testimony of the survivors of the Hiroshima and Nagasaki bombings of August 6 and 9 in 1945 having provided some of the most persuasive evidence. One witness recalls her experience as a young girl in a small town outside Hiroshima being at the temporary first-aid station that was set up in her school. She describes the bombing victims, well away from the epicentre of the explosion, lined up and waiting for help:

> The victims' hair was frizzled, and their faces bloated and dark red from burns. Pieces of their skin were hanging down from open wounds, and their clothing was scorched. They were covered with blood. Many of them were brought in on shutters that served as stretchers. They looked like ghosts, lying there, their internal organs bulging through their hands. Some people were simply moaning. Others were calling out the names of family members, and still others begged, "Water, please. Give me water," as they were carried out on stretchers or in wheelbarrows. It was an indescribably hideous scene.
>
> All the Women's National Defense League members could do was attempt to comfort the victims, since there was no medicine whatsoever. When victims stopped moaning, we knew that they had died. As the dead increased in number, hole after hole was dug on the grounds of the crematorium. Pine boughs were placed on top of the corpses, oil was poured over them, and they were cremated. Day after day, from morning to late at night, the air was filled with smoke and the stench of rotting flesh.[1]

Any state that threatened to carry out mass assaults with conventional weapons on civilian populations meant to produce those kinds of results would be immediately accused of having made the intention to commit war crimes and crimes against humanity core elements of its security policies. But nuclear deterrence is precisely that – the declared intention under certain circumstance to launch massive assaults on civilian populations, on civilian infrastructure, and on the global ecosystem. Yet states with large arsenals of nuclear weapons designed to produce untold numbers of these "hideous scenes" are not global pariahs. Of course, the rejoinder from nuclear weapon states and their nuclear umbrella allies is that the whole point of nuclear deterrence is to prevent such threats from ever being carried out (even as they keep those weapons on high alert and available for firing within minutes of an order to do so). The intent, they say, is to make the actual use of nuclear weapons so incalculably costly and hideous that all who possess them will be deterred from using them. Indeed, they explain, nuclear weapons are really "political weapons." They are thus "symbols," as three former but eminent American national security officials patiently explained in the *Washington Post* in mid-2014, "a visible symbol to friend and potential foe of the US commitment to defend NATO with all the military power it possesses."[2] They didn't add that "all the military power it possesses" would, once employed, successfully incinerate vast areas of the planet with not the slightest regard for distinctions between civilians and combatants or the niceties of international humanitarian law.

Meanwhile, growing international demands that nuclear weapon states speed up implementation of their solemnly made disarmament commitments, or at the very least take their weapons off high alert so as to reduce the dangers of inadvertent attacks, are as often as not met with the kind of bland assurance that NATO repeats in its most recent (2012) defence posture review: "The supreme guarantee of the security of the Allies is provided by the strategic nuclear forces of the Alliance."[3] You get a clear sense of the kind of security world we inhabit when the phrase, "the supreme guarantee of security," is used to summarize a policy that, if carried out, would accomplish the mass, irredeemable destruction of friend and foe alike and make much of the planet uninhabitable.

Nuclear weapons are not symbols. They are deployed as active and ongoing threats, and, as with any threats, they serve a real function only if they are genuinely believable. Nuclear threats are believable only if there is an undoubted capability and willingness to make good on those threats in particular circumstances, a willingness to launch an attack of indiscriminate mass destruction on another society, even when such an attack would guarantee retaliation in kind. The two leading – that is to say, the two most brazen – nuclear powers go to great lengths to keep their weapons on the highest possible alert levels, capable of being launched within a few minutes of an order to do so, constantly updating and modernizing them, even if overall numbers are reduced. An estimated eighteen hundred American and Russian warheads are on that high alert, ready for immediate launch from land- or sea-based ballistic missiles – and once a missile and its warheads have been launched, there is no calling them back. The smallest of these warheads has an explosive power of one hundred kilotons. Clusters of three or four, in some cases more, sit atop individual missiles, so the launch of a single such missile would send those three or four warheads to three or four separate targets – each with an explosive power at least equivalent to more than a half-dozen Hiroshima bombs. The single Hiroshima bomb resulted in immediate deaths of some one hundred thousand. Do the macabre math and it is clear that the launch of even a single missile – and no planned attack would be kept to only one missile – with four warheads then headed toward any four military or civilian targets would obliterate upwards of a million lives immediately, ignite fires no fire departments could hope to control, cause injuries no emergency rooms could treat, and spread radiation with untold long-term health effects on millions more. And instead of that being cited as a plan to commit mass crimes against humanity, official NATO describes the threat of such attacks, except on a much grander scale than a single launch, as a positive good, a protective "umbrella" under which its member states are allowed to huddle, even though the real guarantee is that instead of the huddled masses under the figurative umbrella being protected, they would themselves the object of a counter attack. ICAN, the international campaign to ban nuclear weapons, cites scientific studies showing that in an all-out nuclear war in which five hundred warheads hit major US and Russian cities, one hundred million people would die in the first half hour and tens of millions more would be fatally injured. Radioactive fallout would cover large swaths of both countries.[4]

It would be possible to go on at length in a similar vein, calling on more testimony from the survivors of Hiroshima and Nagasaki, reprising the various scenarios and likely consequences, including nuclear winter, of even the most limited of nuclear strikes, but we can forgo all that and just rely on Nikita Khrushchev's conclusion – in the event of a nuclear attack, said the late Soviet leader, the living would envy the dead. Enough said. Every day we rely on nuclear deterrence we inexplicably affirm that the threat of indiscriminate destruction beyond all precedent is a rational and moral security policy.

Not surprisingly, it is not a posture that builds public confidence, and accordingly public support for the abolition of this logic and the weapons that spawn it is high and is building. Large swaths of civil society and religious communities have long insisted, as articulated in a 2010 Canadian Council of Churches letter to Prime Minister Stephen Harper, that "to rely on nuclear weapons, to threaten nuclear attack as a foundation for security, is to acquiesce to spiritual and moral bankruptcy."[5] In 2009, former US Secretary of State Henry Kissinger made essentially the same point, using the rather more secular and utilitarian language of diplomacy: "Any use of nuclear weapons is certain to involve a level of casualties and devastation out of proportion to foreseeable foreign policy objectives."[6] More recently a large group of governments have emphasized the humanitarian case against nuclear weapons with the starkly practical and understated point that, given the catastrophic effects of nuclear weapons detonation, it is doubtful that "these weapons could ever, under any circumstances, be used in conformity with international law."[7]

There is now a slow convergence of morality and political realism insisting that nuclear weapons use, and therefore possession and threatened use, cannot be reconciled with international humanitarian law and cannot continue to be regarded as sources of security and stability. That convergence in turn compels the international community to collectively "seek," in the words of President Barack Obama, "the peace and security of a world without nuclear weapons." Two troubling realities in addition to the horrors of Hiroshima and Nagasaki have emerged to give greater impetus to the pursuit of nuclear weapons abolition. The attacks of 9/11 graphically hint at the exponentially greater destruction that would be possible were non-state groups bent on spreading terror to gain control of nuclear explosive devices rather than just civilian airliners. In fact, the US Department of Homeland Security has studied that possibility in some detail, concluding that if a Hiroshima-sized (that is to say, small by today's standards) nuclear explosion were to be set off at ground level a few blocks north of the White House, there would be 45,000 immediate deaths, 323,000 injuries, four hospitals within the area would cease to function and another four would be subjected to dangerous radioactive fallout.[8] The other dawning reality, reinforced by the two cases of North Korea and Iran, is that nuclear materials and knowledge are spreading. And even when that spread is in full compliance with international rules and focused on civilian power generation and medicine, those materials and technologies carry with them weapons options. The full range of nuclear materials and know-how, and thus nuclear options, can no longer be realistically confined to a select few.

The capacity to build a nuclear weapon is spreading primarily by lawful means, and the only real way to prevent the conversion of that capability into actual weapons is to persuade states that it is in their best interests to eschew nuclear weapons.

It is a vexing but inescapable reality that while compliance with international nuclear rules and obligations can be vigorously encouraged, it is ultimately voluntary. When it comes right down to it, compliance with existing prohibitions on nuclear weapons is chosen rather than imposed. The essential rules of the nuclear road are, of course, legally binding, and the international community does have formidable powers of investigation, persuasion, and coercion to try to ensure that the rules are honoured. It is also true that these international rules, and the pressures to abide by them, are critically important factors in persuading states that their best interests are served by compliance. But, in the end, sovereign states decide whether or not to comply, and some are willing to absorb the diplomatic, economic, and security costs of noncompliance, notably North Korea. And when a state chooses noncompliance, effective enforcement, in the sense of the international community "forcing" compliance when persuasion fails, is hard to come by.

That is obviously not an argument for abandoning enforcement efforts, but it does mean that the global nuclear control regime that is constructed relies on the respect and political support it earns as a fair, non-discriminatory system that serves the common global interest. Domestic law enforcement is possible when the overwhelming majority of citizens voluntarily comply because they regard the laws as fair and in their own and the community's best interests, leaving "enforcement" to focus on the few outliers. The same is true of the international community. International law becomes real and enforceable when the overwhelming majority of states regard it as fair and consistent with their own interests. The problem is that the rules governing the use of nuclear materials and technology for weapons purposes are widely regarded as discriminatory. The idea that a discriminatory system – in which the vast majority of states eschew nuclear weapons, while the few states that already have them can continue to build, modernize, and deploy them, can threaten indiscriminate destruction against all others, and can wield the political and military intimidation that attends those arsenals – will enjoy ongoing respect without generating irresistible proliferation pressures is no longer credible. That is why total abolition has become the formal and universally agreed on goal of the international community.

That leads to another sobering truth. While prohibition is now the only realistic option, it is not a permanent "solution" to the nuclear threat.

There is no permanent, once-and-for-all solution. The abolition of nuclear weapons would not eliminate the nuclear threat. Abolition cannot eliminate either nuclear materials or nuclear know-how, and it certainly can't eliminate human folly. Even when the weapons are universally prohibited and that prohibition is broadly respected, an elaborate system of verification will still have to be permanently in place because human folly will always be present in the form of some outliers wanting to get around the prohibition. But prohibition is the best, the most realistic, ground from which to stand guard against the enduring nuclear threat.

In the meantime, the top priority policy imperative is to stay lucky. Gareth Evens has put it bluntly: "It is not statesmanship, or good professional management, or anything inherently stable about the world's nuclear weapons systems that has let us survive so long without catastrophe, but rather sheer dumb luck. It simply cannot be assumed that luck will continue indefinitely."[9] But it was the golf great Ben Hogan who offered the best advice on how to make luck a priority: "Golf is a game of luck," he said, "and the more I practice, the luckier I get." The more the world does to practise restraint, to respect international humanitarian law and the minimum imperatives of morality, and to control dangerous substances, the longer our good luck is apt to last.

There are three categories of urgent actions for the long-term management of the nuclear threat: pursue measures to reduce the risk that existing weapons will be used, deliberately or by accident; continue to pursue disarmament on the way to abolition by a specified date; and strengthen the non-proliferation regime to ensure the non-diversion of nuclear materials and technologies from peaceful to military purposes. Risk reduction, disarmament, and nonproliferation are the three priorities, along with promoting the kinds of political conditions most conducive to advancing those priories.

As a matter of formal, or at least rhetorical, policy, essentially all 193 member states of the United Nations have declared their support for these priorities and the goal of a world without nuclear weapons. The 185 states that have already disarmed and signed on to the Nuclear Non-Proliferation Treaty (NPT) have agreed to remain permanently disarmed and to submit to independent verification of their compliance with that pledge. Only one of those states, North Korea, has overtly reneged on that commitment and now has nuclear weapons. One state, Iran, had by certain clandestine actions cast doubt on its commitment, but in 2015 extensive negotiations were proposing measures Iran would take to restore international confidence in its declared rejection of nuclear weapons. Five states (China, France, Russia, the United Kingdom, and the United States) already had nuclear weapons when they signed on to the NPT, but by accepting Article VI of the treaty they have assumed a legal obligation to disarm and to eliminate their nuclear arsenals, though without yet committing to any firm timeline. That is not to say they haven't made some impressive progress, having reduced their collective total nuclear warhead inventory from about seventy thousand at the height of the Cold War to just over sixteen thousand in 2014. But that's where the good news now ends – all five now pursue modernization of their arsenals and show little inclination to take serious steps towards elimination. Then there are three states with nuclear weapons – India, Israel, and Pakistan – that have never signed on to the NPT and thus are formally outside the primary nuclear weapons control and non-proliferation regime. All three have nevertheless rhetorically joined in aspirational declarations of support for universal nuclear disarmament. Obviously, these rhetorical commitments are heavily qualified and compromised by their current pursuits (expanding nuclear arsenals) and circumstances.

The NPT, the primary nuclear disarmament and non-proliferation agreement, awaits universality and full implementation. Accomplishing that requires final settlement of the North Korean and Iranian issues, bringing the three states still outside the treaty under its disarmament obligation, fulfilling the Article VI disarmament mandate, and continuing to strengthen the International Atomic Energy Agency (IAEA) safeguards system. In the meantime some states have begun to focus on the need to develop a new and overarching legal framework or umbrella convention that would link a time-specific prohibition on nuclear weapons with the several measures, such as a testing ban and controls over fissile materials for weapons purposes, that are widely agreed on and central to making abolition real. Just as separate treaties set out the universal prohibitions on chemical and biological weapons, all the measures under the broadly agreed disarmament agenda must finally be brought into a single and comprehensive legal framework. But there is no shortcut, and the reality is that the basic deal that was struck in 1968 when the NPT was negotiated is still the one that needs to be implemented. The global norm is now clear. States without nuclear weapons need to stay that way, and states with nuclear weapons need to get rid of theirs.

In the latter case, another likely reality is that states with nuclear weapons will largely have to disarm together. No state with nuclear weapons is inclined to disarm unilaterally, and most think they should be the last to disarm. There are two possible exceptions – the Democratic People's Republic of Korea (DPRK) and the United Kingdom. In the North

Korean case, international pressure on it to pull back from its nuclear adventures will not relent. North Korea is a weak state and will not – cannot – prevail in this struggle. If the international community proves incapable, or capable only with great difficulty, of disarming a state as dysfunctional and as far out of the global mainstream as North Korea, the prospects for persuading the other eight states with nuclear weapons to disarm will be rather dim. The UK (and why not France) should be a candidate for unilaterally relinquishing its nuclear arsenal, on grounds that whatever security benefits the nuclear umbrella is perceived to bring would remain with the UK as a NATO state whether or not it has a nuclear weapons capability of its own. Furthermore, the main achievement of the UK arsenal is crippling cost and the distinction of being a primary, rather than just a secondary, target for the nuclear arsenals of others. The estimated $100 billion that Trident renewal could cost may yet persuade parliamentarians to bow to fiscal restraint and free the UK of its continuing nuclear folly. Israel might logically also be persuaded to divest itself of its unacknowledged (by Israel) nuclear arsenal ahead of universal nuclear disarmament as part of a comprehensive and durable Middle East peace accord – a prospect, it is safe to say, that is not within anyone's current definition of imminence. All other states with nuclear weapons (China, France, India, Pakistan, Russia, and the United States) will have to be treated as inter-linked and brought into a coordinated disarmament process, once Russia and the US, where the primary onus now rests, accomplish significant additional reductions in their arsenals.

The Agreed Disarmament Agenda

As of early 2015, the nine states with nuclear weapons together were in possession of just over 16,000 nuclear warheads. Some 93 per cent of those were in the arsenals of the US and Russia, about 7,200 and 8,000 respectively, of which about 2,100 and 1,600 respectively were deployed and operational. The US and Russia each keep 1800 or so of their warheads stockpiled and available for deployment, while the rest are retired and awaiting dismantling. France, the UK, and China have arsenals within the 200–300 warhead range, while India and Pakistan are estimated to have more than 100 warheads each – Pakistan slightly more than India – and Israel is assumed to have just under 100 warheads. The DPRK has tested nuclear devices, but it is not known whether it has an inventory of warheads; if it does it would certainly be fewer than 10.[10]

The disarmament commitment of the five nuclear weapon states within the NPT is explicit. While Article VI, the disarmament article, is replete with ambiguity and clumsy syntax, successive NPT Review Conferences have issued clarifying judgments, all with the consent of the nuclear weapon states. In the 2010 conference the nuclear weapon states signed on to the "unequivocal undertaking to accomplish, in accordance with the principle of irreversibility, the total elimination of their nuclear arsenals leading to nuclear disarmament, to which all States parties are committed under article VI of the Treaty."[11] The UN Security Council also confirmed in 2009 that the intent of Article VI is a world without nuclear weapons, and NATO's Strategic Concept uses the same phrase.[12] That formal commitment has been elaborated in successive agreements by the NPT Review Conferences: the "Principles and Objectives" agreed to in 1995,[13] the "practical steps" agreed to in 2000,[14] and the sixty-four specific "actions" agreed to in 2010.[15] These were consensus agreements, meaning that all the states parties to the NPT, including the nuclear weapons states, supported the disarmament agenda set out.

To reduce the risk of use (deliberate or accidental) of existing arsenals, states made commitments in principle on the need to de-alert all deployed weapons systems, on diminishing the role of nuclear weapons in national security strategies, and on providing legally binding negative security assurances (commitments not to use or threaten to use nuclear weapons against non-nuclear weapons states). Disarmament commitments included declarations of the need for steady progress in verifiable and irreversible reductions in existing arsenals, leading to the total elimination of nuclear weapons; support for the entry into force of the Comprehensive Nuclear-Test-Ban Treaty; the negotiation of a fissile materials treaty; support for greater transparency from nuclear weapons states with regard to their existing arsenals, including commitments to provide regular reports and document progress made toward full implementation of Article VI of the NPT; and a commitment to pursue universality of the NPT (so as to extend the legal obligation to disarm to states not within the NPT – notably through a non-discriminatory nuclear weapons convention). In addition to having elaborated a broad disarmament agenda, the international community has also elaborated a basic approach to non-proliferation.

De-alerting

The two states with the largest nuclear arsenals have so far failed utterly to meet the minimum requirement for reducing the risk of using existing weapons. They keep weapons on high alert, ready for virtually instantaneous launching, even in response to unexplained blips on radar screens if someone decides it's a real danger. It needn't be so. One minimal but simple move would be for the US and Russia to adopt a firm no-first-use policy – that is, to declare that they will never be the first to introduce a nuclear attack into a conflict. Both claim, of course, that they retain weapons only as a last resort, to be used only in the most exceptional of cases, but they still refuse to offer this simple no-first-use pledge. But beyond that declarative change, an absolute minimum requirement for disarming conflict is to manage existing nuclear arsenals in such a way as to make them verifiably unavailable for quick use in any conflict. Today we have the utterly irresponsible and dangerous opposite – the US and Russia maintain large arsenals on land- and sea-based missiles available for immediate firing. In 2000, they formally agreed to consider reducing the operational status of their nuclear weapons systems (de-alerting, step 9d). Presidents George W. Bush and Barack Obama have both described "high alert" postures as relics of the Cold War, but neither acted to change them.[16] So it remains entirely possible to launch an immediate retaliatory strike in response to a false warning of an attack (that unexplained blip on a radar). The typical strategic justification for such a launch-on-warning policy is that, if the missiles were not launched in response to a warning of attack, they could be destroyed in their launch silos (the use 'em or lose 'em argument). But in today's strategic environment there can be no possible justification for such a dangerous, reckless posture since the weapons are dispersed in multiple systems, with those in submarines especially invulnerable to an adversary's preemptive first strike.

De-alerting nuclear forces involves the imposition of physical impediments to an immediate launch and the most reliable measure is to separate warheads from their delivery vehicles. Bruce Blair, a former intercontinental ballistic missile launch control officer and currently at Princeton University and Global Zero, describes other measures to ensure that missiles would require twenty-four to seventy-two hours to be readied for firing.[17] These technical obstacles to launching include delays in communications, positioning submarines in ways that would preclude immediate launch, and installing pins in land-based missiles, which would require maintenance crews to enter missile silos before a launch could take place. It would also be possible, says Blair, to "remov[e] all of the existing wartime targets from ballistic missile submarine databases and the land-based missile computers," one more measure helping to make it impossible to maintain launch-on-warning postures and to launch a missile in response to a false warning. With appropriate verification, mutual de-alerting by the US and Russia "would remove the threat of a sudden first-strike or decapitation strike."

All the US and Russia really have to do is follow the model of other states with nuclear weapons. The United Kingdom, for example, reports that the Trident submarine (there is usually only one on patrol at a time) "is normally at several days' notice to fire."[18] China already keeps its warheads separated from their delivery systems. States that possess nuclear weapons but have not signed the NPT – India, Israel, and Pakistan – are at even lower levels of alert, do not under normal circumstances deploy any nuclear weapons with military forces, and keep warheads separated from their delivery missiles and aircraft. It is the conventional wisdom that newer nuclear powers are bound to have less reliable weapons management systems, but in fact it is they that provide the more sensible model for nuclear weapons' management and deployment.

Reducing Existing Arsenals

Logically and practically, however, the only way to prevent the use of nuclear weapons is to eliminate them. And progress toward that end requires movement on two key measures, among others: a ban on testing nuclear warheads by nuclear weapon states (non-nuclear weapon states are already barred from testing) and an agreement on strict international controls over the production and possession of fissile materials. The major part of the work on a ban on testing, which puts major limits on the development of new warheads by nuclear weapon states and prevents states that might at some point aspire to developing their own warhead capability from testing their designs, has already been done. The treaty has been negotiated, more than 180 states have signed and more than 160 have ratified it, including three states with nuclear weapons (Russia, France, and the UK). Those states with nuclear weapons that have yet to ratify the treaty are essentially complying with it. But the final steps still need to be taken – all states with either military or civilian nuclear programs must ratify it before it can enter into force. The current holdouts are five states that have signed the treaty but not ratified it (the US, China, Israel, Iran, and Egypt) and three states that have neither signed nor ratified it (North Korea, India, and Pakistan). In the meantime, the Comprehensive Nuclear-Test-Ban Treaty (CTBT) organization is developing a test ban verification regime that is already partly operational. The system is capable of detecting any nuclear explosion anywhere on earth, whether underwater, underground, or in the atmosphere. A monitoring system of more than three hundred installations worldwide, supported by on-site inspections within member countries, it is also used to detect undersea earthquakes that can cause tsunamis, underwater volcanic eruptions, and the breaking up of sea ice. With extremely sensitive sensors to detect radioactivity, the CTBT system can detect the dispersal of radioactivity from sources other than nuclear explosions.[19] But it will be fully operational and allow for such provisions as on-site inspections only after the treaty's entry into force.

The fissile materials challenge is quite another story.[20] Since 1993 it has been the formal intention of the international community, universally agreed by virtue of a 1993 UN General Assembly resolution (48/75), to negotiate "a non-discriminatory, multilateral, and international and effectively verifiable treaty banning the production of fissile material for nuclear weapons and other nuclear explosive devices." Negotiations have yet to begin. The major nuclear weapons states agreed to the proposed negotiation because they already have far more fissile material than they need, but other states like India and Pakistan are still actively producing fissile materials for weapons purposes. Pakistan, supported by many states of the non-aligned movement, insists that fairness requires that agreement to halt production must include measures to radically reduce existing stockpiles. For Pakistan, the issue is decidedly local inasmuch as a halt in production would leave it permanently with a much smaller stockpile than India.

The most significant recent disarmament achievement of the major nuclear powers was the 2010 ratification of the New START Treaty.[21] The treaty limits the Russian and US deployed warheads to 1,550 each, but that has not stopped them, along with all other states with nuclear weapons, from extensive "modernization" of their arsenals. The "nuclear notebook" of the *Bulletin of the Atomic Scientists*, through the work of Hans M. Kristensen and Robert S. Norris, is the preeminent source on nuclear weapons developments and their 2014 account of "endless nuclear weapon modernizations" is a detailed listing of contemporary nuclear folly. "All the nuclear-armed states," they report, "have ambitious nuclear weapon modernization programs in progress that appear intended to prolong the nuclear era indefinitely."[22] Indeed, the rate by which arsenals are being numerically reduced has slowed substantially, and the extent of modernization of nuclear weapons and the development of new capacities calls into question the commitment to reduce the operational role of nuclear weapons in national security policies and practices.

Preventing Horizontal Proliferation

The primary mechanism for avoiding the spread of nuclear weapons is established by the NPT and requires all states without nuclear weapons to enter into monitoring and verification (safeguards) agreements with the International Atomic Energy Agency (IAEA) to confirm that they are not in any way trying to acquire nuclear weapons. While that has been an effective control program – North Korea is the only state that signed on to the NPT that subsequently violated its central commitment not to acquire a nuclear weapon – states have collectively agreed on a number of measures needed to bolster the nonproliferation regime.

Inspections undertaken by the IAEA are largely confined to confirming the accuracy of declarations made by states about their nuclear materials and activities related to peaceful purposes – the only kinds of materials and activities that non-nuclear weapons states party to the NPT are permitted. These traditional inspections allow the IAEA to judge whether or not materials from declared facilities are being diverted for weapons purposes, but traditional inspections are too limited to allow the IAEA to develop confident judgments as to whether or not a state has undeclared nuclear materials or facilities. In order to increase IAEA inspection capacity, an Additional Protocol to IAEA agreements has been developed to extend standard IAEA safeguard agreements to provide for broader and more intrusive inspections and monitoring. Once an Additional Protocol is in place the IAEA is able to draw more confident conclusions, not only to confirm the non-diversion of materials from declared facilities, but also about the presence or absence of any undeclared nuclear materials or activities.[23] Most states now agree that the provisions of the Additional Protocol should be the minimum standard for safeguard agreements.

The nuclear suppliers group is an informal yet powerful network of nuclear supplier states set up to place co-ordinated restraints on trade in nuclear materials, aimed at limiting the export of nuclear materials and technology to civilian purposes (as required under the NPT, which prohibits the transfer of any materials or technology that are weapons-related) and to states that adhere to full-scope safeguards administered by the IAEA – meaning full inspections of all of a country's nuclear facilities. Indeed, in 1995 this rule became a global norm when the 189 states in the NPT adopted and expanded the principle in a decision that said "acceptance of the agency's full-scope safeguards and internationally legally binding commitments not to acquire nuclear weapons" is "a necessary precondition" for civilian nuclear co-operation. In a major blow to both nonproliferation and disarmament, India was later exempted from this central principle.

The greater the number of states that enrich uranium and reprocess spent nuclear fuel, the greater the number of states with expertise and opportunity to divert nuclear materials for weapons purposes. It follows that, if the more sensitive elements of fuel production (those which have application for weapons purposes) can be confined to a very few countries, the capacity to detect and prevent diversion will improve. At the same time, the restriction of these technologies and materials cannot credibly be pursued as one more double standard or class division. Uranium enrichment and plutonium reprocessing cannot be wide open and simply left to national prerogatives, but neither can it be allowed to remain the monopoly of a few states. The sensible objective pursued by some is multilateral control of the fuel cycle to ensure that all states that meet safeguard requirements have equal access to the legal product of those technologies (e.g., civilian reactor fuel) on a nondiscriminatory basis. If the international community is to move beyond the double standard between "haves" and "have nots" in the development of multilateral controls on fuel cycle technologies, it will have to find a way to develop collective controls that have the confidence of states that are asked to forgo national development of relevant technologies. Iran, for example, is suspected of insisting on developing its own technology and expertise in uranium enrichment so that it can in the future apply it to weapons production if it so decides, but it is also the case that Iran and other countries seeking nuclear power claim that they are not confident that they can rely on external sources for fuel. For Iran and others to give up their nuclear technology ambitions, they would have to have confidence that the international community, through a system of multilateral controls over enrichment and reprocessing, would respect and honour their legitimate nuclear energy ambitions.

Other items on the agreed nonproliferation agenda include a call on nuclear weapons states to place their excess fissile materials under IAEA safeguards, and for all others to take further measures to ensure the security and safety of physical nuclear materials and facilities. In 2004, for example, UN Security Council Resolution 1540 focused on legally binding measures against "any form of support to non-State actors that attempt to develop, acquire, manufacture, possess, transport, transfer or use nuclear, chemical or biological weapons and their means of delivery." All states are required to establish national laws and regulations toward that end and to report to the Security Council's "1540 Committee," and the UN Office of Disarmament Affairs offers assistance, funded by a special trust fund, to states in their efforts to meet their obligations under 1540. Ten years after the resolution was passed, the editor of a 1540 journal undertook an extensive review of the successes and failures. While calling it a mixed record, he nevertheless concluded that the resolution and the infrastructure that is emerging around it are performing an important role in preventing non-state access to weapons of mass destruction.[24]

In all of these measures, verification is obviously critical. Disarmament has to happen at a particular time, but verification is forever. There will not be a time in foreseeable human history when it won't be necessary to verify nuclear disarmament and the compliance of all states with the coming prohibition on nuclear weapons possession and use. Vigilance of that magnitude depends on technical monitoring capacity, but above all on transparency. Monitoring is possible in a world of strained superpower relations, but amity among major powers would make transparency feasible and thus monitoring more effective and believable. And that speaks to the urgent need to build the political conditions for disarmament.

Building Conditions for a World Without Nuclear Weapons

Support for urgent and concrete action has emerged from new and sometimes surprising sources. The "gang of four,"[25] including former US Secretary of State Henry Kissinger, has since 2007 argued persuasively that action on specific disarmament measures and commitment to the final goal of a world without nuclear weapons are inseparable:

> Reassertion of the vision of a world free of nuclear weapons and practical measures toward achieving that goal would be, and would be perceived as, a bold initiative consistent with America's moral heritage. The effort could have a profoundly positive impact on the security of future generations. Without the bold vision, the actions will not be perceived as fair or urgent. Without the actions, the vision will not be perceived as realistic or possible.[26]

Expectations for significant progress in implementing that agenda were raised when, in 2009, US President Barack Obama told a Prague audience:

> Today, I state clearly and with conviction America's commitment to seek the peace and security of a world without nuclear weapons. I'm not naive. This goal will not be reached quickly - perhaps not in my lifetime. It will take patience and persistence. But now we ... must ignore the voices who tell us that the world cannot change. We have to insist, "Yes, we can."[27]

Countless other current and former security officials, diplomats, and politicians have joined civil society organizations and security experts around the globe in also calling for a world without nuclear weapons and urging decisive action on nuclear disarmament. Civil society has from the dawn of the nuclear age – through research, expertise, advocacy, and moral witness – been the primary and persistent carrier of the vision of a world without nuclear weapons.

Soured relations between the US and Russia, as well as the recalcitrance of the US Congress in the face of President Obama's ambitious disarmament objectives, have generally dimmed the optimism that accompanied the Obama Administration's commitment to action and the successful 2010 Review Conference of the NPT. Nevertheless, the universal formal commitment to a world without nuclear weapons and broad international agreement on the essentials of the nuclear disarmament agenda continue to make this a propitious moment to make significant progress toward the final abolition and prohibition of nuclear weapons.

Progress in advancing toward the goal of a world without nuclear weapons is all about reshaping the context. Shultz, Perry, Kissinger, and Nunn made this essential point when they said "a world without nuclear weapons will not simply be today's world minus nuclear weapons."[28] While it is true that a world without nuclear weapons will have to be different in some fundamental ways from a world with many, it is also true that today's international security environment is already fundamentally different from what it was when nuclear arsenals were at their peak in the 1970s.[29] The Cold War is over. We now have greater awareness of the proliferation incentives generated by existing arsenals. There are heightened concerns about non-state groups getting their hands on the bomb.[30] All of these changed conditions have helped to galvanize a new constituency of support for nuclear abolition.

The lesson is that the world security environment can and does change, even for the better. Furthermore, while it is clear that a world without nuclear weapons will require significant changes to big power security arrangements and to regions of conflict that have been nuclearized, it is also true that credible progress toward zero nuclear weapons is itself transformative. So the point is not only that accelerated nuclear disarmament depends on a transformed security environment, but also that advances in nuclear disarmament contribute enormously to that transformation – a positive feedback loop. But there is no disputing the unavoidable fact that security arrangements conducive to a world without nuclear weapons do depend in particular on changing big power relations. It is worth noting that while there is an ample literature on the disarmament steps needed to reach zero, much less attention has been paid to the security arrangements that are needed to encourage and attend disarmament progress.

Long before the US and Russia get close to zero nuclear weapons, the current NATO-Russia conventional imbalance will become an impediment to further progress. Combined, the US and NATO have well over ten times the military capacity of Russia, measured in total military spending.[31] It is unlikely that Russia will divest itself of all its nuclear weapons with that military imbalance intact or without some forms of security guarantees, which could only be possible and credible in a radically altered Russia/US/Europe relationship. The most recent US *Nuclear Posture Review* (NPR)[32] is entirely oblivious to that reality. While it articulates a welcome reduction in US reliance on nuclear weapons, it proposes to replace nuclear deterrence gradually with what it calls "the growth of unrivalled U.S. conventional military capabilities." While it cites other factors as facilitating reduced reliance on nuclear deterrence, notably the easing of Cold War tensions and the development of missile defences, it cites "the advent of US conventional military pre-eminence" and "the prospect of a devastating conventional military response" as the alternative to nuclear deterrence. The NPR repeatedly links declining reliance on nuclear weapons with the pledge to "continue to strengthen conventional capabilities."[33] In other words, it proposes that deterrence by weapons of *mass* destruction be replaced with deterrence by weapons that are *massively* destructive – military planners will say that modern weapons are more accurate and more precisely targeted, but precise hits on multiple targets rapidly amount to massive destruction.

Contrary to the NPR, American conventional military preeminence is an impediment, not a means to nuclear disarmament. High levels of competing offensive conventional military forces are also a primary source of horizontal nuclear proliferation pressure. And those pressures will not vanish with nuclear disarmament. Nuclear materials and technology will continue to exist and spread through civilian programs, and states that feel an existential threat from militarily superior powers will be no less tempted to acquire a nuclear weapons capability than are some states now. Threats of mass destruction, whether by conventional or nuclear means, generate pressures to acquire an antidote or a strategic trump. So, massive accumulations of conventional weapons inevitably generate nuclear proliferation pressures. In other words, reducing the demand for nuclear weapons will require reductions in conventional arms as well. The point is that conventional arms restraint, not escalation, is essential to continuing progress in nuclear disarmament and to reducing the demand for nuclear weapons. To that end, NATO's 2010 Strategic Concept includes a welcome nod toward "keep[ing] armaments at the lowest level for stability" – and given NATO's disproportionate share of global military spending, there is plenty of room to cut to get to that lowest level.

The NPR's insistence that missile defences reduce reliance on nuclear deterrence is a dangerous fantasy. US and NATO ballistic missile defence systems, current and planned, are allegedly aimed only at defending against so-called rogue state missiles – until recently referring to both North Korea and Iran, but now (since the 2015 framework agreement) with Iran less likely to acquire a nuclear weapon. But the Russians clearly have another view. US missile defences have been part of what has led them to upgrade and add to their own missile defence systems, made them wary of any more reductions in their arsenals, and persuaded them to rely more on a threatening posture which makes the US more, not less, reliant on nuclear deterrence.

A nuclear weapons convention, bolstered by a more effective and comprehensive verification system, is key to building an effective supply-side constraint on nuclear proliferation, but a durable nonproliferation regime also requires demand-side remedies. Nonproliferation in a world without deployed nuclear weapons will require security arrangements that promote stability, reduce threats, and thus reduce demand for a means of neutralizing or topping conventional threats. The point is not that nuclear disarmament must await a totally transformed world, but it must be accompanied by the progressive emergence of a new security environment reflected in conventional arms control and military spending reductions (in essence, disarming conflict through implementation of Article 26 of the UN Charter). Demand reduction strategies include the movement from deterrence to reassurance in major power security relationships,[34] conflict resolution in the regional conflicts that have been nuclearized (North Asia, South Asia, and the Middle East), and transformation of defence alliances into mutual security arrangements.[35]

In calling for deliberate efforts toward a world without nuclear weapons, President Obama has always insisted that as long as nuclear weapons remain, the United States will maintain a credible deterrent.[36] And it is true that as long as nuclear weapons remain deployed they will have a basic deterrent effect against other nuclear weapons. But if other states also feel genuinely intimidated by US conventional dominance, they will, as the late American academic and strategic analyst John Steinbruner has reminded us, have "a strong incentive to pursue asymmetrical deterrent strategies." It is in the US interest, therefore, to "reassure the [militarily] disadvantaged to prevent these asymmetrical deterrent strategies." Thus, he calls for arms control and security strategies to be focused on developing force structures, along with co-operation and confidence building measures, designed not to deter adversaries but to reassure them. "It is not only the imposing nuclear deterrent of the United States that creates a need for reassurance," he says, "but its increasingly intrusive and inherently more usable capacity for precise conventional attack as well." US conventional capacity intimidates a broad range of states and, as Steinbruner says, "the stark imbalance in capacity that has developed today will assuredly not be accepted as equitable, and the implications of inequity are likely to be relentless."[37] Reassurance and co-operation are obviously not possible, or even logical, if the main purpose of military force is to prepare for war, but if, as Mikhail Gorbachev's "new thinking" had it, the role of nuclear arsenals and military forces more broadly is to prevent war, then all of these reassurance measures become eminently sensible.

That is the central point of non-offensive defence or mutual defence postures: for states to seriously consider the security needs of their adversaries because they understand their own security will be enhanced if their adversary feels more secure. Hence, says Bjorn Moller in his study of non-offensive defence,

> states should take into serious consideration the security concerns of their opponents, because neither side can be really secure unless both are (and perceive themselves to be so). The theory, of course, is to be able to mount an effective defence that says to a potential adversary that it will not be able to launch a successful attack, but with defences structured so as not to pose a counter threat to the adversary. To opt for a military posture that would deliberately eschew posing threats to opponents is the only logical answer to this requirement, since this would enhance the opponent's security and, by doing so, improve that of the first party as well.[38]

Besides generally building stability into the international system, non-offensive defence force structures have particular relevance for promoting stability in crisis situations. In downplaying offensive capabilities, incentives for preemption are obviously reduced. It is a posture that recognizes that because war has become so unremittingly horrible, the purpose of military forces, as Bernard Brodie said in 1946 and Gorbachev said in 1987, must be to avert wars rather than to win them. A military establishment, says Moller, "can have no other useful purpose."

Seventy years into the nuclear weapons era, says Noam Chomsky, "we should be contemplating with wonder that we have survived. We can only guess how many years remain."[39] Luck is not a strategy. But as long as the world refuses nuclear abolition, luck remains a primary requirement. To transition from luck to security we will have to see the world's steady evolution into a security community in which there develops the credible expectation that states will not go to war with each other for the purpose of resolving conflicts between and among them. And such a community could be nearer at hand than we've allowed ourselves to imagine. States have not gone to war with each other to resolve an interstate conflict since the Eritrea-Ethiopia War at the turn of the millennium. They haven't stopped preparing for such wars, and they haven't stopped preparing for nuclear war – but to do so, to stop preparing for nuclear war, is the eminently sensible and doable next step. Building on the record of fifteen years of avoiding interstate warfare, perhaps this fledgling global security community could manage to extend the record of seven full decades without combat use of nuclear weapons.

9

When Prevention Fails

Protecting the Vulnerable

THE SMALL SINGLE-ENGINE AIRCRAFT weaved and shuddered its final descent to the grass airstrip in southwestern Sudan. People from the internally displaced persons (IDP) camp that was our destination could already be seen making their way to the edge of the strip. The unkempt grass that thrashed and tangled in the landing gear brought the plane to a quick stop, the engine was cut, the door opened, and we stepped down to a scene of utter quiet. There was no wind, and especially there were no voices, even though scores of people had by then moved onto the grass strip. There was none of the excited chatter or murmuring that one would expect from an assembled crowd that had come to see the far from routine arrival of foreign visitors. The local welcomers stood tall and motionless, some without clothes, all bones and angular, shielding the sun with their hands. The long gently waving grass and the thatched huts in the distance lent an idyllic flare to the unfolding picture, but the silence of those assembled owed to one simple reality – an energy-sapping hunger so thorough and debilitating as to extinguish all casual conversation and certainly all excitement.

The world knew them as IDPs; they knew themselves as abandoned by the world, friends and enemies alike. In flight from their burned homes and bombed villages in Western Upper Nile, they had crossed the swamps to the west of the Nile delta to neighbouring Bahr El Gazal, where they were now ignored and trying to survive on innutritious water lilies and a few fish from the swamps. So there we, a small assessment team, also stood silent, in shirts boasting the latest in UV protection ratings and sturdy shoes, water bottles holstered and ready at our belts. Slowly, one of the elders detached himself from the onlookers to welcome the visitors with a slight bow and then handshakes. The visiting delegation indicated it would be useful for our subsequent reporting back to our respective agencies to take a tour of the camp and observe the conditions firsthand. Wandering through the encampment we were surprised at the number of university-educated camp residents. They had been forced to flee Juba or

171

one of the other larger urban centres and return to their home region where life was supposed to have been safer away from the main action of Sudan's decades-long war, but they had found themselves once more on the run, and in a questioning mood. "Why isn't the Christian West helping us?" was the most frequent question – although it was an accusation rather than a question. Were they, the southern Sudanese, not Christians too? How could the world we represented abandon them so? We must go home and immediately, some told us, urge the United States or the United Nations or whoever could or would listen to send in military forces to protect those who had been denied all protection.

In fact, southern Sudan at the time was the textbook for the kinds of extraordinary circumstances that are widely regarded as warranting military intervention to protect people in great peril. The Canadian-sponsored International Commission on Intervention and State Sovereignty (ICISS) had set the intervention bar very high. In its influential 2001 report, entitled *The Responsibility to Protect*, ICISS said intervention should be contemplated only in circumstances of real or impending harm to people in the form of "large scale loss of life, actual or apprehended," or "large scale 'ethnic cleansing,'" including "forced expulsions" – conditions that apply to very few cases.[1] But those were in fact the conditions that had existed in Sudan for well over a decade at that point. Two million people had died and several millions more were displaced. Furthermore, the right kind of UN-sanctioned military intervention in Sudan – to enforce a no-fly zone, as some were proposing – would most probably have worked in the sense that it would have brought enormous relief to the southern Sudanese, with minimal risk to the interveners and no risk of escalating the fighting in the civil war. Government of Sudan bombing of civilians and the forced expulsion of people from their homes were two prominent features of the war against the separatist southerners. The bombing, the purpose of which was to terrorize the civilian population and set it on the run, was carried out by slow-flying turboprop aircraft, delivering crude bombs, sometimes simple drums of gasoline with lighted wicks, airborne Molotov cocktails kicked out of the tailgate. Declaring and enforcing a southern no-fly zone, with UN relief flights the only exception, would have stopped the bombing. A relatively small number of fighter/patrol aircraft could have handled the enforcement. One immediate source of danger and terror to civilians in the south would have been eliminated and the numbers of displaced radically reduced – in other words, the humanitarian payoff would have been huge and immediate.

The framers of the UN Charter envisioned a world in which individual states would keep their national arsenals and forces to "the lowest possible level" and that rogue aggressors, such as Sudanese forces bombing southern civilians, would be dealt with collectively. States together, under the authority of the UN Security Council, would assure international peace and security and would protect individual states from aggression. And notably, as promised in the 2005 UN General Assembly's global summit that adopted the Responsibility to Protect (R2P) doctrine, the international community would collectively undertake to protect individuals from the war crimes of their governments. Of course, it is more than an understatement to say it hasn't quite worked out that way. Many states have not kept their use of public resources for security purposes to a minimum, the Security Council has been less than stellar as an impartial arbiter of disputes or in delivering collective security assistance to those facing aggression, and individuals and communities continue to endure the vilest of violations of human rights and international humanitarian law without any effective response from the international community. To be fair to the Security Council, most of the vexing security questions it has faced in the last quarter century, like the still persistent ones in Sudan and now South Sudan, have not been about disputes between states but immensely complex disputes within states, and the UN Charter offers little guidance on when and how to intervene in intrastate conflict.

That said, collective security has not been an unmitigated failure. The resort to collective force in support of international peace and security is ordained by the United Nations Charter (Chapter VII), but it was designed for restoring peace between states, and so especially following the end of the Cold War it had to be adapted for also restoring peace within states. The 2005 summit in effect broadened the commitment to collective engagement to include intrastate conflicts by setting out a role for the international community, through the UN, in protecting the vulnerable when national governments have lost either the capacity or the will to do so. The Summit, taking its cue from the ICISS report, declared that states are "prepared to take collective action," under the authority of the UN Security Council, "in a timely and decisive manner" to protect populations when "peaceful means [are] inadequate and national authorities are manifestly failing to protect their populations from genocide, war crimes, ethnic cleansing and crimes against humanity."[2]

Despite this comprehensive mandate for collective action, the international community's response to egregious human suffering due to such crimes is inconsistent and woefully inadequate. Collective military action initiated specifically in support of international law and/or humanitarianism is certainly not uncommon, yet it is the explicit failures to act effectively (whether through peaceful or coercive measures) in support of masses of people in extraordinary peril that stand out – Myanmar, Zimbabwe, Somalia, Darfur (Sudan), Northern Uganda, Rwanda, Syria, and southern Sudan. The resort to force in pursuit of a clear national interest obviously comes more easily to states than do sacrificial interventions on behalf of populations at risk in places where neither national nor broad strategic interests of the interveners are in play. In Kosovo (1999), Afghanistan (2001), Iraq (2003), and Syria (2014), collective military operations – multilateral wars – were initiated without the formal consent of the international community acting through the Security Council and were primarily a response to perceived threats to the interests of the force leaders, rather than the vulnerability of the people of the states that were attacked.

The remedy, however, is obviously not a simple matter of more energetic military intervention. Afghanistan, Iraq, Libya, and Syria are by now icons of the delusions of military power, and they challenge the assumption that military force remains a security trump. When diplomacy fails, the resort to armed force cannot override political and social impediments to agreement and bring rogues to heel. It can't force particular political outcomes, and cannot on its own protect the vulnerable. The assumption in all of these cases was that force could solve fundamental problems that had no other apparent solutions – and the lesson taught, if not necessarily learned, is that when there is no other solution, military force will also fail. The point of the lesson is not to question the skills or dedication of the soldiers who risk their lives in carrying out the commands of their civilian masters and military managers. Nor does it question the real impact that military operations have on political outcomes, including peace negotiations, or cast doubt on the effectiveness with which tactical objectives are achieved. The simple point of the history of multilateral military intervention in Afghanistan, Iraq, and Libya is that all the military skills and sophistication in the world and a virtually unblemished record of tactical battlefield successes cannot be relied on to produce strategic success – political stability and protection of the vulnerable – if the right political and social conditions are not present or pursued with equal determination. The truth that winning battles doesn't win either the war or the peace is nowhere more true than in the "good war" in Afghanistan. National forces arrayed against determined rebels or multilateral military forces sent in to stabilize a chaotic and violence-laden environment are not self-sufficient, no matter how powerful. Their effectiveness depends heavily on a broad range of conditions that make up the social-political context. The impact or role of military force depends ultimately both on the way in which it is prosecuted and on the political, social, and cultural contexts in which it is pursued.

As already discussed in chapter 5, the distinction between peace support missions on the one hand and warfighting on the other is central to the challenges facing protection operations, and that distinction comes more clearly into focus in the post-2001 security assistance intervention in Afghanistan. It was not conceived as, and certainly not run as, an operation to protect vulnerable civilians, but it most certainly was to make Afghans safer. But in time, the focus switched from supporting security and public safety to defeating the enemy. The argument of course was that the latter was essential to achieving the former, but the latter wasn't possible and thus the Afghan experience became a primary lesson in the consequences of moving from a peace support or security assistance operation that enjoys strategic consent from all the key players to heavy focus on military combat operations trying to defeat a party to a civil war.

Strategic Consent

The post-9/11 attack on Afghanistan, launched October 7, 2001, was clearly not a peace support operation. It was a hi-tech, high explosive war on the Afghan regime of the day – to do what modern, technically advanced military forces do best, which is to destroy the existing order. The attacker, the United States, joined at that point by only a few others, declared itself to be fighting a war of self-defence against a pernicious Taliban regime that was a world leader in human rights violations, had never managed to control all of the territory of Afghanistan, and had harboured the architect of the 9/11 attacks on the US. The aim was to remove the Taliban regime in the hope it would be replaced with a stable regime run by the Americans' Northern Alliance partners in the attack. The first part of that aim, the removal of the Taliban, was quickly achieved; the second part, a stable replacement regime, turned out to be rather more of a challenge. The job of reconstituting a new government was taken up in Bonn, Germany. In early 2002, with the Taliban regime apparently defeated, the Bonn process led to a peace agreement and the establishment of an interim government, along with an electoral process and other measures designed to disarm non-state groups and legitimize and support the new government. The agreement prominently included provisions for a multinational peace support force. The new interim government, the quickly assembled creation of the victors, the US and their Afghan Northern Alliance partners, not only consented to the presence of international security forces in Afghanistan but also requested and needed them. The UN-authorized International Security Assistance Force (ISAF) initially largely followed the established peacekeeping/ peace support operation model, the main difference being that it was not UN-commanded, although the UN immediately established a major political/humanitarian resence in the country.

The newly established interim government had a rather significant shortcoming in that it did not include the political party or movement that had been in control of most of the country just a few months earlier. And UN guidelines are clear about the risk that such an omission, the absence of full strategic consent, places on the whole enterprise: "in the absence of such consent, a [multilateral peace support] operation risks becoming a party to the conflict; and being drawn towards enforcement action, and away from its intrinsic role of keeping the peace," or support-ing the extension of state authority throughout the country.[3] But at the time it was not entirely clear that the Bonn process did not meet the requirements for a fully inclusive or comprehensive peace agreement. At the time, the victors were still confident that the vanquished Taliban had been consigned to history, never to return. The Northern Alliance probably would not have allowed the Taliban a place at the table, and at the time it appeared not to be necessary. In that sense, the all-important strategic consent was deemed to be in place when ISAF began operations in 2002. In other words, there was, in fact, an assumed effort to set a constructive political context within which the international security assistance forces were to operate. A new political order was under construction and was seen to be so, as preparations for elections began.

The focus of the multilateral military forces in ISAF, operating under a climate of basic acceptance, was to be restraining the spoilers. Even in cases where there is a comprehensive peace accord, there is clearly no guarantee of an end to all violence. Afghanistan had for more than two decades been in a state of full-blown civil war, first against Soviet inter-vention, next in competition for control in the immediate post-Soviet era, and then in ongoing armed resistance to Taliban rule. No one could have expected in early 2002 that the legacy of that violence and discord would dissolve overnight into a tranquil new order. Even with strategic consent for foreign security assistance forces in place, there can still be challenges to the new order by spoilers – smaller pockets of communal resistance, anxious to boost their standing in the new order, or even orga-nized criminal elements eager to take advantage of the fragility and the absence of mature security institutions. The UN *Principles and Guide-lines* document puts it this way:

The fact that the main parties have given their consent to the deployment does not necessarily imply or guarantee that there will also be
consent at the local level, particularly if the main parties are internally
divided or have weak command and control systems. Universality of
consent becomes even less probable in volatile settings, characterized
by the presence of armed groups not under the control of any of the
parties, or by the presence of other spoilers.[4]

A multilateral force that enjoys strategic consent may still be required
to conduct tactical combat operations to deal with such spoilers, but, by
virtue of the peace agreement, the context is expected to be one of broad
public support for the newly established authority and support for controlling the spoilers. That is essentially what multilateral security forces
did in Afghanistan in the period from 2002 to 2005. In 2003 political violence was the lowest it had been for more than two decades. But, as the
world now knows, that early period was also characterized by escalating
levels of "spoiler" activity. And that should have raised the key question of
when, at what threshold of escalating violence, does the escalation of tactical action against spoilers amount in effect to the loss of strategic consent? When the challenges from spoilers escalate, and when international
security forces are increasingly pulled into ongoing combat with well-
organized forces that have become an existential challenge to the new
order, there comes a point to recognize that strategic consent is no longer
in place. As the UN guidelines document puts it, "consent, particularly if
given grudgingly under international pressure, may be withdrawn in a
variety of ways when a party is not fully committed to the peace process."[5]
When the spoilers are transformed into a broad-based political opposition
movement that can boast a significant constituency of political support,
then there has in reality been the de facto withdrawal of consent at the
strategic level. At that point the military operation has switched from a
peace support operation to a peace enforcement operation – that is, a
multilateral war against insurgents. So, when strategic consent is no
longer available, multilateral forces can find themselves in full combat
with a significant opposition force that can, with some credibility, claim to
be fighting on behalf of a significant element of a population that has lost
confidence in the political agreement produced by the original peace
agreement.

The temptation in such a situation, as history and a myriad of specific cases illustrate, is to intensify the military fight and to try to recover
strategic consent through force. But that is where the evidence of the
past twenty-five years of intrastate warfare ought to be acknowledged –
the recovery of strategic consent by force doesn't work. When peace support morphs into war to defeat an insurgency, the chances of victory are

slim. When the need is to build, not dismantle, a social-political order that can earn the confidence and trust of the people, military force is remarkably impotent. Overwhelming military superiority can readily destroy an existing order, but it cannot by force create political consensus in support of a new order. You can't force people to trust a government. Some 85 per cent of intrastate wars in the past quarter century had to move from the battlefield to the conference table or other political alternatives to find the political consensus that would end the fighting, and the story of Afghanistan after 2005 was largely the wilful refusal to acknowledge that the same thing would have to happen there.

The reality of these unavoidable limits on the utility of force is that military force is neither autonomous nor self-sufficient. Armed force and coercion can reinforce stable and peaceful social orders, but only when at least minimally respected political, social, and law enforcement institutions are in place to legitimize and consolidate enforcement actions. The effectiveness of enforcement is shaped by the environment in which it functions, just as effective economic development depends on the environment in which it is pursued. The point bears emphasizing that there are limits to the effectiveness of force that cannot be overcome simply by the application of greater force. And it is a recognition that at long last became the conventional wisdom in Afghanistan. By 2010, President Obama had shifted the focus on Afghanistan – belatedly if not too late – to include the pursuit of a political track and announced the commitment to end the military mission in 2014. That there is no military solution to Afghanistan's chronic political divides became a common assertion. Making it happen will take a lot longer.

What escalating combat operations in Afghanistan failed to recognize was that a peace agreement and the strategic consent it reflects is not a once-and-for-all achievement, even when based on a comprehensive peace agreement. Strategic consent needs to be constantly and continually renewed through political engagement and credible governance. Again, the UN guidelines make the same point: "In the implementation of its mandate, a United Nations peacekeeping operation must work continuously to ensure that it does not lose the consent of the main parties, while ensuring that the peace process moves forward."[6]

It is also a much larger point. The legitimacy of a new political order or new government is not established once and for all – it is earned and renewed, or eroded, on a daily basis. And, by the way, the same goes for the intervening peace support or security assistance forces – their credibility is not settled once and for all by a Security Council resolution. Rather, it is earned or eroded daily by virtue of their conduct and impact.

The critical point bears repeating: when strategic consent and national consensus are lost, central to their recovery is a new and comprehensive peace process leading ultimately to a new political agreement or framework that has the confidence of the people and the trust needed to sustain a renewed national consensus. After 2005, the international forces in Afghanistan tried to recover strategic consent by military means, and it never came close to working. It takes a political process to reestablish a political context in which security forces can return to their role as peace support forces that may still have to deal with spoilers, but are no longer engaged in an effort to militarily defeat an element of the national political/social constituency.

Protecting the Vulnerable

Multilateral military intervention in the affairs of sovereign states and the importance of the distinction between peace support and warfighting will potentially become more prominent as the international norm of R2P becomes more deeply entrenched. But the basic reality that foreign intervention forces can expect to advance stability and restrain lawlessness only in the context of strategic consent, or at least the active pursuit of it, poses special challenges for operations specifically intended to protect vulnerable people in the midst of a war and chaos. Typically, populations in extreme peril are also caught in a context of political disintegration in which public institutions have lost all credibility. How then to meet the responsibility to protect the vulnerable when strategic consent is prominently absent, when prospects for the political pursuit of a climate of consent are remote, and when prospects for military settlement of the conflict are as remote as they consistently have been over the past quarter century?

The responsibility to protect doctrine has obviously not been formulated and accepted because it will be easy to implement. At the moment, given the experience to date, it seems to be largely impossible to honour the commitment to vulnerable people in any context of extreme peril, but that is not a shortcoming of the emerging norm. The norm holds that national governments clearly bear the primary and sovereign responsibility to provide for the safety of their people. Indeed, a state's sovereignty is to some extent conditional on its capacity to carry out the responsibility to protect and serve the welfare of its people. When there is egregious failure to carry out that responsibility, whether through neglect, the lack of capacity, or deliberate assaults by the state on its own citizens, the international community, as determined by the new UN doctrine adopted in

2005, has the duty to override sovereignty and intervene in the internal affairs of the state in the interests and safety of the people. It is important to add that the international community's responsibility is a collective one – intervention is neither the duty nor the right or prerogative of individual states acting on their own authority when there is not consent from the state whose citizens are to be protected. The responsibility to protect is collective and must include UN authorization when it involves coercion. Unilateral military coercion, no matter how noble the claimed reasons may be, is aggression under the Charter and thus illegitimate.

Military interference in the internal affairs of sovereign states to protect people from extreme harm has, of course, been debated for a long time. The Biafran war of the late 1960s led to an early R2P-style intervention – the civilian mercy flights violated the sovereignty of Nigeria in order to come to the aid of the people of the breakaway effort in southeast Nigeria who faced an extraordinary humanitarian disaster. In 1978, Tanzania invaded Uganda to rid its people of the murderous regime of Idi Amin and thus to end the state of extreme instability on its border. In 1979, Vietnam invaded Cambodia to depose the last vestiges of another murderous regime. Because security and well-being within individual states are inextricably linked to conditions in neighbouring states and ultimately to global stability and prosperity, many states have a history of responding to security concerns beyond their borders when there are serious strains on the stability of the regional and global systems on which they ultimately depend.

The current doctrine evolved following the Rwandan genocide of 1994, the 1995 massacre in Srebrenica, and the unauthorized intervention of NATO in Kosovo in 1999, and in response to a 1999 speech by then UN Secretary-General Kofi Annan, in which he challenged the idea that state sovereignty can be a legitimate barrier to access by the UN and the international community to people caught in humanitarian crises. "If humanitarian intervention is, indeed, an unacceptable assault on sovereignty," he said, "how should we respond to a Rwanda, to a Srebrenica – to gross and systematic violations of human rights that affect every precept of our common humanity?" Then he challenged states: "Surely no legal principle – not even sovereignty – can ever shield crimes against humanity.... The sovereignty of States must no longer be used as a shield for gross violations of human rights."[7]

That speech was a prompt to action, and Africa played a particularly important and catalytic role in mainstreaming the R2P doctrine.[8] Under the Organization of African Unity, the African political convention was to be adamantly suspicious of any moves to interfere in the domestic or internal affairs of African states, but African leaders increasingly feared that the non-interference doctrine had become a mechanism through which sovereignty became a curtain behind which corrupt regimes felt free to engage in extraordinary violations of human rights, ethnic conflict, and official indifference to humanitarian crises. That changed under the African Union, which replaced the OAU in 2002. The AU Constitutive Act asserted "the right of the Union to intervene in a Member State pursuant to a decision of the Assembly in respect of grave circumstances, namely war crimes, genocide and crimes against humanity."[9] As African leaders characterized it at the time, it was a change from a policy of non-interference to one of non-indifference. The AU upholds a strict prohibition on any one Member State interfering in the internal affairs of another, so it is only collective and duly authorized interference in cases of gross violations of the rights of citizens of a state that is to be countenanced. Under the R2P doctrine, the obligation on individual nation states to help protect the citizens of other countries applies only to peaceful means under Chapter VI (that is, with the consent of the host state). Any military coercion to protect people of other states must be carried out collectively under Chapter VII on the basis of Security Council authorization and according to the UN Charter. It is not individual states acting on their own authority that have the responsibility to protect under Chapter VII; rather, the responsibility is that of the international community collectively.

For ICISS, the basic formula was to shift the debate away from the rights of the intervener to the rights and needs of the vulnerable. It said "that sovereign States have a responsibility to protect their own citizens from avoidable catastrophe – from mass murder and rape, from starvation – but that when they are unwilling or unable to do so, that responsibility must be borne by the broader community of States." The UN system then addressed the issue in two reports,[10] resulting ultimately in an extraordinary level of global consensus in support of the final 2005 adoption of the R2P doctrine. It accepts a "responsibility to protect populations" from four particular threats: genocide, war crimes, ethnic cleansing, and crimes against humanity. In other words, it is a limited responsibility, but it is now clear that states have agreed to broaden the Security Council's mandate under the UN Charter. The Security Council can override the national sovereignty of a state not only if events internal to the state are judged to be a threat to international peace and security (such as apartheid in South Africa), but also in response to the presence of or threat of the four listed perils (genocide, war crimes, ethnic cleansing, and crimes against humanity) within that state.

Since then, the international community has shown itself to be extremely reluctant to meet that responsibility. The formal R2P doctrine as adopted by the UN is ambiguous on direct intervention. States did not accept a responsibility to intervene, but declared themselves "prepared to take collective action, in a timely and decisive manner, through the Security Council . . . on a case-by-case basis."[11] The Security Council, in particular, has rarely found agreement on the question and prospects for that soon changing are remote. So Kofi Annan's dilemma remains. If intervention can be legitimate only under Security Council authorization, then the principle of sovereignty will continue to shield crimes against humanity and gross violations of human rights. Resolving questions of the conditions and authority under which the international community can, or must, take protective action in support of vulnerable people, even if that means overriding a state's sovereignty, remains a primary challenge to the R2P doctrine. Protection operations are obviously extremely difficult to carry out. They are complex because they must by definition be undertaken in societies that are chronically troubled, where the chances of failure are great, so states are reluctant to get involved. Many states want to make a clear exit strategy a basic condition for becoming involved in peace support and protection operations, but, of course, there is no such thing as a constantly available exit strategy – once involved, the international community has little opportunity to simply walk away.

But force is, and is intended to be, the exception in protecting vulnerable populations. The doctrine's primary commitment is to "use appropriate diplomatic, humanitarian and other peaceful means, in accordance with Chapters VI and VII of the Charter, to help protect populations."[12] The resolution in that sense acknowledges that the active and persistent pursuit of human security offers the most reliable prospect for protecting people and preventing the kinds of human-made humanitarian catastrophes that we now witness in Syria, Libya, the Democratic Republic of the Congo, Somalia, the Central African Republic, and elsewhere, and that we saw earlier in Rwanda, Southern Sudan, Cambodia, and many other locations of acute insecurity. All are reminders that insecurity is experienced most immediately as unmet basic needs, political exclusion and the denial of basic rights, social and political disintegration, and the related escalation of criminal and political violence. Thus the prevention of armed conflict depends on measures that address and mitigate the ways in which people and communities experience insecurity – by meeting basic economic, social, and health needs; respecting fundamental rights and freedoms; controlling the instruments of violence and prohibiting the means of mass destruction; and honouring the dignity and worth of all people.

At the same time, in calling on the international community to come to the aid of vulnerable people, even those most wary of military interventions are not prepared to say that it is never appropriate or never necessary to resort to the use of lethal force.[13] This refusal to preclude the use of force as a matter of principle is based not on a naive belief that force can be relied on to solve otherwise intractable problems. The point instead is that if the primary obligation is to the welfare of people, it would be irresponsible to preclude in principle any resort to force when, in much more stable and much less perilous circumstances, we do not on principle preclude an appeal to armed police for protection in extraordinary circumstances. The resort to force in conflict settings is first and foremost the result of the failure to prevent what could have been prevented with the appropriate foresight and actions. But having failed, the world needs to do what it can to limit the peril experienced by people as a consequence. Just as individuals and communities in stable and affluent societies can call on armed police to come to their aid in an emergency, people in much more perilous circumstances should have access to protectors. Therefore, it is not assumed that armed force can never be effective in trying to bring at least a short-term reprieve. The formal R2P doctrine thus also acknowledges that the collective responsibility to protect people in peril does not end when peaceful means fail – it is simply not acceptable to simply abandon them to their tormentors.

So there are and will continue to be disastrous circumstances in which force appears to be the only available option – circumstances of imminent or full-blown violence that leave civilians in genuine peril. That certainly doesn't mean that the resort to lethal force can guarantee success. It means only that, having run out of options, military action will sometimes be authorized because the world has failed to find any other means of coming to the aid of those in desperate situations – for the world has promised, after all, to come to the aid of those in extreme peril. But the resort to military protection missions is not an assertion that lethal force will forge the political solution that will bring in the new order of peace and safety. The long-term solutions that are required – that is, the restoration of societies to conditions in which people are for the most part physically safe, basic economic, social, and health needs met, fundamental rights and freedoms respected, the instruments of violence controlled, and in which the dignity and worth of all people are affirmed – cannot be delivered by force. Limiting the resort to force to protective operations embodies the understanding that the distresses of deeply troubled societies cannot be quickly alleviated by either military means or diplomacy and that in the long and slow process of rebuilding the conditions for sustainable peace, those that are most vulnerable are entitled to protection from at least the most egregious of threats. The use of force for humanitarian purposes is not the attempt to find military solutions to social and political problems, to militarily engineer new social and political realities. Rather, it is intended to mitigate imminent threats and to alleviate immediate suffering while long-term solutions are sought by other means.

For force to be effective, it has to be used as has been argued here, in the context of a broad spectrum of economic, social, political, and diplomatic efforts to address the direct and long-term conditions that underlie the crisis (as discussed in chapter 5). For military interventions to have a chance at being effective, they have to be accompanied by independent humanitarian relief efforts and include the resources and will to stay with people in peril until essential order and public safety are restored and there is a demonstrated local capacity to build conditions of durable peace. The ICISS report envisioned the responsibility to protect to include a responsibility to rebuild.

That the force deployed and used for the protection of vulnerable people is, as in multilateral interventions generally, to be distinguished from military warfighting methods and objectives is reinforced by the ICISS report. While noting that peacekeeping was designed to monitor ceasefires between belligerent states, the ICISS report says, "the challenge in this context is to find tactics and strategies of military intervention that fill the current gulf between outdated concepts of peacekeeping and full-scale military operations that may have deleterious impacts on civilians."[14] Later it makes the point that "military intervention [for protection purposes] involves a form of military action significantly more narrowly focused and targeted than all out warfighting."[15] Winning the acceptance of civilian populations, it says, "means accepting limitations and demonstrating through the use of restraint that the [military] operation is not a war to defeat a State but an operation to protect populations in that State from being harassed, persecuted or killed."[16] Such intervention is more related to policing – though not necessarily in the level of force required since it is inevitable that protection forces sometimes face heavily armed, unrestrained, adversaries. But military operations to protect people are analogous to policing in the sense that the armed forces are not employed to "win" a conflict or defeat a regime. They are there only to protect people in peril and to try to maintain some level of public safety while other authorities and institutions pursue solutions to underlying problems. Increasingly, UN peace support operations are specifically mandated to protect civilians through such quasi-constabulary operations. These are fraught undertakings and force-contributing countries still need collectively to find the operational tactics and rules of engagement to do this effectively.

The protection of vulnerable civilians means being willing and able to intervene in situations of extreme instability and violence. However, as we have seen, intervention in such contexts, even with massively superior military force, is no guarantee that stability will ensue – indeed, the odds suggest that it will not. It is one of the most profound moral and political dilemmas of our time. Morality and empathy inevitably and properly translate into overwhelming political pressure to "do something" in support of vulnerable populations under imminent threat of attack or in disastrous humanitarian circumstances. Such crises rarely yield to short-term diplomacy, yet military engagement, even if it is successful in staving off an attack (as in Benghazi in Libya or Kobane in Syria), invokes long-term consequences that are unknowable but can be reliably taken to lack promise. The responsibility to protect is a relatively new doctrine. Efforts to employ multilateral military forces to implement it have at best faltered. The likelihood is that the international community will continue to respond on a case-by-case basis, trying, when good will prevails, to make the best of impossibly complex situations. By definition, circumstances in which people need protection from extreme violence are complex and defy easy solutions. Mistakes will continue to be made, some with severe consequences, but it is also likely that the experience gained will be informative and will gradually improve prospects for constructive protection operations – much as peacekeeping lessons learned have gradually informed and improved peace support actions. The Security Council regularly invokes R2P to acknowledge the international community's grave responsibility to come to the aid of vulnerable people under extreme conditions. A growing number of states, almost fifty, have appointed officials to act as "focal points" for protection and atrocity prevention efforts. A similar group of states has at the UN formed a "friends of R2P group focused on exploring more effective means of operationalizing the R2P norm."[17]

It is to the discredit of major powers like Russia and the United States that they have, on occasion, used the R2P doctrine to justify unilateral attacks. It is, nevertheless, to the credit of the international community that it came together to unanimously adopt the doctrine of the responsibility to protect. It is a doctrine that has yet to be made effectively operational, so that is now the challenge – to implement it by means of the peaceful methods it prescribes, and when those fail, to resort to coercive measures in ways that will mitigate suffering rather than escalate and prolong it.

10

Peace after the Sun Goes Down

I<small>T WAS JUST 9:30 P.M.</small> at Kenya's Mombasa airport, but that was more than two full hours after nightfall and the instructions had been clear – do not drive from the airport to the coastal hotel and conference venue after the sun goes down. Two former senior Kenyan diplomats and I were on our way to a conference at the hotel but had arrived late in Mombasa due to a four-hour flight delay in Nairobi. So now the question was, should we heed the instruction not to make the one-hour drive after dark and instead find a place to stay the night in Mombasa and then head out after sunrise? Or should we chance it? One colleague was part of the conference opening, so was keen to get there sooner rather than later. A van was still available and the driver was willing, although he admitted there was some risk. Though the Mombasa coast was a major destination for tourists, night-time travel along the coastal road was certainly discouraged. For some time, extra police patrols had been sent to the route, but even so, after the sun went down armed bandits and some more sinister extremist elements were on the prowl. But we decided to take the chance. It was only an hour, and my colleagues knew of others who had made the drive after dark without incident.

The night was clouded and thus very dark, and once on the narrow but paved roadway there were no street lights of any kind and no traffic. "We'll make it fast," said the driver and set the van whining down the empty highway. We passengers had just begun to settle in when there was a sudden sharp swerve and in the same instant a loud bang and the driver jamming the accelerator to the floor. The engine's whine turned to a high pitch, and now we were leaving a dramatic trail of sparks in our wake. A tray of metal spikes had been put in our path. The driver was on the lookout for just such devices and at the last moment moved to avoid it, but the rear tire caught the spikes and burst. So now we were on three tires and one rim and still speeding along. To stop would have exposed us to the bandits or political extremists, whoever it was who had put the spikes on the road. At the same time, it was clear we couldn't keep going indefinitely on the rim; sooner or later we would have to stop to change the tire. Then, some distance ahead, lights came into our view. The driver slowed to a cautious advance and explained our likely situation. The road would be blocked, and we would face two possibilities. It would be either a police patrol or the bandits or extremists linked to the planted spikes. In either event, we would have to stop. If it turned out to be the bandits or worse, it would not be pleasant. If it were the police we would face another two possibilities – either they would be helpful, or they would demand payoffs and rifle through our belongings before sending us along on our uncertain way. As it turned out, we got lucky on two counts. It was the police, and they were nothing but very helpful. They helped change the tire and then escorted us the rest of the way to the hotel.

In the 2014 *Global Peace Index* (GPI), Kenya ranks 132 out of 162. It is among the 20 per cent of the world's least peaceful states. And on the Mombasa coastal road we found out why. If, after the sun goes down, it's unsafe to drive along a prominent country road, walk down major city streets, or stroll about in the suburbs, peace does not prevail. Kenya is also the site of ongoing state failure armed conflict, according to the definition used here, but the country's low ranking on the peace index is due especially to high levels of public insecurity. After the sun goes down, Nairobi, Mombasa, the Mombasa coast, and many other locations are simply not safe places. In 2015, years after our Mombasa road incident, the Government of Canada's travel advisory counselled "a high degree of caution due to the increasing number of terrorist attacks and incidents of crime." Nairobi and the Coast region, including Mombasa, were noted for particular care. In one sense, such cautions are a touch melodramatic. Most Kenyans live fully productive lives under those conditions, and many business people and tourists visit Nairobi and other centres daily without incident. If basic precautions are taken, and if one is slightly more sensible than we three conference-goers were, Kenya is a largely safe and highly compelling place to visit. But a combination of limited law enforcement capacity, an abundance of corruption, prominent cleavages in Kenyan society, and adverse economic and housing conditions in the major centres also make it a place of unrest and, at night in particular, uncertainty. At hotels and suburban homes, police, security guards, and alarm systems keep visitors and residents safe. But peace, negative or positive, has a higher threshold than that.

The GPI makes the negative peace/positive peace distinction. Negative peace is measured by the absence of violence or the fear of violence. Kenya does not score well. High crime rates and frequent attacks by Somalia-based al Shabaab militants make violence very present and the fear great. The al Shabaab militants hit Kenyan targets, they say, in retaliation for Kenyan forces entering Somalia, but the radical Islamist group also seeks support and influence within Kenya's ethnically Somali communities. For any state ranking low on the negative peace scale, positive peace remains aspirational. The GPI measures positive peace according to the presence of key "pillars of peace" – notably a well-functioning government, a sound business environment, equitable distribution of resources, acceptance of the rights of others, good relations with neighbours, free flow of information, a high level of human capital, and low levels of corruption – and of course, the list of countries challenged to varying degrees on many of these counts is long.

The prominent lesson of contemporary warfare is that peace can't be won on the battlefield and that peace after the sun goes down won't be assured by extra police patrols. A quarter century of warfare has accumulated persuasive evidence that while winning wars is the rarest of events, winning peace is never the product of fighting. Not only does warfighting not resolve the political conflicts that gave rise to it, but as long as it is pursued it remains an unqualified obstacle to any peacebuilding process or agenda.

Furthermore, expanding and perfecting military capacity, though the effort continues to hold an inexplicable fascination for security planners, serve more to advertise weakness than to prevent or terminate war. That high school teacher in Kabul had it right. Unless authorities actually earned the trust of Afghans, he said, unless families could manage to meet basic needs of food and shelter, and unless all the key ethnic communities could rely on equal and fair treatment, there would never be enough fighter aircraft or tanks to make Afghanistan safe – or, he might have added, to make the Kenyan coastal road safe to travel after sundown. The deep insecurities felt in Afghanistan, parts of Kenya, and all the other states that rank among the lowest on the GPI and that year after year make the armed conflicts list are not the kinds of threats and vulnerabilities that aircraft and tanks, or even extra police patrols, can alleviate. There is certainly a sense in which peace needs to be defended more effectively, notably by improving community law enforcement, including road patrols by accountable police, but it is just as obvious that sending more police into deeply troubled economic, social, and political environments is not what will produce safety.

Enforcing peace and fighting for peace have become post–Cold War oxymorons. Whatever the historical merits of going to war in order to secure peace or freedom or democracy, in the past twenty-five years it hasn't been working – though not for want of trying. Superior military force can destroy regimes, including very bad regimes, and it unavoidably destroys infrastructure, but it obviously doesn't build replacement regimes. And superior military force almost never defeats insurgencies.

From the Philippines to Iraq to Sudan to Colombia, governments and multilateral forces that undertake to neutralize dissidents by military force face very long odds. Vastly superior force cannot even reliably impose negative peace, that is, ensure the absence of violent conflict, let alone convert negative into positive peace. Multilateral coalitions bent on ending wars and driving defined political outcomes have just as assuredly found that the resort to force, though it be superior in every way to the forces it is seeking to marginalize and defeat, turns out to be more effective in spreading insecurity than establishing it. These are the limits to force that are unavoidable, but still not sufficiently recognized.

Facing the Zealots

But does that mean the international community gets to ignore zealots? It is true that acts of terrorism – more accurately, deadly attacks on civilians, crimes against humanity, war crimes, and violations of human rights and international humanitarian law – are committed primarily in contexts of war, and it is also true that wars are not settled by superior force. But they don't settle themselves, either, and extremists in the mode of Islamic State surely cannot simply be left to their own devices in the hopes they will burn themselves out.

Having implanted itself in the global consciousness through a succession of videos showing deaths of hostages by beheadings and burning, in early 2015 Islamic State had become the focus of reporting on the wars in Iraq and Syria, and inevitably the object of air attacks by another multilateral coalition. But isolating IS as a particularly pernicious group warranting extraordinary attention seemed to ignore the reality that hundreds of groups were engaged in sectarian violence and infighting in which friends and foes were indistinguishable and among which war crimes were ubiquitous. Few advocates of intervention expected IS to be "defeated" or could say with any confidence what the impact of "degrading" IS might be in the context of chaos in Syria. So, to say again that there are no military solutions to the multiple armed conflicts in Syria is not an ideological statement. It's about as close to hard-nosed realism as it is possible to get and is supported by a quarter century of warfare evidence that is largely devoid of examples of clear battlefield outcomes. Syria's crowded battlefields are unlikely to produce the exception. Nor is the American-led coalition likely to make Syria an exception to its succession of spectacular military failures. Fareed Zakaria, the prominent author, writer, and television broadcaster for mainstream media like *Newsweek*, the *Washington Post*, and *CNN*, concludes that "the solution does not lie in more American military intervention in the Middle East."[1] The American scholar and political philosopher Michael Walzer agrees that IS and other "zealots" perpetrating heinous crimes in Syria and Iraq will not be defeated by war or a series of wars; rather, he says, "this is a fever that will have to burn itself out." But there is a callousness to that conclusion, and Walzer immediately acknowledges that "there is a deep difficulty with this view," for "many people will suffer in the burning."[2]

The international community has real responsibilities in the face of such crimes against humanity, the promise to try to protect those who "suffer in the burning," but the evidence still suggests that largely Western military interventions are unlikely to be the means by which those responsibilities will be met. Experience suggests the war in Syria – the war whose fog has created the cover for IS and others like it – will not be won, not by foreign powers or by any local group or group of groups. Instead, it is likely to end in the same tragic way in which most wars have ended over the past twenty-five years – namely, when exhaustion and diplomacy finally combine to persuade enough of the belligerents, and all at the same time, that continued fighting is likely to produce far greater harm and much less advantage than would ever be risked at a conference table. In early 2015 few were holding out hope for a diplomatic surge. There was obviously little evidence that IS or its many counterparts were open to talking to anyone. Some voices were at least encouraging more determined political engagement among states in the region, the international coalition, and other influential powers. There was also insistence that at least the failure of diplomacy should not continue to be matched by humanitarian failure. In 2014, the UN received only half of the funds requested for humanitarian response to the Syrian war, and the prospects for meeting the $2.9 billion requirement for 2015 were grim. By comparison, the US Center for Strategic and Budgetary Assessment estimated in a September 2014 report that at its then current levels of operations, the cost of the US military operations, never mind all the other forces involved, against IS would run at $2.4 to $3.8 billion per year. Should the Americans enter into higher-intensity air operations, that cost could grow to $4.2 to $6.8 billion annually.[3] The cost of major ground forces would be exponentially higher. We can be sure that the prospects of funding those operations, at whatever level, would not be in doubt – the deficit wary but "chickenhawk" (see below) US Congress would happily print or borrow all the money needed.

Neither the US Congress nor the international community more broadly showed any inclination to mount diplomatic, humanitarian or military missions on behalf of the people of northeast Nigeria. The radical

Islamist movement Boko Haram – which means, literally, "Western education is forbidden" – declared itself to be fighting against democracy and Christians and had pledged to kill all Muslims who "follow democracy."[4] In 2014, Boko Haram attacks and the government's counterattacks killed at least 10,000 Nigerians, some 1.5 million were internally displaced and 200,000 Nigerians fled to neighbouring countries. A Security Council Presidential Statement describes Boko Haram's "violence against civilian populations, notably women and children, kidnappings, killings, hostage-taking, pillaging, rape, sexual slavery and other sexual violence, recruitment of children and destruction of property."[5] Initially confined to hit and run raiding parties, in 2014 Boko Haram began seizing and holding territory, rendering northeast Nigeria ungovernable and entirely cut off from humanitarian assistance. Nigeria's security forces in response also engaged in serious human rights violations and extrajudicial killings of suspected Boko Haram members.

The Multi-National Joint Task Force, which was set up initially in 1998 with troops from Nigeria, Chad, and Niger to fight trans-border crime in the Lake Chad region, had more recently begun operations against Boko Haram, and in 2015 it was reformed by the African Union to mandate Chad, Cameroon, Benin, and Niger, to join Nigeria in combating Boko Haram.[6] The Task Force was claiming success in its military operations to regain towns and territory that had fallen to Boko Haram, and there was evidence to support the claim.[7] Unlike the situation in Syria, in northeast Nigeria it was clear who would fill the void in any area from which Boko Haram was expelled – it was the Government of Nigeria. The Nigerian government has its failings, but it is also recognized and welcomed in the region as the legitimate authority, and its authority is respected by neighbouring states. The Multi-National Joint Task Force operations were thus much closer to the model of a peace support operation – engaged in combat operations, to be sure, but focused on controlling particularly egregious spoilers rather than fighting on one side of a civil war. Even so, it was clear that in the long-term, the Nigerian government would have to attend to the roots of such chaos, which include poor governance, corruption, lack of any credible economic prospects, and deep religious and ethnic divisions. A meeting of the UN Human Rights Council in April 2015 made it clear that "military operations alone were not sufficient to effectively address the problem or defeat Boko Haram." The Council urged Nigeria to address the "root causes of this terrorism," interrupt Boko Haram funding, and bring to justice the perpetrators and their supporters.[8]

A 2013 US Institute for Peace (USIP) survey of why young people join

Boko Haram offers an interesting take on the role of religion. The survey found that police excesses in dealing with the movement were a factor, and that criticism of security forces was prominent among opinion leaders who cited "unlawful killings, dragnet arrests, extortion, and intimidation,"[9] actions that actually built support for Boko Haram.[10] But in some communities, the top factor in leading young people to adopt extreme religious views was ignorance of the real teachings and the sacred texts of the religion.[11] Illiteracy and the lack of religious education and education generally leave people particularly vulnerable to independent itinerant clerics with distorted appeals. Researchers also found unemployment and poverty to be factors, not in directly driving young people to extremist views and organizations, but because deep frustrations that accompany long-term economic marginalization leave young people more vulnerable to recruiters for extremist causes. The strategy for combatting extremism is basically to reverse those conditions that promote it – by regulating religious instruction (it's not often that theological education is put forward as a major war prevention tool), establishing job creation programs, undertaking programs for child welfare, promoting literacy and education generally, including peace education, and getting serious about combatting corruption, especially in security services. The USIP study concludes that reversing conditions that drive insurgent recruitment is key to the northeast's recovery – an essential strategy, but one that obviously fails on the level of short-term protection. [12] In the meantime, those who "suffer in the burning" still need help. The international community has the means to be more helpful, but not the means to determine outcomes.

The Fatal Attraction

The prevailing pattern is for long-term amelioration efforts to be neglected while short-term "cures" default to military prowess that makes the cure worse than the disease. Though the big powers centred in Brussels, Washington, and Moscow fail in warfare against insurgents, extremist or otherwise, just as certainly as do small powers based in Khartoum or Manila, enthusiasm for expensively assembled and deployed hi-tech military power seems undiminished. It is an enthusiasm that persists in spite of the fact that, for all practical purposes, it has become impossible to fight and win a war so that winning actually means something – namely that the political problems that prompted war in the first place are thereby solved. To be sure, even the military forces of the smallest of governments fighting insurgencies win their share of battles; it's just that they are destined to lose the wars. Yet, military forces and institutions are lionized, just as surely as their utility declines. It is genuinely puzzling why governments, officials, and security experts steeped in "realist" calculations of national interests remain so drawn to military responses to conflict when the only realistic outcome is that they won't work. The most reliable effects of deploying military forces against ill-defined adversaries in deeply rooted political conflicts are the escalation of political violence, further entrenchment of insurgencies, and further loss of credibility of the governments those military forces are ostensibly defending.

Though the example of Libya was still fresh in 2014, notably the political and military chaos that followed the use of NATO military air power to aid the destruction of the Gaddafi regime, Washington's chosen, if now more reluctant, response to Islamic State (IS) attacks in Iraq and Syria was to again turn to air power to degrade a new version of an ill-defined enemy. Military actions hinged on the vague objective of bolstering the government in Iraq and the opposition in Syria by degrading the Islamic State forces in both countries – but without knowing with any confidence just who would actually be bolstered in the process. In early 2015, the question most asked – but never answered – about multilateral attacks on IS strongholds in Syria was who would occupy those areas if IS were successfully removed.

At the same time in Europe, even though it was clear that a direct NATO military challenge to Russia would not and could not reduce tensions, much less resolve differences over Russia's 2014 annexation of Crimea and support to eastern Ukrainian rebels, the response chosen by NATO was to raise the threat of direct military action. A Very High Readiness Joint Task Force would now be launched to enable NATO to do in forty-eight hours, instead of five days, what it would be utter folly to do at all – namely, engage in direct combat with Russia and raise the spectre of escalation to nuclear weapons use. German Chancellor Angela Merkel chose realism over posturing. Adamant that lethal arms not be shipped to the Ukraine, she said: "I cannot imagine any situation in which improved equipment for the Ukrainian army leads to President Putin being so impressed that he believes he will lose militarily."[13] Nor was the switch from "high" to "very high" readiness likely to impress him, except to reinforce his already well-entrenched paranoia/hostility toward NATO.

The proclivity for resorting to military actions or threats when there are no military solutions available and when military postures make the politics only more complicated is a habit not easily unlearned. James Fallows, national correspondent for *The Atlantic*, calls this phenomenon in the United States the "chickenhawk nation" – referring to the eagerness with which politicians threaten war "as long as someone else is going."[14] National defence forces, not only in the US, are routinely accorded unqualified praise and then sent into harm's way without any public acknowledgement of past failures or of the military's persistent inability to meet the unrealistic objectives that civilian politicians set for them. And so, standing military forces, always available and always symbols of national virility, become the go-to means of "doing something." In the process, realism in international security slips further and further away from reality.

Consenting to Peace

Two decades ago, when those young and barefoot trainees of the Sudan People's Liberation Army were sure they would soon defeat the oppressive government in Khartoum, the odds were not nearly as steep as they seemed at the time. It turns out that much better armed and organized state forces are routinely unable to prevail against much weaker armed rebels. It's not that the rebels win, it's just that they don't lose – they tend to keep on doing what the SPLA and other South Sudanese rebels did for decade after decade. And the government didn't lose because it was defeated – it eventually lost because it could not win. That's the pattern. Rebels in that sense may view their use of force as effective, but they too must inevitably discover the strict limits of its utility. The SPLA has now discovered the truth of the lesson it taught Khartoum, that persistence in fighting is much better at making a territory ungovernable than it is at governing it. They could fight Khartoum on a shoestring, or even without shoes, but when it comes to making South Sudan safe after the sun goes down, they face a new reality. Even in the earliest days of nascent self-rule, the South Sudan government has fixed on the methodologies of war but is finding them to be radically out of step with the requirements for peace.

During the thick of the war in the late 1990s, not far from the town of Yei, the SPLA held a gathering in a region then under its control, having been recently taken from Khartoum. The late John Garang de Mabior, the charismatic leader of the SPLA at the time, was there with many of the movement's top leaders to consult with community and civil society leaders of the area. The people were represented primarily by churches, by then almost the only surviving civil society institutions in a land where most of the population had been displaced and traditional structures had been badly disrupted. It was a gathering of some three hundred people, well guarded by young SPLA fighters. The people had walked long distances, many days en route, to the conference site, constructed in a wooded area almost entirely, including the tables and benches where we sat and conferred, out of bamboo held together by local vines. The participants were invited to engage with SPLA leadership in a series of public sessions, highlighted by two public forums with Garang himself. And when they had a chance to talk to their leader, they didn't hold back. The gathering included only a small number of non-Sudanese observers, and what we observed was a population in full solidarity with the SPLA, but profoundly troubled by events following their area's "liberation." Bandits continued to raid villages, cattle rustlers were more active than ever, and SPLA soldiers regularly came to remote villages to claim the spoils of war – including the attentions of girls and women. One elder told Garang, "Our liberators have become our tormentors."

Twenty years later, after the southerners ended the war, largely on their own terms through a negotiated peace agreement and a referendum, they got their prized independence but they couldn't stop the fighting. There were still plenty of provocations from Khartoum, and once again they felt forced into a defensive mode, but the truly fatal missteps were internal attempts to manage and manipulate the affairs of their new state through exclusionary identity politics, backed up ultimately by guns. And so by late 2013, only two short years since full independence, they were back into full-fledged combat. The fighting, still active in early 2015, was over key political issues of openness, inclusion, and power sharing – to some extent delineated by a persistent Dinka/Nuer split – with the factions led respectively by Salva Kiir and Riek Machar. But the conflict was further complicated by a proliferation of militia groups, up to two dozen by some counts in early 2015. Most aligned with one of the two main sides, resulting in tens of thousands of civilians killed and some 1.5 million displaced from their homes.

So in 2015, the new government faced its own rebels bent on making the south ungovernable for as long as the SPLA-dominated rulers tried to accomplish what they had ensured the government in Khartoum could not: keeping control by means of superior military capabilities. They will not succeed. Even the assumption of the government's superior military capability is no longer obvious, following mass defections from its ranks. Both sides are now in the familiar no-win situation of civil war.

Persisting in wars that no side will win is the costly failure to recognize the limits of force. Bringing wars to an end is the job of diplomats, not soldiers. It is an extraordinarily daunting task to persuade bitter enemies in conflicts that involve multiple parties to all come, at the same time, to the realization that no military solutions are available and that each party's interests would be best pursued through negotiations and renewed political processes. The political/diplomatic task is made all the more daunting for lack of serious resources to devote to it. Requests for funding major humanitarian programs and the resettlement of people displaced by war are chronically underfunded. The costs of official and citizen diplomacy, reconciliation initiatives, and community engagement are extremely modest compared to military engagement costs, but the same governments that are willing to pay for unwinnable wars balk at providing serious levels of funding for conflict resolution diplomacy – activities in which non-governmental organizations, with their deep roots in the social and economic lives of societies in distress, are essential participants.

While security forces remain prominent in supporting the rule of law and peacemaking efforts, the evidence still shows that sheer force is of limited utility or counter-productive. Even enforcement must ultimately be based more on consent than coercion. Without a dominant culture of support for the prevailing order, in which enforcement manifests itself primarily in actions against spoilers, enforcement quickly becomes the attempt to *force* particular political outcomes – not a promising prospect, if the experience of the past twenty-five years is admitted as evidence. That recalls once again the essential distinction between warfighting and peace support operations: "warfighting" operations try to override political processes to force particular outcomes where no consensus is available whereas "peace support" operations attempt to support an environment conducive to the political pursuit of negotiated outcomes. UN-mandated peace support operations thus can and do sometimes involve significant levels of combat, but in those cases the operations are still under basic strategic consent. Combat operations by UN-authorized multilateral forces pursue tactical advantages over spoilers, but tactical military gains mean something only if a supportive political climate and credible social institutions are available to consolidate the gains. In Syria, tactical military gains against IS are not supported by credible public institutions to consolidate gains in areas vacated by IS. In Nigeria, there is a government, albeit weak, especially in the northeast, that can begin to fill the vacuum with a stable presence in areas from which Boko Haram is expelled. For national and collective military force to contribute constructively to sustainable human safety and well-being, it must be accompanied by certain social, political, and economic conditions or measures that can integrate tactical military advances into a gradually maturing political and economic order. That kind of context makes a peace support military operation possible. Without that context, a military operation is a warfighting operation that tries to overcome the limitations of the context by force – again, not a promising endeavour in the past twenty-five years.

Stopping and preventing the fighting, which is the basic prerequisite for serious efforts to build and entrench peace, is not a pipe dream. In the past twenty-five years, after all, seventy wars ended, not because they were won, but because it finally became clear that no one could win. And prevention is improving. Over the past quarter century new wars began at the rate of about 2.5 per year, but in the past ten years (2005 through 2014), the rate of the onset of new wars as defined here is down to just over one per year (eleven new wars in ten years, including the most recent onsets in Libya, Mali, Syria, and Ukraine). Furthermore, there have been no new interstate wars in more than a decade. The foundation of security – and also the best defence against extremism – is ultimately not enforcement, but consent. A secure society relies ultimately on the active consent of a population confident that its laws are just and fairly applied, and that its security policies and practices are relevant to the ways in which insecurity is most directly experienced. Consent can be formally confirmed through elections, but it is politically sustained through concerted and non-discriminatory efforts to create economic, social, and environmental conditions conducive to peace and stability. Peace is built. It isn't won on the battlefield.

Notes

Introduction

1 Khalid Abdelaziz and Ulf Laessing, "Sudan's President Omar Hassan al-Bashir Promises to Teach South Sudan a 'Final Lesson by Force'," *National Post* (Reuters), April 19, 2012, news.nationalpost.com.

2 Rupert Smith, *The Utility of Force: The Art of War in the Modern World* (London: Penguin, 2006), 4.

3 "UN Passes Leaner 2012–2013 Budget Amid Economic Turmoil," Reuters, December 25, 2011, uk.reuters.com.

4 The term "peace support" is used here to refer to multi-dimensional, UN authorized interventions, usually involving a combination of humanitarian, diplomatic, and military efforts from traditional peacekeeping to "robust peacekeeping," the latter defined by the UN as including tactical level combat operations that are designed to restore and support conditions of peace and stability.

5 Institute for Economics and Peace, *2014 Global Peace Index*, www.visionofhumanity.org.

6 Stephen Kinzer, "Conventional Military Has Lost Power," *Boston Globe*, August 1, 2014.

1: A Quarter Century of Failed Warfare

1 The term "war," as used here, is interchangeable with "armed conflict," as defined in the text.

2 Project Ploughshares has been tracking wars or armed conflicts according to these criteria since 1987. Definitions, detailed conflict descriptions, and an annual *Armed Conflicts Report* are available at www.ploughshares.ca. The Department of Peace and Conflict Research at Sweden's Uppsala University defines armed conflicts as follows: "A conflict, both state-based and non-state, is deemed to be active if there are at least 25 battle-related deaths per calendar year in one of the conflict's dyads. . . . A one-sided actor is deemed to be active if an organized group incurs at least 25 deliberate killings of civilians in a year." Uppsala Conflict Date Program, www.pcr.uu.se. Summaries of conflict trends are published in the yearbook of the Stockholm International Peace Research Institute. For the most recent report, in the 2012 yearbook, see chapter 2, "Armed Conflict," and chapter 3 at www.sipri.org. The annual *Peace and Conflict* publication of the Center for International Development and Conflict Management at the University of Maryland relies on data from the Uppsala University project for assessing global conflict trends (p. 25 of the 2012 edition) but produces its own "Peace and Conflict Instability Ledger" which ranks countries according the level of risk each faces of experiencing future political instability and armed conflict. See J. Joseph Hewitt, Jonathan Wilkenfeld, and Ted Robert Gurr, *Peace and Conflict 2012* (Boulder, Colorado: Paradigm Publishers, 2012) and Monty G. Marshall and Benjamin R. Cole, *Global Report 2014: Conflict, Governance, and State Fragility* (Vienna, Virginia: Center for Systemic Peace, 2014), www.systemicpeace.org.

3 Now housed at Penn State University, the Correlates of War project maintains data on

wars since 1815 in the interests of providing publicly available and reliable data – "the original and continuing goal of the project has been the systematic accumulation of scientific knowledge about war." See www.correlatesofwar.org.

4 Meredith Reid Sarkees, "The COW Typology of War: Defining and Categorizing Wars (Version 4 of the Data)," n.d., www.correlatesofwar.org.

5 Uppsala Conflict Date Program Overview, www.pcr.uu.se.

6 Anouk S. Reigterink, "New Wars in Numbers: An Exploration of Various Datasets on Intra-state Violence," MPRA Paper No. 45264, March 2013, mpra.ub.uni-muenchen.de.

7 Marshall and Cole, *Global Report 2014*.

8 ploughshares.ca/programs/armed-conflict/armed-conflicts-report/.

9 Gilles Olakouilé Yabi, *The Role of ECOWAS in Managing Political Crisis and Conflict: The Cases of Guinea and Guinea-Bissau* (Nigeria: Friederish Ebert Stiftung, 2010), library.fes.de.

10 Bill Whitaker, "Mexico's Drug War Adopts Al Qaeda Tactics: Car Bombs, Mass Killings Part of Increasing Violence Related to Drug Cartels," *CBS News*, July 23, 2010, www.cbsnews.com.

11 "What Is At Stake in the Colombian Peace Process," *BBC News*, January 15, 2015, www.bbc.news.

12 Monty G. Marshall and Benjamin R. Cole, *Global Report 2011: Conflict, Governance, and State Fragility* (Vienna, Virginia: Center for Systemic Peace, 2011), www.systemicpeace.org.

13 Marshall and Cole, *Global Report 2014*.

14 Human Security Report Project, *The Decline in Global Violence: Evidence, Explanation, and Contestation* (Vancouver: Simon Fraser University, 2014), www.hsrgroup.org.

15 Lotta Themner and Peter Wallensteen, "Armed Conflicts, 1946–2012," *Journal of Peace Research* 50, no. 4 (2013): 509–21.

16 These types were drawn from the Uppsala University Department of Peace and Conflict Research in Sweden. The Department no longer uses them. www.pcr.uu.se.

17 Melissa Zisler, "Globalizing Contemporary War," *Journal of Alternative Perspectives in the Social Sciences* 1, no. 3 (2009): 870–82.

18 Haruna Umar, Associated Press, "Extremists Kidnap 40 Males in Northern Nigeria," *FOX 11 Online*, January 3, 2015, fox11online.com.

19 Sinan Salaheddin and Sameer N. Yacoub, Associated Press, "Clashes With IS in Iraq Kill 23 Troops, Allied Fighters," *Seattle Times*, January 6, 2015, seattletimes.com.

20 "Somalia Violence: Deadly Car Bomb Near Mogadishu Airport," *BBC News*, January 4, 2015, www.bbc.com.

21 Alastair Jamieson, "Suicide Bomb Attack in Istanbul Tourist District Wounds Police," *NBC News*, www.nbcnews.com.

22 Marshall and Cole, *Global Report 2014*.

23 For 2009 estimates see www.photius.com.

24 *The Geneva Declaration on Armed Violence and Development, Global Burden of Armed Violence 2011*, 43–44, www.genevadeclaration.org.

2: Wars and Rumours of Wars

1 Richard Jackson, "Towards an Understanding of Contemporary Intra-state War," review of *Rethinking the Economics of War: The Intersection of Need, Creed, and Greed*, by Cynthia J. Arnson and I. William Zartman, eds., *Cadair*, Aberystwyth University Open Access Repository, cadair.aber.ac.uk.

2 Gareth Evans, "What We Know about Preventing Deadly Conflict: A Practitioner's Guide," International Crisis Group, January 2, 2006, www.crisisgroup.org.

3 Thomas Ohlson, "Understanding Causes of War and Peace," *European Journal of International Relations* 14, no. 1 (2008): 133–60, ejt.sagepub.com.

4 Alex J. Bellamy, "Mass Atrocities and Armed Conflict: Links, Distinctions, and Implications for the Responsibility to Prevent," Policy Analysis Brief, The Stanley Foundation, February 2011, www.stanleyfoundation.org.

5 S. M. Murshed and M. H. Tadjoeddin, "Revisiting the Greed and Grievance Explanations for Violent Internal Conflict," MICROCON Research Working Paper No. 2 (Brighton: MICROCON, 2007), www.un.org.

6 Thania Paffenholz, "Underdevelopment and Armed Conflict: Making Sense of the Debates" (paper, International Studies Annual Convention, San Francisco, March 26–29, 2008).

7 Maria Kett and Michael Rowson, "Drivers of Violent Conflict," *Journal of the Royal Society of Medicine* 100, no. 9 (2007): 403–6.

8 S. Bakrania and B. Lucas, "The Impact of the Financial Crisis on Conflict and State Fragility in Africa," Emerging Issues Paper commissioned by AusAID, Governance and Social Development Resource Centre (Birmingham: University of Birmingham, 2009), www.gsdrc.org.

9 Kett and Rowson, "Drivers of Violent Conflict."

10 See Francisco Gutierrez and Gerd Schönwälder, eds., *Economic Liberalization and Political Violence: Utopia or Dystopia?* (Ottawa: Pluto Press/International Development Research Centre, 2010), 339.

11 Alex de Waal, "Nile Deal Signals Regional Reset among Egypt, Sudan and Ethiopia," *World Politics Review*, Briefing, March 27, 2015, www.worldpoliticsreview.com.

12 A. Blundell, "Forests and Conflicts: The Financial Flows that Fuel War" (Washington DC: Program on Forests, 2010), www.profor.info.

13 "Liberia Timber Profits Finance Regional Conflict," *Global Witness*, May 4, 2001. www.globalwitness.org.

14 Cynthia J. Arnson and I. William Zartman, eds., *Rethinking the Economics of War: The Intersection of Need, Creed, and Greed* (Washington, DC & Baltimore: Woodrow Wilson Center Press/Johns Hopkins University Press, 2005).

15 A. Kok, W. Lotze, and S. V. Jaarsveld, "Natural Resources, the Environment and Conflict" (Durban, South Africa: ACCORD/Madariaga College Foundation, 2009), www.accord.org.za.

16 Vanda Felhab-Brown, "The Drug-Conflict Nexus in South Asia: Beyond Taliban Profits and Afghanistan," in *The Afghan-Pakistan Theater: Militant Islam, Security, and Stability*, ed. Daveed Gartenstein-Ross and Clifford D. May, 90–112 (Washington, DC: Foundation for Defense of Democracies, 2010), www.brookings.edu; United Nations Office on Drugs and Crime (UNODC) Studies and Threat Analysis Section, "Drug Trafficking as a Security Threat in West Africa" (Vienna: UNODC, 2008), www.unodc.org.

17 Murshed and Tadjoeddin, "Revisiting the Greed and Grievance Explanations for Violent Internal Conflict."

18 Göran Holmqvist, "Inequality and Identity: Causes of War?" Discussion Paper, Nordiska Afrikainstitutet, Uppsala, 2012.

19 Jackson, "Towards an Understanding of Contemporary Intra-state War."

20 I. Atack, "Peace Studies and Social Change: The Role of Ethics and Human Agency," *Policy & Practice: A Development Education Review* 9 (Autumn 2009): 39–51, www.developmenteducationreview.com.

21 Socheat Som, "Pol Pot's Charisma," *Cambodia: Beauty and Darkness*, December 2001, www.mekong.net.

22 Atack, "Peace Studies and Social Change."

23 Jackson, "Towards an Understanding of Contemporary Intra-state War."

24 Ohlson, "Understanding Causes of War and Peace."

25 Human Security Report Project, *Human Security Report 2009/2010: The Causes of Peace and the Shrinking Costs of War* (Vancouver: HSRP, 2010), www.hsrgroup.org (forthcoming in print from Oxford University Press).

26 "Kenya Violence: Deadly Mix of Politics and Old Grudges," AlertNet, www.trust.org.

27 Robert Fisk, "The Historical Narrative That Lies Beneath the Gaddafi Rebellion," *The Independent*, March 3, 2011, www.independent.co.uk.

28 Michelle Maiese, "Causes of Disputes and Conflicts," BeyondIntractability.org, October 2003, www.beyondintractability.org.

29 Freedom C. Onuoha, "Why Do Youth Join Boko Haram?" United States Institute of Peace, 2014, USIP.Org.

30 Maiese, "Causes of Disputes and Conflicts."

31 Interview, *PBS News Hour*, February 12, 2007, www.pbs.org.

32 Maiese, "Causes of Disputes and Conflicts."

33 Maiese, "Causes of Disputes and Conflicts."

34 T. Lyons, "Conflict-generated Diasporas and Transnational Politics in Ethiopia," *Conflict, Security and Development* 7, no. 4 (2007): 529–49, www.gsdrc.org.

35 Many thousands of children, some as young as nine years, are mobilized in today's wars. Coalition to Stop the Use of Child Soldiers, www.child-soldiers.org.

36 The ICRC challenges the commonly advanced figure that 80 to 90 per cent of war casualties are civilians. The ICRC uses two sources to produce more conservative estimates. Its own surgical database, begun in 1991, shows that reports of persons admitted for weapons injuries showed 35 per cent to be female, or males under sixteen and over fifty years of age – in other words, 35 per cent of injuries were to persons who could properly be assumed to be non-combatants. A second ICRC study found that 64 per cent of fatalities tabulated were considered to be civilians. The ICRC concludes that both figures for civilian casualties highlight the need for greater efforts toward special protection for civilians in conflict, and the evidence suggests the proportion of civilian deaths in conflicts has been increasing over the twentieth century. ICRC, *Arms Availability and the Situation of Civilians in Armed Conflict* (Geneva: ICRC, 1999), 16–17.

37 United Nations Security Council, Report of the Secretary-General on the Protection of Civilians in Armed Conflict (S/2009/277), May 29, 2009, unispal.un.org.

38 Bobby Ghosh, "Rage, Rap and Revolution: Inside the Arab Youth Quake," *Time Magazine*, February 17, 2011, www.time.com.

39 Duncan Green, "What Caused the Revolution in Egypt?" PovertyMatters Blog, *The Guardian*, February 17, 2011, www.guardian.co.uk.

40 Jennifer Wells, "Young and Restless Means Africa is At Risk," *Toronto Star*, February 27, 2011.

41 Holmqvist, "Inequality and Identity: Causes of War?"

42 Gutierrez and Schönwälder, *Economic Liberalization and Political Violence*, 339.

43 Glen Smith and Hélène Bouvier, "Crosscutting Issues in the Kalimantan Conflicts," *Communal Conflicts in Kalimantan: Perspectives from the LIPI-CNRS Conflict Studies Program* (Jakarta, Indonesia & Villejuif, France: PDII-LIPPI/LASEMA, 2006), 207–23.

44 Bellamy, "Mass Atrocities and Armed Conflict."

45 This and the following points are from the Stanley Foundation. The Stanley Foundation encourages use of our resources for educational purposes. Any part of the material may be duplicated with proper acknowledgment. www.stanleyfoundation.org.

3: How Civil Wars End

1 The Human Security Report Project out of Canada's Simon Fraser University says that "most of the conflicts that have started in recent years have been of short duration," but that seeming contradiction is largely a matter of definition. The HSR data defines armed conflicts or conflict episodes as starting when a twenty-five combat death threshold is crossed in a single year and ending when the combat death toll drops below that threshold in a calendar year. That results in intermittent fighting being recorded as multiple conflicts or conflict episodes – showing fighting to be of more limited duration, but also recurring more often. Human Security Report Project, *Human Security Report 2012* (Vancouver: Simon Fraser University, 2012), www.hsrgroup.org.

2 Uppsala Conflict Data Program, *Armed Conflict Dataset v.4–2010* (Uppsala, Sweden/Oslo: Uppsala University Centre for the Study of Civil War/International Peace Research Institute, 2010), www.pcr.uu.se.

3 *Human Security Report 2012*.

4 *Human Security Report 2012*, 176.

5 *Human Security Report 2012*, 177.

6 *Human Security Report 2012*, 181.

7 *Human Security Report 2012*, 175–76.

8 Vicenc Fisas, *2014 Yearbook on Peace Processes* (Barcelona: Universitat Autonoma de Barcelona School for a Culture of Peace, 2014), 17, escolapau.uab.

9 "Angolan Civil War," *Wikipedia*, en.wikipedia.org/wiki/Angolan_Civil_War.

10 US State Department, *Country Report on Human Rights: Sri Lanka* (US State Department, 2010), www.state.gov.

11 *Report of the Commission of Inquiry on Lessons Learnt and Reconciliation* (Sri Lanka, November 2011), www.priu.gov.lk.

12 United Nations Office of the High Commissioner for Human Rights, "Human Rights Council Concludes Nineteenth Session," Human Rights Council Roundup, March 23, 2012, www.ohchr.org.

13 US State Department, *Country Report on Human Rights: Sri Lanka*; Bruce Vaughn, *Sri Lanka: Background and US Relations*, Congressional Research Service (RL31707), June 16, 2011, www.fas.org; "Sad Political Situation in Sri Lanka," *Sri Lanka Guardian*, March 23, 2010, www.srilankaguardian.org.

14 J. S. Tissainayagam, "Hold the Champagne in Sri Lanka," *Foreign Policy*, January 13, 2015, foreignpolicy.com.

15 Allan Woods, "Bob Rae's Sri Lanka Nightmare," *Toronto Star*, June 11, 2009, www.thestar.com.

16 "Flashback: The 1991 Iraqi Revolt," *BBC News*, August 21, 2007, news.bbc.co.uk.

17 Lawrence E. Cline, "The Prospects of the Shia Insurgency Movement in Iraq," *Journal of Conflict Studies* 20, no. 2 (2002), journals.hil.unb.ca/index.php/jcs/article/view/4311/4924; Jim Ruvalcaba, "Understanding Iraq's Insurgency," *al Nakhlah* (Spring 2004), Article 7.

18 "Flashback," 2007.

19 John Wendle, "One Year On, Could Russia and Georgia Fight Another War?" *Time*, August 7, 2009, content.time.com.

20 Jim Nichol, "Russia-Georgia Conflict in August 2008: Context and Implications for US Interests," Congressional Research Service Report, March 3, 2009, www.fas.org.

21 Maria J. Stephan and Eric Chenoweth, "Why Civil Resistance Works: The Strategic Logic of Nonviolence," *International Security* 33, no. 1 (Summer 2008): 7–44; Erica Chenoweth and Maria J. Stephan, *Why Civil Resistance Works: The Strategic Logic of Nonviolent Conflict* (New York: Columbia University Press, 2013).

22 *Human Security Report 2012*, 184.

23 *Human Security Report 2012*, 184.

24 Comments from a policy symposium titled "Sierra Leone One Year After the Peace

Accord: The Search for Peace, Justice and Sustainable Development," Ottawa, June 21–23, 2000.

25 "Sierra Leone One Year After the Peace Accord."

26 www.hrw.org/legacy/backgrounder/eca/tajikbkg1005.htm#aftermath.

27 Benjamin Valentino, Paul Huth, and Dylan Balch-Lindsay, "'Draining the Sea': Mass Killing and Guerrilla Warfare," *International Organization* 58, no. 2 (Spring 2004): 375–407.

28 "El Salvador, Civil War," *Encyclopedia Britannica*, www.britannica.com.

29 Cynthia J. Arnson, ed., *El Salvador's Democratic Transition Ten Years after the Peace Accord* (Washington, DC: Woodrow Wilson International Center for Scholars), www.wilsoncenter.org.

30 "Aceh: Peacemaking after the Tsunami," WorldWatch Institute, www.worldwatch.org.

31 Gemima Harvey, "The Human Tragedy of West Papua," *The Diplomat*, January 14, 2014, thediplomat.com.

32 Glen Smith and Hélène Bouvier, "Crosscutting Issues in the Kalimantan Conflicts," www.internal-displacement.org.

33 news.bbc.co.uk; www.globalsecurity.org.

4: How International Wars End

1 Drawn from GlobalSecurity.Org's online summary account of the Iran-Iraq War, www.globalsecurity.org.

2 Jan Zwierzchowski and Ewa Tabeau, "The 1992–95 War in Bosnia and Herzegovina: Census-Based Multiple System Estimation of Casualties Undercount," Conference Paper for the International Research Workshop on "The Global Costs of Conflict," The Household in Conflict Network and the German Institute for Economic Research, Berlin, February 1–2, 2010.

3 "Barak: Hezbollah 3 Times Stronger Than at End of War," *Israel News*, November 24, 2008, www.ynews.com.

4 Besty Pisik, *Washington Times*, July 31, 2006.

5 The US Army Center of Military History has produced an account of the American presence in Somalia, including greater details on this particular incident. *The United States Army in Somalia: 1992–1994*, CMH Pub 70–81–1, www.history.army.mil.

6 Iraq Body Count, www.iraqbodycount.org.

7 www.libyabodycount.org.

8 "Bosnia War Dead Figure Announced," *BBC News*, June 21, 2007, news.bbc.co.uk/2/hi/europe/6228152.stm.

9 Internal Displacement Monitoring Centre, December 31, 2013, www.internal-displacement.org.

10 New York University Center for International Cooperation, *Annual Review of Global Peace Operations 2013* (New York: Lynne Rienner, 2013).

11 Nathalie Baptiste, "Haiti's Chief Foreign Import: Meddling," *Foreign Policy in Focus*, June 11, 2014, fpif.org.

5: The Limits of Force

1 www.oxfordresearchgroup.org.uk.

2 Richard Jackson, "Towards an Understanding of Contemporary Intra-state War," review of *Rethinking the Economics of War: The Intersection of Need, Creed, and Greed*, by Cynthia J. Arnson and I. William Zartman, eds., *Cadair*, Aberystwyth University Open Access Repository, cadair.aber.ac.uk.

3 United Nations Security Council, "The Situation in Afghanistan and Its Implications for

International Peace and Security: Report of the Secretary-General," December 10, 2010 (A/65/612 – S/2010/630), para 55, and June 20, 2012 (A/66/855 – S/2012/462), daccess-dds-ny.un.org.

4 United Nations Assistance Mission in Afghanistan, "Civilians Casualties Rise by 24 per cent in First Half of 2014," July 9, 2014, unama.unmissions.org; Kate Clark, "The Human Cost of the Afghan War," Afghanistan Analysts Network, February 18, 2015, www.afghanistan-analysis.org.

5 www.unknownnews.org/casualties.html.

6 www.iraqbodycount.org.

7 Gilbert Burnham, Riyadh Lafta, Shannon Doocy, and Les Roberts, "Mortality After the 2003 Invasion of Iraq: A Cross-sectional Cluster Sample Survey," *The Lancet*, October 11, 2006, www.thelancet.com.

8 "Iraq 2014: Civilian Deaths Almost Doubling Year On Year, *Iraq Body Count*, January 1, 2015, www.iraqbodycount.org.

9 "Inside the Advocacy Group That Keeps Track of Syria's War Casualties," *Huffington Post*, November 24, 2014, www.huffingtonpost.com.

10 Monty G. Marshall and Benjamin R. Cole, *Global Report 2014: Conflict, Governance, and State Fragility* (Vienna, Virginia: Center for Systemic Peace, 2014), www.systemicpeace.org.

11 www.everycasualty.org.

12 The *Global Burden of Armed Violence* reports are detailed studies of armed violence in all its forms, published in 2008 and 2011 by the "Geneva Declaration." The Geneva Declaration on Armed Violence and Development is a diplomatic initiative by more than one hundred countries aimed at addressing the interrelations between armed violence and development. www.genevadeclaration.org.

13 *Armed Conflicts Report 2010*, www.ploughshares.ca.

14 The Canadian *Human Security Report 2009*, www.hsrgroup.org.

15 "South Sudan Clashes Force 20,000 to Flee: Official," AFP, February 18, 2010, www.google.com.

16 Nicholas Kulish, "South Sudan's Forces Clash with Rebels Near UN Base," *New York Times,* February 18, 2014, www.nytimes.com.

17 "Tens of Thousands Displaced by Clashes in Somalia," UNHCR news release, October 26, 2010, www.unhcr.org.

18 UNHCR, *UNHCR Statistical Yearbook 2012*, www.unhcr.org.

19 "War's Human Cost: UNHCR Global Trends 2013," www.unhcr.org.

20 Stephen Kaufman, "Clinton – Rape of Civilians was 'Horrific Attack'," *AllAfrica.Com*, August 26, 2010, allafrica.com.

21 "Prosecute to Help Stop Rape in Congo" (Editorial), *Globe and Mail*, September 4, 2010, www.theglobeandmail.com.

22 More information about the number of rapes and orphans can be found on the UNICEF website, www.unicef.org.

23 Valerie M. Hudson, Bonnie Ballif-Spanvill, Mary Caprioli, and Chad F. Emmett, *Sex and World Peace* (New York: Columbia University Press, 2012).

24 Valerie M. Hudson, "What Sex Means for World Peace," *Foreign Policy*, April 24, 2012, www.foreignpolicy.com.

25 Office of the Special Representative of the Secretary-General for Sexual Violence in Conflict, www.un.org.

26 Linda J. Bilmes, "The Financial Legacy of Iraq and Afghanistan: How Wartime Spending Decisions Will Constrain Future National Security Budgets," Faculty Research Working Paper Series, Harvard Kennedy School, March 2013, RWP13–006, web.hks.harvard.edu.

27 The Costs of War project (costsofwar.org) is the work of a broad range of academic researchers led by Professors Neta C. Crawford and Catherine Lutz of Boston University

and Brown University respectively, and Andrea C. Mazzarino, a researcher at Human Rights Watch.

28 Scott Gates, Havard Hegre, Havard Mokleiv Nygard, and Havard Strand, "Development Consequences of Armed Conflict," *World Development* 40, no. 9 (2012): 1713–22.

29 Barney Frank, "Cut the Military Budget," *The Nation*, March 2, 2009, www.thenation.com.

30 Robert Pollin and Heidi Garrett-Peltier, *The U.S. Employment Effects of Military and Domestic Spending Priorities* (Amherst: University of Massachusetts Institute for Policy Studies, October 2007), www.peri.umass.edu.

31 Dean Baker, *The Economic Impact of the Iraq War and Higher Military Spending* (Washington, DC: Center for Economic and Policy Research, May 2007), www.cepr.net.

32 Nobel Peace Laureate Óscar Arias, president of Costa Rica 1986–1990 and 2006–2010, in a message for the 2012 Global Day of Action on Military Spending. April 17, 2012, www.commondreams.org.

33 "All Members shall refrain in their international relations from the threat or use of force against the territorial integrity or political independence of any state, or in any other manner inconsistent with the Purposes of the United Nations." Article 2(4), UN Charter.

34 United Nations General Assembly, *2005 World Summit Outcome*, Resolution A/Res/60/1, October 24, 2005, paras. 138–39.

35 Center on International Cooperation, *Annual Review of Global Peace Operations 2013* (Boulder: Lynne Rienner, 2013).

36 The Multinational Force in Iraq was first authorized by the UN Security Council in October 2003 (Security Council Resolution 1511), six months after the initial unauthorized US-led attacks on Iraq.

37 Rupert Smith, *The Utility of Force: The Art of War in the Modern World* (London: Penguin, 2006).

38 UN Security Council Resolution 2098, March 28, 2013.

39 UN Security Council Resolution 2164, June 25, 2014.

40 amisom-au.org/amisom-mandate.

41 United Nations Department of Peacekeeping Operations, Department of Field Support, *United Nations Peacekeeping Operations: Principles and Guidelines*, 2008, un.org. Emphasis added.

42 Authorized by Security Council Resolution 678 (November 29, 1990).

43 Charles T. Call and Elizabeth M. Cousens, *Ending Wars and Building Peace*, Coping with Crisis Working Paper Series (New York: International Peace Academy, 2007).

44 International Commission on Intervention and State Sovereignty, *The Responsibility to Protect* (Ottawa: International Development Research Centre, 2001).

45 Mary Kaldor, *Beyond Militarism, Arms Races and Arms Control* (New York: Social Science Research Council, 2001), www.ssrc.org.

46 Gerald W. Schlabach, ed., *Just Policing, Not War: An Alternative Response to World Violence* (Collegeville, Minnesota: Liturgical Press, 2007).

47 These definitions are taken from Amitav Acharya, *Constructing a Security Community in South East Asia: ASEAN and the Problem of Regional Order*, 2nd ed. (London: Routledge, 2009), 18–21. Acharya's definition is an elaboration of Karl Deutch's foundational discussion of "security communities."

48 Acharya, *Constructing a Security Community in South East Asia*, 18–21.

49 Taylor B. Seybolt, *Humanitarian Military Intervention: The Conditions for Success and Failure* (Oxford: Oxford University Press, 2007).

6: Disarming Security

1 Steven Pinker, *The Better Angels of Our Nature: Why Violence Has Declined* (New York: Viking, 2011); Joshua S. Goldstein, *Winning the War on War: The Decline of Armed Conflict Worldwide* (New York: Dutton, 2011); Ian Morris, *War! What is it Good For? Conflict and the Progress of Civilization From Primates to Robots* (New York: Farrar, Straus and Giroux, 2014).

2 Pinker, *The Better Angels of Our Nature*, Preface.

3 The UN Security Council, for example, regularly addresses issues of war prevention in specific cases, as well as more generally, as part of its mandate to maintain international peace and security. In September 2011 the Council agreed to a Presidential Statement on issues of conflict prevention that include early warning, preventive deployments, mediation, peacekeeping, local disarmament, and attention to the economic, social, and political roots of conflict. Statement by the President of the Security Council, September 22, 2011 (S/PRST/2011/18), www.securitycouncilreport.org.

4 Michael Mandelbaum, "Learning to be Warless," *Survival / IISS Quarterly* (Summer 1999): 150.

5 Gareth Evans, "What We Know about Preventing Deadly Conflict: A Practitioner's Guide," January 2, 2006, International Crisis Group, www.crisisgroup.org.

6 Evans, "What We Know about Preventing Deadly Conflict."

7 Resolution 2171 was passed at United Nations Security Council, Meeting 7247 on Conflict Prevention on August 21, 2014. The record of the debate is available in UN Security Council meeting document S/PV.7247 of the same date.

8 "Kyrgyzstan: Promoting Peace by Improving Access to Water," n.d., www.undp.org.

9 T. Addison et al., "Ending Violent Conflict and Building a Social Compact," Chapter 6 in *Escaping Poverty Traps* (Manchester: Chronic Poverty Research Centre, 2008).

10 T. Addison et al., "Ending Violent Conflict and Building a Social Compact."

11 Francisco Gutierrez and Gerd Schönwälder, eds., *Economic Liberalization and Political Violence: Utopia or Dystopia?* (Ottawa: Pluto Press/International Development Research Centre, 2010), 339.

12 "Briefing Security Council, Senior Officials Urge UN System-Wide Approach to Early Warning, Conflict Prevention," *UN News Centre*, August 21, 2014, www.un.org.

13 Chetan Kumar and Jos De la Haye, "Hybrid Peacemaking: Building National 'Infrastructure for Peace'," *Global Governance* 18 (2011): 13–20.

14 Chetan Kumar, "Building National 'Infrastructures for Peace': UN Assistance for Internally Negotiated Solutions to Violent Conflict," www.undp.org.

15 The Institute for Economics and Peace, "Structures of Peace: Identifying What Leads To Peaceful Societies," n.d., www.economicsandpeace.org.

16 Ernie Regehr and Peter Whelan, "Reshaping the Security Envelope: Defence Policy in a Human Security Context," Ploughshares Working Paper 04–04, www.ploughshares.ca.

17 Human Security Report Project, *Human Security Report 2009/2010: The Causes of Peace and the Shrinking Costs of War* (Vancouver: HSRP, 2010), www.hsrgroup.org (forthcoming in print from Oxford University Press).

18 Human Security Report Project, *Why the Dramatic Decline in Armed Conflict? Human Security Report 2005*, 150–55, www.hsrgroup.org.

19 Adopted August 21, 2014.

20 United Nations Security Council, S/PV.7247, August 21, 2014.

21 Mr. Pearson's vivid aphorism was from another era – namely, "that we prepare for war like precocious giants, and for peace like retarded pygmies." Our sense of appropriate language has improved, but the reality remains the same.

22 Ban Ki-moon, "The World is Over-Armed and Peace is Under-Funded," *UN Office for Disarmament Affairs*, August 30, 2012, www.un.org.

23 OECD Development Assistance Committee, *Guidelines on Conflict, Peace and*

Development Co-Operation (Paris: Organisation for Economic Co-operation and Development, 1997), 9. Available at: www.fas.org.

24 Jean-Marie Guehenno, "The Impact of Globalization on Strategy," *Survival / IISS Quarterly* (Winter 1998–99), 10.

25 Oliver P. Richmond, "Failed Statebuilding versus Peace Formation," *Cooperation and Conflict* 48, no. 3 (2013): 378–400.

26 James Eayrs, *Fate and Will in Foreign Policy* (Toronto: Seven Talks for the Canadian Broadcasting Corporation, 1967), 84.

7: Disarming Conflict

1 www.transparency.org.

2 The Stockholm International Peace Research Institute (SIPRI, www.sipri.org) is the preeminent authority on international arms transfers – on the numbers and details, but also on analysis and related political and arms control developments. The following analysis draws on SIPRI and further references refer to specific publications.

3 SIPRI provides a list of states in which military spending more than doubled over the past decade. *Doubled*: Belarus, Armenia, Russia, China, Vietnam, Cambodia, Oman, Bahrain, Saudi Arabia, Swaziland, Namibia, Angola, Algeria, Argentina, Paraguay, Ecuador; *Tripled*: Georgia, Kazakhstan, Iraq, Ghana, Honduras; *Five-fold increase*: Azerbaijan; *Six-fold increase*: Afghanistan.

4 Sam Perlo-Freeman and Carina Solmirano, "Trends in World Military Expenditure, 2013," SIPRI Fact Sheet, April 2014, www.sipri.org.

5 The 20 per cent figure is necessarily a very rough estimate. In the United States in 2012, procurement was less than 20 per cent of the Department of Defense budget. SIPRI's December 2014 Fact Sheet on the top one hundred arms producing and services companies reports 2013 sales at $402 billion, just over 20 per cent of world military spending (noting that those sales also included services). In low-income countries procurement costs are relatively higher because of lower personnel costs.

6 The following review of military spending and arms trade trends relies on two primary sources: the annual publication of the US Congressional Research Service and the annual reports of SIPRI. See Richard F. Grimmett and Paul K. Kerr, *Conventional Arms Transfers to Developing Nations, 2004–2011*, Congressional Research Service, August 24, 2012; Simon T. Wezeman and Pieter D. Wezeman, "Trends in International Arms Transfers, 2013," SIPRI Fact Sheet, March 2014; Sam Perlo-Freeman and Carina Solmirano, "Trends in World Military Expenditures, 2013," SIPRI Fact Sheet, April 2014.

7 Compiled by Paul Holtom and Mark Bromley, "Next Steps for the Arms Trade Treaty: Securing Early Entry Into Force," *Arms Control Today*, June 2013, as summarized in Bromley and Holtom, "Arms Trade Treaty Assistance: Identifying a Role for the European Union," Discussion Paper, February 2014, EU Non-Proliferation Consortium.

8 Tom Arendshorst, "Small Arms Trade," *Beyond Intractability*, April 2005, www.beyondintractability.org.

9 The final document of the 2005 United Nations Global Summit. UNGA 2005 A/60/1, paras 139–39.

10 Thomas Countryman, US Assistant Secretary of State for International Security and Nonproliferation, quoted by Jeff Abramson, "Special Report: UN General Assembly Adopts Arms Trade Treaty in Overwhelming Vote," *Arms Control Today*, May 2013, Arms Control Association, Washington, www.armscontrol.org.

11 Tom Countryman, "The Arms Trade Treaty: Just the Facts," speaking at a "briefing for reporters" at the Stimson Center in Washington, November 7, 2013, The Arms Control Association, www.armscontrol.org.

12 International Institute of Strategic Studies, *The Military Balance 2013* (London: International Institute of Strategic Studies, 2013).

13 Human Rights Watch, "Country Summary: Saudi Arabia," January 2013, www.hrw.org.

14 F. Gregory Cause, "Saudi Arabia in the New Middle East," Council Special Report, December 2011, Council of Foreign Relations, cfr.org.

15 "Estimating Civilian Owned Firearms," Research Notes, *Small Arms Survey* 9 (September 2011).

16 "UN Arms Trade Treaty Remains Paradigm Shift," *Deutsche Welle*, n.d., www.dw.de.

17 Sylvester Domasa, "Small Arms Threaten Africa's Peace – VP," *IPP media*, May 30, 2014, www.ippmedia.com.

18 www.australiagroup.net/en/index.html.

19 www.nuclearsuppliersgroup.org/en.

20 www.wassenaar.org.

21 These points draw on "Transparency and Accountability in Military Spending and Procurement," a report on the SIPRI publication *Budgeting for the Military Sector in Africa*, by Wuyi Omitoogun and Eboe Hutchful, SIPRI, n.d., www.sipri.org.

8: Disarming the Bomb

1 Testimony of Yasuhiko Taketa, a survivor of Hiroshima and member of the Hiroshima Prefectural Confederation of Atomic Bomb Sufferers' Organization, www.gensuiukin.org/english/taketa.html.

2 Brent Scowcroft, Stephen J. Hadley, and Frank Miller, "NATO-based Nuclear Weapons are an Advantage in a Dangerous World," *Washington Post*, August 17, 2014, www.washingtonpost.com.

3 *Deterrence and Defence Posture Review*, May 12, 2012, www.NATO.int.

4 "The Radioactive Incineration of Cities," ICAN, www.icanw.org.

5 Canadian Council of Churches, Letter to Prime Minister Harper, June 25, 2010, www.ploughshares.ca.

6 Henry Kissinger, Speech to the 45th Munich Security Conference, delivered February 6, 2009, www.americanrhetoric.com.

7 2015 Review Conference of the NPT, "Working Paper on the Humanitarian Impact of Nuclear Weapons" (working paper, NPT/CONF.2015/WP.30, April 22, 2015, www.un.org).

8 "Nuclear Scenario: US Studies Attack on Washington," *The Hamilton Spectator*, Associated Press, May 27, 2012.

9 Gareth Evans, "Nuclear Weapons As a Threat to Global Peace" (speech at the UNI Global Union 3rd World Conference, Nagasaki, Japan, January 11, 2010), gevans.org.

10 The "Nuclear Notebook" in the *Bulletin of the Atomic Scientists*, prepared by Hans M. Kristensen and Robert S. Norris, is the preeminent public source of up-to-date information on global nuclear arsenals, nuclear modernization, and disarmament. See bos.sagepub.com/cgi/collection/nuclear notebook. The *Yearbook of the Stockholm International Peace Research Institute* (SIPRI, www.sipri.org) is a similarly comprehensive source. The Centre for Nuclear Non-Proliferation and Disarmament at the Australian National University has produced, in co-operation with SIPRI, a comprehensive report on the "state of play" of nuclear weapons and disarmament efforts. Gareth Evans, Tany Ogilvie-White, and Ramesh Thakur, *Nuclear Weapons: The State of Play 2015* (Canberra: Centre for Nuclear Non-Proliferation and Disarmament, Australian National University, 2015), cnnd.crawford.anu.edu.au.

11 Nuclear Non-Proliferation Treaty (NPT) Review Conference, *2010 Review Conference of the Parties to the Treaty on the Non-Proliferation of Nuclear Weapons: Final Document*, vol. 1, para 79, www.un.org.

12 United Nations Security Council, Resolution 1887, "Maintenance of International Peace and Security: Nuclear Non-proliferation and Nuclear Disarmament," September 24, 2009.

13 United Nations Office for Disarmament Affairs, "Decision 2, Principles and Objectives for Nuclear Non-Proliferation and Disarmament," NPT/CONF.1995/32 (Part I), Annex, Review and Extension Conference of the Parties to the Treaty on the Non-Proliferation of Nuclear Weapons, 1995, www.un.org.

14 NPT Review Conference Final Document, 2000, 14–15, www.un.org.

15 United Nations General Assembly, "Conclusions and Recommendations for Follow-on Actions," 2010, 19–29, www.un.org.

16 Hans M. Kristensen and Matthew McKinzie, "De-alerting Nuclear Forces," *Bulletin of the Atomic Scientists*, June 19, 2013, thebulletin.org.

17 Global Zero U.S. Nuclear Policy Commission, *Modernizing US Nuclear Strategy, Force Structure and Posture, Global Zero*, May 2012, www.globalzero.org.

18 Statement by Ambassador David Broucher, United Kingdom, NPT Preparatory Committee, May 3, 2004, www.fco.gov.uk/ukdis.

19 www.ctbto.org.

20 "Fissile Material Cut-off Treaty," *Reaching Critical Will*, www.reachingcriticalwill.org.

21 The New Strategic Arms Reduction Treaty between the United States and the Russian Federation was ratified by the US Senate in December 2010 and entered into force in February 2010.

22 Hans M. Kristensen and Robert S. Norris, "Slowing Nuclear Weapon Reductions and Endless Nuclear Weapon Modernizations: A Challenge to the NPT," Nuclear Notebook, *Bulletin of the Atomic Scientists* 70, no. 4 (2014): 94–107.

23 "How We Implement Safeguards," International Atomic Energy Agency, www.iaea.org.

24 Igor Khripunov, "A Work in Progress: UN Security Resolution 1540 After 10 Years," *Arms Control Today*, May 2014, www.armscontrol.org. Khripunovis is a distinguished fellow and adjunct professor at the Center for International Trade and Security at the University of Georgia.

25 George P. Shultz, William J. Perry, Henry A. Kissinger, and Sam Nunn, *Wall Street Journal*, January 4, 2007, www.2020visioncampaign.org.

26 Shultz, Perry, Kissinger, and Nunn.

27 Remarks by President Barack Obama, Hradcany Square, Prague, Czech Republic, April 5, 2009, www.whitehouse.gov.

28 George P. Shultz, William J. Perry, Henry A. Kissinger, and Sam Nunn, "Deterrence in the Age of Nuclear Proliferation: The Doctrine of Mutual Assured Destruction is Obsolete in the Post–Cold War Era," *Wall Street Journal*, March 7, 2011, online.wsj.com.

29 James Doyle makes the compelling point that the Perkovich/Acton paper on nuclear abolition does "not give enough emphasis to the transformed nature of the security environment and the implications of that transformation for traditional nuclear strategies." James E. Doyle, "Eyes on the Prize: A Strategy for Enhancing Global Security," in *Abolishing Nuclear Weapons: A Debate*, ed. George Perkovich and James M. Acton (Washington: Carnegie Endowment for International Peace, 2009), www.carnegieendowment.org.

30 In fact, in the current security environment, as pointed out by Mohamed ElBaradei some time ago, the only actors on the international stage that could "rationally" use (that is, actually detonate) a nuclear weapon to their perceived advantage would be a non-state extremist group. Mohamed ElBaradei, "In Search of Security: Finding an Alternative to Nuclear Deterrence," Speech to the Stanford University Center for International Security and Cooperation, November 4, 2004, www.iaea.org.

31 International Institute for Strategic Studies, *The Military Balance 2013* (London: Oxford University Press, 2013), 543–56.

32 US Department of Defense, *Nuclear Posture Review Report*, April 2010, www.defense.gov.

33 US Department of Defense, *Nuclear Posture Review Report*, ix.

34 John Steinbruner, "Renovating Arms Control through Reassurance," *Washington Quarterly* 23, no. 2 (Spring 2000): 197–206, www.twq.com.

35 ElBaradei argues that mutual security arrangements require renewed efforts to build what he calls "a functional system for collective security," which in turn calls for changes to the Security Council's membership, more active preventive diplomacy, and more effective enforcement. ElBaradei, "In Search of Security."

36 In his 2009 Prague speech he said, "Make no mistake: As long as these weapons exist, the United States will maintain a safe, secure and effective arsenal to deter any adversary, and guarantee that defense to our allies." President Barack Obama, Prague, April 5, 2009.

37 John Steinbruner, "Renovating Arms Control through Reassurance."

38 Bjorn Moller, *Common Security and Nonoffensive Defense: A Neorealist Perspective* (Boulder: Lynne Rienner, 1992).

39 Noam Chomsky, "Hiroshima Day 2014," *TomDispatch*, August 5, 2014, www.truth-out.org.

9: When Prevention Fails

1 International Commission on Intervention and State Sovereignty (ICISS), *The Responsibility to Protect: Report of the International Commission on Intervention and State Sovereignty* (Ottawa: International Development Research Centre, 2001).

2 ICISS, *The Responsibility to Protect*.

3 United Nations Department of Peacekeeping Operations and Department of Field Support (DPKO), *United Nations Peacekeeping Operations: Principles and Guidelines*, 2008, pbpu.unlb.org, 32.

4 DPKO, *United Nations Peacekeeping Operations: Principles and Guidelines*, 32–33.

5 DPKO, *United Nations Peacekeeping Operations: Principles and Guidelines*, 32.

6 DPKO, *United Nations Peacekeeping Operations: Principles and Guidelines*, 32.

7 Kofi Annan, "Two Concepts of Sovereignty," *The Economist*, September 18, 1999; Annan, *We the Peoples: The Role of the United Nations in the 21st Century* (Millennium Report of the Secretary-General) (New York: UN Department of Public Information, 2000), 48.

8 The following notes on the AU and R2P rely on Greg Puley, "The Responsibility to Protect: East, West, and Southern African Perspectives on Preventing and Responding to Humanitarian Crises," Ploughshares Working Paper 05-5, www.ploughshares.ca.

9 www.africa-union.org/root/au/AboutAu/Constitutive_Act_en.htm.

10 *A More Secure World: Our Shared Responsibility*, the 2004 report of the High-level Panel on Threats, Challenges and Change, was the work of a panel of eminent persons convened by the UN Secretary-General. The panel "endorse[d] the emerging norm that there is a collective international responsibility to protect, exercisable by the Security Council authorizing military intervention as a last resort, in the event of genocide and other large-scale killing, ethnic cleansing or serious violations of international humanitarian law which sovereign Governments have proved powerless or unwilling to prevent." It joined the ICISS report in naming the Security Council as the source of authority for any intervention. Then, a year later, the UN Secretary-General's own report, *In Larger Freedom: Towards Development, Security and Human Rights for All*, supported both the ICISS and High-Level Panel reports on the responsibility to protect and urged the international community to act on it at the forthcoming 2005 Global Summit.

11 United Nations General Assembly, Resolution 60/1, "2005 World Summit Outcome," A/RES/60/1, September 16, 2005, paras 138–39.

12 United Nations General Assembly, Resolution 60/1, "2005 World Summit Outcome."

13 The following relies on the author's summary of a World Council of Churches consultation on humanitarian intervention, which was drawn on to draft the WCC's historic resolution on protection passed at the 2006 Puerto Allegro Assembly. Ernie

Regehr, "Endorsing the Responsibility to Protect as a Global Norm," in *The Responsibility to Protect: Ethical and Theological Reflections*, ed. Semegnish Asfaw, Guillermo Kerber and Peter Weiderud (Geneva: World Council of Churches, 2005), 105–107.

14 ICISS, *The Responsibility to Protect*, 5.

15 ICISS, *The Responsibility to Protect*, 37.

16 ICISS, *The Responsibility to Protect*, 63.

17 Evan Cinq-Mars, "In Support of R2P: No Need to Reinvent the Wheel," *OpenCanada.Org*, March 18, 2015, opencanada.org.

10: Peace after the Sun Goes Down

1 Fareed Zakaria, "The West's Four-Part Strategy to Deal With Radical Islam," January 23, 2015, fareedzakaria.com.

2 Michael Walzer, "Islamism and the Left," *Dissent*, Winter 2015, thirdnarrative.org.

3 Todd Harrison, John Stillion, Eric Lindsey, and Jacob Cohn, "Estimating the Cost of Operations Against ISIL," *Center for Strategic and Budgetary Assessments*, September 29, 2014, csbaonline.org.

4 This description of Boko Haram is taken from the *R2P Monitor* 19, January 15, 2015, www.globalr2p.org.

5 "Security Council Presidential Statement Demands Cessation of Hostilities by Boko Haram in Nigeria, Release of Hostages, Including 276 Girls Abducted in April," United Nations Meetings Coverage, January 19, 2015, www.un.org.

6 Thomas Fessy, "Can Regional Force Beat Nigeria's Militant Islamists?" *BBC News*, March 3, 2015, www.bbc.com/news.

7 Ejike Ejike, "Insurgency: Hunger Killing IDPs in Borno, Adamawa Mountains," *Leadership Newspaper*, April 10, 2015, leadership.ng/features.

8 UN Human Rights Council Session, April 1, 2015, www.ohchr.org.

9 Freedom C. Onuoha, "Why do Youth Join Boko Haram?" Special Report, US Institute of Peace, June 2014, www.usip.org.

10 "Spiraling Violence: Boko Haram Attacks and Security Force Abuses in Nigeria, Human Rights Watch, 2012, www.hrw.org.

11 "Crisis in Nigeria: A Case for RtoP's Second Pillar," *ICRtoP Blog*, May 21, 2014, icrtopblog.org.

12 Onuoha, "Why do Youth Join Boko Haram?"

13 Joanna Slater, "Angela Merkel: The Indispensable Woman," *Globe and Mail*, February 14, 2015.

14 James Fallows, "The Tragedy of the American Military," *The Atlantic*, January/February 2015, www.theatlantic.com.

Index

Note: "n" after a page number indicates an endnote; "nn" after a page number indicates two or more consecutive endnotes

Abkhazia. *See* Georgia

Aceh. *See under* Indonesia

Afghanistan, 33, 35, 48, 57; civilian deaths in, 97–98, 109; combat deaths in, 5; costs of, 101–2, 136; multilateral forces in, 4, 29, 36, 79–80, 88–89, 93–94, 100, 104, 174; security assistance in, 175, 189; and the Taliban, 3, 35, 79, 88, 98, 109, 175, 176; United States attack on, 30–31, 36, 54, 85, 87, 175–79

Albania, 27. *See also* Kosovo

al-Bashir, Omar Hassan, 2

Algeria, 15, 32

al Qaeda, 35, 47, 115

al Shabaab, 22, 105, 188

Angola, 46, 58, 62, 133, 138, 208n3

Annan, Kofi, 180, 182

Arab Spring, 10, 11, 27, 41, 47, 53, 55, 97

Arias, Óscar, 103, 206n32

Aristide, Jean-Bertrand, 92

Armenia. *See* Armenia-Azerbaijan War

Armenia-Azerbaijan War, 27, 83–84, 208n3

arms. *See* nuclear weapons; small arms. *See also* Arms Trade Treaty; military spending

Arms Trade Treaty, 135–49

Arnson, Cynthia, 45

Azerbaijan. *See* Armenia-Azerbaijan War

Ban, Ki-moon, 127

Bangladesh, 78

Biafra, 61–62

Blair, Bruce, 160

Boko Haram, 9, 13, 34, 35, 49, 109, 126, 191–93, 197

Bosnia-Herzegovina, 30, 36, 65, 87, 90–91, 92, 93, 94

Burma. *See* Myanmar

Burundi, 68–69, 119

Bush, George H. W., 87

Bush, George W., 3, 160

Cambodia, 45, 46, 182, 208n3. *See also* Vietnam-Cambodia War

Canada, 93, 129, 142, 143, 145, 154

the Caucasus. *See under* Russia

Center for Systemic Peace, 22, 28, 35, 98

Central African Republic, 27, 32, 121, 182

Chad, 26, 27, 192

Charlie Hebdo, 34

Christianity, 9, 49, 73, 75–76, 172, 192

civil wars. *See* intrastate wars

Cold War, 26, 28, 108, 115, 132–33, 137, 139, 157, 160, 167. *See also* Soviet Union

Colombia, 27, 33, 57, 100, 119, 138, 190

Comprehensive Nuclear-Test-Ban Treaty, 159, 161, 162

conflict mediation. *See* negotiation

Correlates of War Project, 22

Cote d'Ivoire, 45

crimes against humanity, 2, 11, 104, 140–41, 152, 153, 173, 180. *See also* Bosnia-Herzegovina; Cambodia; genocide; Rwanda; Serbia

criminal activity, 8, 13–14, 24, 25, 32, 45, 93, 123, 176, 177. *See also* law enforcement

Croatia, 44, 65, 90–91

Darfur. *See* Sudan

deaths: civilian, 23, 35, 51, 61–62, 84, 95–99, 109, 119, 192, 196,